3

THE TERRITORIAL BASIS OF GOVERNMENT UNDER THE STATE CONSTITUTIONS

STUDIES IN HISTORY, ECONOMICS AND PUBLIC LAW

EDITED BY THE FACULTY OF POLITICAL SCIENCE OF
COLUMBIA UNIVERSITY

Volume XL]   [Number 3

Whole Number 106

THE TERRITORIAL BASIS OF GOVERNMENT UNDER THE STATE CONSTITUTIONS

Local Divisions and Rules for Legislative Apportionment

BY
ALFRED ZANTZINGER REED

AMS PRESS
NEW YORK

98539

COLUMBIA UNIVERSITY
STUDIES IN THE
SOCIAL SCIENCES

106

The Series was formerly known as *Studies in History,
Economics and Public Law.*

Reprinted with the permission of Columbia University Press
From the edition of 1911, New York
First AMS EDITION published 1968
Manufactured in the United States of America

Library of Congress Catalogue Card Number: 68-56685

AMS PRESS, INC.
New York, N.Y. 10003

PREFACE

In the extremely elaborate political structure of the United States, as, indeed, of any nation, the local units within which governmental and party organs operate constitute, in more senses than one, the foundation lines of the entire edifice. The division of the Union into States is, of course, the prime fact in our political life; but of hardly less importance than this is the division of the States themselves into counties and towns, and into districts for legislative representation. The purpose of this study is to present, in form convenient for reference, and with due regard to their historical relationship with one another, those provisions of our American State Constitutions which bear upon the formation of these, and other, interior districts.

I should like to explain why I have chosen a subject of enquiry which, on its surface, seems far removed from the pressing political problems of the day; and why, having chosen it, I have treated it in a highly technical manner.

The constitutional history of government is the veriest dry-bones of an exceedingly human topic. It is not merely that Constitutions contain only a small portion of the law on the subject, needing to be supplemented by judicial construction, by legislative enactment, by those party regulations which are as much a part of our common law as the customs of the British Constitution. Law itself is meaningless until we include the dominating personality who works within its forms, influencing legislators, cajoling the popular vote, making those evershifting combinations which we term "majorities", evoking and making active those powers, in short, which of themselves merely " reside " in plural organs. All this on the side of structure alone. There remain the procession of external events which determine this structure, in large part, and determine entirely the problems which it has to face—the cast of popular thought and feeling, without adjustment to which no political system can long endure —the consideration, finally, that politics itself is only a means to an end, and that the question of what the government of a people shall be is of infinitely small importance compared with the question of what happens to the people thus governed. What value has any system of government except as a means for conserving free institutions? On what does our belief, not merely in democratic rule, but in law and order itself depend, other than a conviction that these afford the only sure guarantees for freedom? No one who is incapable of seeing the topic of government as a whole is fit to treat any part of it.

Because the topic should be seen as a whole, however, it by no means follows that it should be so treated. Quite the reverse. Politics is an exceedingly technical profession —how technical, I think few understand who have not had even a slight practical acquaintance with it. It is a pity that it must to some extent always be so, because of the complexity of modern life. It is a defect of our system of government that it is needlessly so, because of unpruned excrescences and traditional deadwood. But there is nothing to be gained by blinking facts and thinking that it can be pursued on an old-fashioned amateur basis. Those who accomplish most in it are those who have studied it most carefully in all its wearisome and often degrading detail. And even they usually know very little about it. It is a profession to be practiced by experts, and only pseudo-experts exist—the men who have picked up an empirical knowledge

of its present-day intricacies, but are rarely capable of enacting broad remedial measures, because the broader aspect
of their profession is one they have had little time or oppor-
tunity to study. They are the nearest approach to experts
we possess, and it is fortunate that they exist. They accomplish wonders in simply making a cumbersome system
work. Our government would go to pieces if the guiding
hand of the professional politician were removed from it.
But his deficiencies are well known. Until he, or his successor has been put in possession of the truths which study
of past experience reveals, his hold upon the present will
only lead to further groping. A wider horizon, on the part
of those who are in a position to put their views into practical effect, seems to me the great need of American politics.

It is because I have in mind this specialized class, rather
than the average citizen who, in the intervals of a busy life,
aspires to take an intelligent interest in politics, that I
have picked out a small topic, and treated it in a manner
calculated to enhance, rather than to veil, its essential tech-
nicality. In particular, I have tried to include every relevant
constitutional provision, with precise references to each, for
the following perfectly concrete purpose. We are likely to
have in New York, for instance, in a few years, one of our
periodic Constitutional Conventions. The New York provision affecting the formation of counties, say, is found to
be decidedly different from the prevailing treatment. Will
it not be of assistance to the particular committee within
whose province this provision falls, to be able to see how
this question has been handled in all the other States, so
that, on the basis of the wide range of suggestions thus
obtained, they may decide what in their judgment is the
wisest treatment? When they have decided what policy
they wish to pursue, will it not be of further assistance to
have at hand precise references to provisions in other States,

so that the most accurate wording may be followed? This, in general, but with a much more limited survey of past instruments, is the way in which most Constitutional provisions have actually been drafted. I seek only to perfect an established procedure. On the general principle that out of a multiplicity of suggestions one or two turn out to be good, I have, it is true, included a few constructive ideas of my own. I have not much belief, however, in the value of irresponsible advice, and know no reason why my own should be considered better than other people's. The man in the Convention or the Legislature—not the man in the study or the street—is the man who, by the exercise of his own judgment, ultimately decides all except the broadest principles. Our best service to him, and, through him, to the community at large, is to put him in a position to decide intelligently.

If my work has been properly done, then, I foresee for it, not a wide appeal, but an immediate practical usefulness.

I have said that it is a small topic which I have chosen to treat in this detailed manner. It is needless to say that, feeling the value of this general method as I do, I should like to see it extended to other elements of the political structure. This takes time, however. Meanwhile, the present instalment, although small in proportion to what might be said, involves questions of fundamental importance— more fundamental than even the suffrage, which is itself defined in terms of political subdivisions—and more in need of our consideration to-day, because, as the following pages will reveal, much farther from being answered. The continuance of amicable relations between country and town; a fair representation of the voters in Legislature and Convention; the protection of minorities against intemperate majority rule; a simplified legal and party system—all these are certainly important ends of political endeavor, and will become pressing ones the moment public opinion chooses so to make them. All depend for their attainment in large degree upon the dry mechanical details of State subdivision.

It would be impossible for me to express, as I should like to, my acknowledgments to all who have helped me, and yet to emphasize, as I must, three especial obligations. Coming to my graduate studies in this university with an, I fear, not too malleable mind—making no secret of convictions, in regard to certain features of our political life, to which I attach perhaps exaggerated importance—I have experienced at all times ready helpfulness and patient consideration. In particular, however, I am indebted to three gentlemen. First, and foremost, Professor Frank J. Goodnow has taught me that the problem of municipal government—that political problem which, to the average city-dweller, comes most nearly home—cannot be approached as a topic by itself, but only as a part of the problem of State government in general. Incidentally, Professor Goodnow has taught me virtually all I know in regard to this broader topic. It was Professor William A. Dunning, again, who first turned my attention to the importance of State Constitutions, and to the comparative neglect of this field of study. My acknowledgments are due to him not only for this, but for the kindly sympathy and encouragement with which he has lightened what has been at times a tedious task. Finally, I owe especial thanks to Professor Charles A. Beard for invaluable suggestions of detail, and for assistance in an unusually laborious task of proof-reading.

A. Z. R.

COLUMBIA UNIVERSITY, 4 APRIL, 1911.

TABLE OF CONTENTS

CHAPTER IV

Urban Districts

CHAPTER V

Districts for General or Judicial Purposes, other than County and Urban

CHAPTER VI

Districts for Special Administrative Purposes

ABBREVIATIONS

For convenience of reference, the Constitutions have been referred to by the year under which they appear in Thorpe's collection, except when, as with the first instruments of West Virginia and Nebraska, Thorpe uses a double date. For these, and for all amendments, the date of final ratification has been used. For the complete Constitutions, Thorpe's numbering has usually been followed; "Articles", however, to which sections are subordinate, are consistently expressed in Roman numerals; e. g. *Kans. Const. 1859, ii, 26;* and in late, serially numbered, instruments, the intermediate "Articles" or "Titles" are omitted; e. g. *La. Const. 1868, 93* (not *1868, vi, 93*). For the amendments, both the year and Thorpe's numbers are used; these sometimes denote the serial number of the amendment as a whole; e. g. *Md. Am. 1807, x;* sometimes the section of the amendment; e. g. *Md. Am. 1837, 10;* sometimes the number of the provision which is amended; e. g. *Pa. Am. 1857, i, 4.* References to provisions not in Thorpe, or not clearly expressed in Thorpe, have an asterisk prefixed; e. g. *Md. * Am. 1799, vi—Cal. * Const. 1879, xiii, 9; Am. 1884—Fla. Const. 1885, viii, 4; * Am. 1900.* See Bibliographical Note at close of paper.

CHAPTER I

POLITICAL SUBDIVISIONS DURING THE COLONIAL PERIOD

FOR purposes of administration, locally limited jurisdictions have always been found necessary. The two most important local divisions, established during the Colonial period, were the urban district and the county. Urban settlements already possessing, or ripe for the acquisition of, special privileges, appeared, before the close of the Colonial period, under the names of towns or cities, in all the Colonies. The more artificial county, serving primarily the general convenience of the Colony, was also early instituted everywhere, except in Georgia, and justified its existence except in South Carolina, where it seems to have been in a precarious position. To this extent, the system of local divisions was fairly uniform when the Revolution occurred, the chief distinction between Colony and Colony being the greater or less development of the urban organization, and the greater or less extent of unsettled lands, to which even the county organization had not yet been extended.

The existence of State territory, lying outside of county lines, was of little importance, being certain to disappear with the movement of population inland. The existence of county territory, however, lying outside of urban lines is a permanent phenomenon, so long as the movement into urban centers endures. A smaller division than the county was needed for the administration of this rural territory, and in the manner in which this need was satisfied the greatest disparity between the colonies appeared. Broadly

speaking, it may be said that, in New England, the movement was from the numerous and vigorous towns outward,
outlying rural territory being brought within the town jurisdiction, so that the tendency was towards a uniform division of the Colony into small areas, containing both urban
and rural territory, out of which the somewhat later county
was aggregated; while elsewhere the tendency was for dis-
tinctively rural areas to appear alongside the few urban
settlements. Towns or townships alone, in New England
—parishes, hundreds, boroughs, beats or districts, elsewhere,
with or without towns and cities as well—was the general
rule, subject to many exceptions.

A detailed account of the various systems of representation in the Colonial Assemblies would be out of place in this
introductory sketch, even if the writer had made of these,
as he has not, a special study. A few simple generalizations,
however, may profitably be kept in mind, while studying
the later development. One is that our modern notion of
a periodically varying district had not even begun to develop; fixed local districts were everywhere the basis of
representation. In New England the towns virtually
monopolized representative privileges, thus establishing a
sectional tradition which is almost unimpaired to-day.
Elsewhere, a favorite plan, just before the Revolution, was
to accord representation to all counties, but also to special
towns, cities or boroughs. This was the English principle,
and produced, in several Colonies, an unsymmetrical, but
historically and practically justifiable, system of representative districts, which we shall see carried over into several
States, before it gave way to a uniform county system.

One other important feature of the Colonial system
should be noted. Control over local divisions was almost
entirely in the hands of the active government. The principal, if not the only exceptions, were some of the urban dis-

tricts, which rested upon Royal or Proprietary Charter. This protection having been swept away by the Revolution, complete power to change existing lines, except in so far as express restrictions were imposed by the Constitutions, was naturally inherited by the State Legislatures. There seems to have been a little uncertainty in regard to this point for a time. In a few States it was thought necessary expressly to vest control of such matters in the Legislatures.[1] Usually, however, this has not been done. The competency of the Legislature, in the absence of restrictions, to alter district lines at will, has never, so far as the writer is aware, been successfully disputed. Doubtless even the three Delaware counties of Newcastle, Kent and Sussex owe their permanence, in a legal sense, to the Legislative policy of this State, and not to the fact that the State itself was formed by the union of these more ancient counties.

The principal inheritance of the States from the Colonies, then, in this matter of political subdivisions, was the existence of the county, as the prime unit of State administration; the use of towns, as units of representation, in New England, and of both counties and urban districts, commonly elsewhere; and the general principle that the Legislature, except as restricted, had full control.

[1] Power to "constitute towns, boroughs, cities and counties," in Pennsylvania (Const. 1776, 9—until 1790) and Vermont (Const. 1777, ii, 8; 1786, ii, 9; 1793, ii, 9).

Power to "divide the State into further and other counties," in New York (Const. 1777, 12—until 1821).

Power to "alter the boundaries of the present counties, and to lay off new ones, as well out of the counties already laid off as out of the other territory belonging to the State," in Georgia (Const. 1789, i, 17; 1798, i, 23—until the War).

CHAPTER II

Rules Incidentally Affecting Local Boundaries

Before we discuss those Constitutional provisions which apply to the formation of the various types of districts, separately, something must be said as to those provisions, in regard to corporations, special bills, local Referenda, etc., which may affect several or all types together. In every State of the Union except Massachusetts, Connecticut, Vermont, New Hampshire, North Carolina and Idaho, provisions of this sort to-day exist, in most cases with an application far broader than the mere bounding of local divisions. The idea of generality, which the framers of Constitutions, even to-day, more or less consciously pursue, has resulted in the grouping together of incongruous objects of legislation, on the strength of some one element or attribute which they have in common.

The corporate characteristics possessed by city or town governments from early times and, more recently, by the inhabitants both of urban and of other districts, have been one fertile source of this confusion. In itself, the possession of corporate powers by persons inhabiting a locality would seem to have no necessary connection with the definition of the locality itself. The venerable custom, however, of including in city charters a description of corporate boundaries, makes provisions regarding corporations in general —first appearing in New York in 1821—apply to the formation at least of this particular type of political division, in this particular way—makes, indeed, the question of how

far such provisions apply to other divisions which are, or
may become, " municipal corporations ", far too abstruse
to be settled except by judicial construction.[1] In a few
States this confusion does not exist. Louisiana, first, in
1845, specially excepted corporations " for political or municipal purposes " from the general corporation provision;
and although this system of imposing restrictions upon the
creation of only non-municipal corporations was abandoned
in this State after the War, it survives in four Southern
States, in Maine, and in three Far Western.[2] In two other
Southern, and four other Far Western States, entirely
separate rules for municipal and for non-municipal corporations are now provided.[3] In Massachusetts, Connec-

---

[1] Counties are expressly stated to be bodies corporate only in Michigan (Const. 1850, x, 1; * 1908, viii, 1), Georgia (Const. 1877, xi, 1),
South Carolina (Const. 1895, vii, 9), Oklahoma (Const. 1907, xvii, 1),
and Arizona (* Const. 1911, xii, 1), Townships, in Michigan (Const.
1850, xi, 2; * 1908, viii, 16), North Carolina (Const. 1868, vii, 4; 1876,
vii, 4), and South Carolina (Const. 1895, vii, 11). This last provision
applies only to townships established prior to 1895.

[2] Municipal corporations excepted from the general rule in:
Louisiana (Const. 1845, 123) until 1852.
Iowa (Const. 1846, viii, 2) until 1857.
Minnesota (Const. 1857, x, 2) until 1881.
North Carolina (Const. 1868, viii, 1; 1876, viii, 1).
Maine (Am. 1876, iv, 14).
Colorado (Const. 1876, xv, 1).
Montana (Const. 1889, xv, 2).
Idaho (Const. 1889, xi, 2).
Rule applicable only to private corporations, in:
Texas (Const. 1845, vii, 30, 31—until the War; Const. 1876, xii, 1).
West Virginia (Const. 1862, xi, 5) until 1872.
Georgia (Const. 1868, iii, 5, par. 5; 1877, iii, 7, par. 18.
Virginia (Const. 1902, 63, par. 18.
[3] Florida (Const. 1885, iii, 25; viii, 8).
North Dakota (Const. 1889, 130, 131).
South Carolina (Const. 1895, viii, 1; ix, 1).
Oregon (Am. 1906, xi, 2).

ticut, Vermont and New Hampshire no rules governing the formation of corporations of any sort have yet appeared. In the remaining thirty States, however, including the important Middle States and almost the entire Mississippi Valley, a general rule applicable to all corporations seems to be in force,[1] supplemented in some cases by additional rules for municipal corporations as such.

Oklahoma (Const. 1907, ix, 38; xviii, 1).

Arizona (* Const. 1911, xiii, xiv).

Florida (Const. 1868, v, 22) and South Carolina (Const. 1868, xii, 1) started with general provisions.

[1] The applicability of the general rule to municipalities is not always perfectly clear from the text. Idaho Const. 1889, iii, 19, is a prohibition of local or special legislation "creating any corporation"; this, however, would seem to be overridden by the clause above cited.

Another question which presents considerable difficulties is whether the clause "except for municipal purposes" qualifies the whole, or only a part, of the general provision. If the language of the successive provisions be examined in chronological order, however, it becomes fairly clear that in the following variants of the original New York provision, "Corporations may be formed under general laws; but shall not be created by special act, except for municipal purposes," the exception does not refer to the first clause:

New York (Const. 1846, viii, 1; 1894, viii, 1).

Illinois (Const. 1848, x, 1) followed by Wisconsin, to-day.

California (Const. 1849, iv, 31) followed by Oregon, to-day.

Nevada (Const. 1864, viii, 1) to-day.

Maryland (Const. 1867, iii, 48) to-day.

[2] Such supplementary rules appear in:

Missouri (Const. 1865, viii, 4, 5) until 1875.

South Dakota (Const. 1889, xvii, 1; x, 1).

Wyoming (Const. 1889, x, 1; xiii, 1).

Washington (Const. 1889, ii, 28, par. 6; xi, 10).

Oregon (Am. 1906, xi, 2).

New Mexico (* Const. 1911, xi, 13; x).

The imposition of supplementary restrictions upon private corporations has been common, and is frequently phrased as an additional general rule from which municipalities are excepted.

To be distinguished from the preceding, but evincing the same tendency, characteristic of the South and Far West, to distinguish, at

A quarter of a century after the launching of this corporation movement, and just at the moment when the advisability began to be felt of discriminating between municipal and non-municipal corporations, New York again gave the initial impulse to a Constitutional generalization of a still broader character. The power possessed by the Legislature to create corporations is only one instance of what are best termed its administrative powers—its power, that is to say, to enact measures applicable to particular persons or to particular localities, as distinguished from measures of general application. Such a power is, of course, peculiarly liable to abuse. Hence the early introduction into Constitutions of rules affecting its exercise in enumerated subjects. But if special safeguards were needed as regards the creation of corporations, the granting of divorces, the changing of a person's name, was it not logical to provide a general rule of procedure for all legislation of a private or local character? We need not here enquire whether this general treatment of subjects, widely distinct, each from each, was wise. We need only point out that, to a generation already compelled, from mere motives of convenience, to print private and local bills apart from general bills, in their session laws, or to omit them altogether from the periodical " Revised Statutes ", the temptation to group all such legislation under a single Constitutional provision was well nigh irresistible. The movement did not spread before the War to more than four (Western) States, but to-day thirty-seven States in all [1] provide more

least formally, between municipal and other corporations, is the express application, to municipalities, of a rule which would appear in any case to apply to them. So California (Const. 1879, xii, 1; xi, 6) and Utah (Const. 1895, xii, 1; xi, 5). So also South Dakota and Wyoming, in addition to the supplementary provisions already cited.

[1] The missing States are Tennessee, and the following ten, all on

or less effective rules for *all* (so-called) "special" legislation.[1]

I. RULES AFFECTING THE FORMATION OF MUNICIPAL CORPORATIONS

Turning now to the content of these provisions, which, in appearance at least, affect legislative control over local boundaries, and leaving, as entirely outside the scope of this study, the question of how far the Courts have as a matter of fact construed them to be applicable, we find, with many variations, five types of provisions affecting municipal corporations. The first and oldest type require more than an ordinary legislative majority for action. This was followed by a class of provisions which, while not disturbing the ultimate control of the ordinary legislative majority, imposed certain safeguards looking towards delay, publicity and careful consideration. Then came an effort to minimize, or prevent, legislative discrimination, by authorizing, or requiring, the passage only of general laws upon the subject. Much more recently, a local Referendum has been imposed upon legislative action; and this, finally, has developed in one State into an absolute removal of the subject from legislative control.

the borders of the Union: The New England States, south of Maine; Delaware, North Carolina, Ohio, Washington and Idaho.

North Carolina is peculiar in possessing, since 1868, a rule applicable to all private legislation only.

[1] The terms "local" and "special" are usually coupled, as distinguished from "general" legislation. In New York and Wisconsin, however, the terms "private" and "local" are used; in Kansas, Maryland (once), Arkansas (once), Minnesota (once), New Mexico (once), and in Missouri, 1865-1875, only "special"; in Maine, South Dakota, and Utah, "private" and "special"; in New Jersey, Virginia, and Alabama, "private," "local," and "special"; and in the last-named State the terms are defined. These variations in phraseology seem to have no force.

(a) *Extraordinary Legislative Majority*

The original New York rule was to require the assent
of two-thirds of the members elected to each house, to any
bill " creating, continuing, altering, or renewing any body
politic or corporate ". Delaware and Michigan, in the
early 30's, followed with similar but weaker rules, requiring
only an ordinary two-thirds majority, and only for the
original act of incorporation. By 1850 the provision was
dropped in the two Northern States. In Delaware, however, it seems to be firmly established, having been reënacted
in 1897 in the form, " No general incorporation law nor
any special act of incorporation shall be enacted without
the consent of two-thirds majority of all the members
elected to each house ". In Iowa, also, since 1857, a curious
survival of the idea can be traced in a requirement of a two-
thirds majority for amending or repealing the (general)
incorporation laws. With these exceptions, the requirement of an extraordinary majority has found no favor.[1]

(b) *Single bills. Deferred action*

Pennsylvania, in 1838, followed many years later by Alabama, took the first step towards preventing " omnibus "
legislation and " grab bills ", by providing that, " No law
hereafter enacted shall create, renew, or extend the charter
of more than one corporation." This particular provision
is now extinct, having succumbed to the third phase of the
corporation movement, with which it is wholly inconsistent.
Rhode Island, however, in 1842, provided that bills creating
corporations should be continued until after a fresh elec-

---

[1] In Delaware, until 1897, corporations could not be created for a
longer term than twenty years.

N. Y. Const. 1821, vii, 9 (until 1846).

Del. Const. 1831, ii, 17; 1897, ix, 1.

Mich. Const. 1835, xii, 2 (until 1850).

Ia. Const. 1857, viii, 12.

tion of the Legislature, notice being given of their pendency; and although, fifty years later, this provision was abolished as a whole, a fragment remains in the requirement that " no corporation shall be created *with the power to exercise the right of eminent domain* . . . except by special act of the general assembly, upon a petition for the same, the pendency whereof shall be notified as may be required by law." Michigan, also, from 1850 until 1908, required that notice should be given for *changing* the charter of any corporation.[1]

With the preceding may be classed also the rule, appearing in the last Florida instrument only, that when any municipality is abolished, provision shall be made for the payment of its creditors.[2]

(c) *General Legislation*

The most widely diffused rule for the treatment of purely private corporations has been absolute prohibition upon their creation by special act. We have seen that in Louisiana, where this idea, in 1845, first received constitutional expression, municipal corporations were excepted from the operation of this provision; and that both here, and in several later States, no substitute was provided. New York, in 1846, however, made a distinction between an authorization to form corporations by general law (to which no exception was made), and a requirement, more or less absolute, that they should be formed only in this way (from which municipalities were excepted). The first half of this provision, with or without the second, and latterly usually strengthened by the requirement that such

---

[1] Pa. Const. 1838, i, 25 (until 1873).
Ala. Const. 1875, xiii, 10 (until 1901).
R. I. Const. 1842, iv, 17; Am. 1892, ix.
Mich. Const. 1850, xv, 16 (until 1908).

[2] Fla. Const. 1885, viii, 8.

general laws shall be enacted, survives, to-day, in eight scattered States; its only importance is that it protects general laws incorporating municipalities in these States from possible attack on the ground that they delegate Legislative power.[1]

Much more commonly, however—in twenty-five States, in all, including, however, only two on the Atlantic seaboard—the preceding distinction has not been preserved, and special legislation creating corporations of any sort has come to be forbidden. Here, again, a distinction must be made between what may be called the Indiana rule, under which special creation, only, is forbidden, and the more stringent Ohio rule, which forbids also special change of charters. The two rules are of equal antiquity, having made their first appearance in these two States in 1851, and each

---

[1] References:

N. Y. Const. 1846, viii, 1; 1894, viii, 1.

Md. Const. 1851, iii, 47; 1864, iii, 51; 1867, iii, 48.

Nev. Const. 1864, viii, 1.

S. C. Const. 1868, xii, 1; 1895, viii, 1.

N. D. Const. 1889, 130, 131.

Wyom. Const. 1889, x, 1; xiii, 1.

R. I. Am. 1892, ix, 1 (not applying to corporations with the power to exercise the right of eminent domain).

* N. Mex. Const. 1911, xi, 13.

Similar provisions existed for a time in:

Ill. Const. 1848, x, 1 (until 1870).

Wisc. Const. 1848, xi, 1 (until 1871).

Cal. Const. 1849, iv, 31 (until 1879).

Mich. Const. 1850, xv, 1 (until 1908).

Or. Const. 1857, xi, 2 (until 1906).

Ala. Const. 1867, xiii, 1; 1875, xiii, 1 (until 1901).

Fla. Const. 1868, v, 22 (until 1885).

The obligation to pass such general laws appears in Florida, North Dakota, Wyoming, New Mexico, and (since 1895) South Carolina. It is quite clear in North Dakota that this is not equivalent to a prohibition upon special legislation.

For the difficulty, in some instances, of determining whether the provision in question falls within the excepting clause, *vide* p. 22, note 1, *supra.*

having been taken up by one other State before the War—
the Indiana rule by Iowa (in addition to the two-thirds
provision, already noted) and the Ohio rule by Kansas.
Since the War, the Indiana rule has spread to the South-
west, including Mississippi, and to West Virginia and Michigan—ten States in all; while the Ohio rule, narrowed, in
some cases, by the exclusion of certain classes of corporations, appears in twelve Northern States, and in three
Southern.[1]

[1] The above is the best digest the writer can give of provisions which
vary much among themselves. The original Indiana rule runs: " Corporations, other than banking, shall not be created by special act, but
may be formed under general laws." In the following States the same
mild rule, in slightly varying language, has appeared from the beginning: Iowa, West Virginia, California, Mississippi, Utah, and Oklahoma. Mississippi supplements the rule by an express declaration, borrowed from its neighbor Arkansas (*vide infra*), that " The Legislature shall have power to alter, amend or repeal any charter . . . that
may hereafter be created."

In Ohio, on the other hand, the more stringent rule appeared: " The
Legislature shall pass no special act conferring corporate powers." Virtually identical provisions have been adopted by Kansas, Nebraska (until
1875), Wisconsin, New Jersey, Minnesota (until 1892), and Washington—
the latter State adding an express prohibition upon the *creation* of municipal corporations. Tennessee, however, in 1870, preferred the following language: " No corporation shall be created, or its powers increased
or diminished, by special laws"; and Illinois, in the same year: " No
corporation shall be created by special laws, or its charter extended,
changed or amended"; and provisions similar to the latter have since
been adopted in Pennsylvania, Nebraska, Louisiana, Minnesota, Kentucky, South Dakota and Alabama. In Illinois, Nebraska, and South
Dakota, however, the provision does not apply to corporations " for
charitable, educational, penal, or reformatory purposes"—*i. e.* certainly not to incorporated school districts; in Louisiana it does not
apply to the organization of levee districts, or parishes, or to New
Orleans, or (since 1898) to any municipal corporation containing as
many as 2,500 inhabitants; in Wisconsin it does not apply to cities;
so also in Minnesota until 1892; and in Alabama it does not apply to
alterations in the boundaries of cities, towns or villages.

Arkansas and Missouri, finally, have to a certain extent changed
places. Arkansas, adopting the original Ohio rule in 1868, re-enacted it

Now, what is a " general " law?   May the intent of the

in 1874 with the limitation reserving to the Legislature the power of
amendment, that Mississippi, later, with less apparent reason, adopted.
At the same time Arkansas excepted charitable, educational, etc., corporations. Missouri, on the other hand, started in 1865 with the Indiana provision, modified by a special rule in regard to large cities. In
1875, however, it came over to the stringent rule in its usual, later
form. This shift of policy between two contiguous States, taken
together with the exceptions made in Louisiana and Alabama, accen-
tuates the tendency of Northern States to impose greater restrictions
upon the Legislature than do the Southern or Southwestern.

The enactment of these general laws is obligatory in Iowa, West
Virginia and Mississippi—in Tennessee, Illinois, Wisconsin, Nebraska,
Minnesota, South Dakota and Alabama.

References:

Ind. Const. 1851, xi, 13.
Ia. Const. 1857, viii, 1.
Mo. Const. 1865, viii, 4, 5 (until 1875).
W. Va. Const. 1872, xi, 1.
Ark. Const. 1874, xii, 2, 6.
Cal. Const. 1879, xii, 1 ; xi, 6.
Miss. Const. 1890, 88, 178.
Utah Const. 1895, xii, 1 ; xi, 5.
Okla. Const. 1907, xviii, 1.
* Mich. Const. 1908, xii, 1, 6.
* Ariz. Const. 1911, xiii, 1.

Ohio Const. 1851, xiii, 1.
Kans. Const. 1859, xii, 1.
Neb. Const. 1866, " Corporations," 1 ; 1875, xi, " Misc. Corps.," 1.
Ark. Const. 1868, v, 48 (until 1874) .
Tenn. Const. 1870, xi, 8.
Ill. Const. 1870, xi, 1.
Wisc. Am. * 1871, iv, 31.
Pa. Const. 1873, iii, 7.
N. J. Am. 1875, iv, 7, par. 11.
Mo. Const. 1875, iv, 53; xii, 2.
La. Const. 1879, 46; 1898, 48.
Minn. * Am. 1881, iv, 33, 34; 1892, iv, 33.
S. D. Const. 1889, xvii, 1 ; x, 1.
Wash. Const. 1889, ii, 28, par. 6; xi, 10.
Ky. Const. 1890, 59, par. 17.
Ala. Const. 1901, 104, pars. 6, 18, and concl.

preceding provisions be evaded, either by passing special in the guise of general legislation, or by the device of classification? To their lists of enumerated cases (including treatment of corporations) in which special legislation was forbidden, Pennsylvania, in 1873, followed by Missouri, two years later, added the requirement, " Nor shall the General Assembly indirectly enact such special or local law, by the partial repeal of a general law; but laws repealing local or special acts may be passed." [1] Minnesota, for a time, also adopted the saving provision in the following words: " But the Legislature may repeal any existing special law relating to the foregoing subdivisions." [2] The distinction between generality and universality, again, first appears in West Virginia, in 1872, in the requirement that laws providing for the organization of corporations shall be " uniform as to the class to which they relate " [3]; it was not until 1889, however, that a safeguard against the abuse of the classification device appears in the South Dakota and Wyoming requirement that " The Legislature shall provide by general laws for the organization and classification of municipal corporations. The number of such classes shall not exceed four, and the powers of each class shall be defined by general laws, so that no corporation shall have any powers, or be subject to any restrictions, other than those of all corporations of the same class." The same provision (but without limitation of the number of classes) was adopted by South Carolina, in 1895. Its applicability to the determination of municipal boundaries is by no means clear, especially in Wyoming and South Carolina, where

[1] Pa. Const. 1873, iii, 7.
   Mo. Const. 1875, iv, 53.
[2] * Minn. Am. 1881, iv, 33 (until. 1892).
[3] W. Va. Const. 1872, xi, 1.

special legislation affecting municipalities is not otherwise forbidden.[1]

(d) *Simple Referendum*

A Referendum, in the original and better sense of the term, is the invoking of popular action in addition to, and as a check upon, the powers over the subject matter normally possessed by the Legislature. County Referenda, as we shall see, had been invoked for boundary purposes for many years, and other local Referenda were also commonly required for particular purposes, before Wyoming, in 1889, provided that " No municipal corporation shall be organized without the consent of the majority of the electors residing within the district proposed to be incorporated."[2]

(e) *Freedom from Legislative control*

Even before this Wyoming provision, an effort had been made in Missouri to free the charters of the larger cities from all Legislative control. This movement culminated, in Oregon, in 1906, in the broad provision, " The legislative assembly shall not enact, amend or repeal any charter or act of incorporation, for any municipality, city or town"; nor in the case of municipalities other than cities or towns, was even any substitute for Legislative action provided. Oklahoma, the year following, did not go quite so far. Although wide privileges in the adoption of local charters are here accorded to cities, the Legislature is not debarred from chartering them, in default of local action; nor is the requirement extended to municipal corporations in general. For the *amendment* of their charters, however, the inhabitants of all municipal corporations, however adopted, have

[1] S. D. Const. 1889, x, 1.
Wyom. Const. 1889, xiii, 1.
S. C. Const. 1895, viii, 1.
[2] Wyom. Const. 1889, xiii, 2.

the privilege of a 25 per cent initiative petition proposing
an amendment, which becomes a part of the charter after a
majority vote and approval by the Governor—the latter
being obligatory, if there is no conflict with the Constitution
and laws of the State.[1]

2. OTHER RULES INCIDENTALLY AFFECTING LOCAL BOUNDARIES

The gradual development of several of the preceding provisions into rules affecting not only corporations, but all
topics of a private or local character, is an interesting study
in comparative constitutional enactment. The points of departure are the Pennsylvania single bill rule of 1838; the
Rhode Island deferred action rule of 1842; the Indiana
general bill rule of 1851; the Pennsylvania interpreting rule
of 1873; and the Wyoming Referendum rule of 1889[2]

(a) Extension of the single bill rule of 1838

Pennsylvania, as we have seen, had provided that no law
should create, renew or extend the charter of more than
one corporation. Within eight years Rhode Island, New
Jersey and New York adopted new instruments. Rhode
Island, we saw, preferred to require notice until after a

---

[1] Oreg. Am. 1906, xi, 2.
Okla. Const. 1907, xviii, 4.
There can be little doubt that these corporation provisions were
never intended to relate to any political divisions other than urban
districts. It has seemed best, however, to distinguish between those
which are applicable only to urban districts, in terms, and those which,
on their face, have a broader application—if only to emphasize the confusion of Constitutional analysis and terminology. For provisions
applicable, in terms, to urban districts, instead of to corporations, or
to municipal corporations, *vide* ch. iv, sec. i, pp. 77-88, *infra*.

[2] It is not intended by this method of treatment to convey the impression that the corporation provisions were the origin of the later
and broader provisions—merely that they are important landmarks
in the development of these latter.

fresh election; but New Jersey pushed the Pennsylvania idea to its logical extreme, by providing that, " To avoid improper influences which may result from intermixing in one and the same act such things as have no proper relation to each other, *every* law shall embrace but one object, and that shall be expressed in the title [1]—a provision which has since been copied in many States, including Pennsylvania itself, and which, as establishing a rule of legislative procedure in any and all cases, carries us outside the bounds of our present enquiry. Its interest for us lies in the modification which New York two years later introduced. With the same moderation which distinguished this State in its treatment of corporations, as such, New York singled out the real evil attendant upon the passage of " omnibus " bills, and enacted the New Jersey provision in the following limited, but far more effective form: " No *private or local* bill, which may be passed by the Legislature, shall embrace more than one subject, and that shall be expressed in the title." This single bill provision, which represents the earliest generalized treatment of special legislation, still survives in this State, and was introduced into Wisconsin (in which it is the only such treatment) two years later.[2]

While this provision is doubtless effective as against " omnibus " bills, it does not meet the evil of special riders to general bills; nor can the original New Jersey restriction of bills to one " object " have any effect in preventing a discriminating treatment of localities, under the guise of general legislation. California, accordingly, the year after Wisconsin, adopted the following provision: " All laws of a general nature shall have a uniform operation "—a rule which has since spread into several Western States, and

[1] N. J. Const. 1844, iv, 7, par. 4.
[2] N. Y. Const. 1846, iii, 16; 1894, iii, 16.
Wisc. Const. 1848, iv, 18.

after the War, to Florida, for a time, and to Georgia, permanently.[1] New Jersey also finally secured the same result in more precise language.[2]

Finally, in a few States, also in the West or extreme Southeast, this uniform operation rule was later introduced with weakened force, being no longer (unless by implication) a general rule of procedure, but only a safeguard against evasion of a rule prohibiting special legislation, and as such applicable only to enumerated topics. While in general the development has been from the enumerated topic outwards, in these States the circle returns upon itself. In the latest application of the rule to this purpose—in South Carolina—a proviso has also been added which would appear to take away all its meaning.[3]

[1] In Ohio, Kansas, Oklahoma, and (since 1877) Georgia, "uniform operation throughout the State". The first Georgia provision was carelessly drawn.

References:

Cal. Const. 1849, i, 11; 1879, i, 11.
Ohio Const. 1851, ii, 26.
Kans. Const. 1859, ii, 17.
Fla. Const. 1868, i, 12 (until 1885).
Ga. Const. 1868, i, 26; 1877, i, 4, par. 1.
N. D. Const. 1889, 11.
Wyom. Const. 1889, i, 34.
Utah Const. 1895, i, 24.
Okla. Const. 1907, v, 59.

[2] "No general law shall embrace any provision of a private, special or local character." N. J. Am. 1875, iv, 7, par. 4.

[3] "Nothing contained in this section shall prohibit the General Assembly from enacting special provisions in general laws." This is also the only State in which the words "throughout the State" are not added.

The rule affects local divisions as follows:

Indiana (Const. 1851, iv, 23), Nevada (Const. 1864, iv, 21), Florida (Const. 1885, iii, 21), designation of places of voting

Iowa (Const. 1857, iii, 30), incorporation of cities and towns.
Wisconsin (Am. 1871, iv, 32), incorporations in general.

(b) *Extension of the deferred action rule of 1842*

The Rhode Island rule had no imitators until 1873, when Pennsylvania, generalizing its own single bill rule into the usual highly rarified form, set up alongside it the requirement that no local or special bill should be introduced without thirty days prior notice " in the locality where the matter or the thing to be affected may be situated ". With some minor variations, this provision has since been adopted by New Jersey, and by eight Southern States, including Oklahoma. [1]

In one of these States—Florida—this is now the only general treatment of special legislation. In Georgia the

Minnesota (Am. 1881, iv, 34), incorporations in general, lines of districts in general, and designation of places of voting.

South Carolina (Const. 1895, iii, 34, par. 12), incorporating or changing the charters of cities, towns or villages; incorporating school districts.

[1] Twenty days notice in Alabama until 1901; since then, four weeks. Four weeks in Oklahoma. Sixty days in Florida. No period prescribed in New Jersey. In Alabama (since 1901) the notice must be in a paper published in the counties, if such exists; in Oklahoma, in a weekly paper published or circulated in the city or counties affected.

Evidence of the notice must in all cases exist. In Missouri and Louisiana, the notice must be recited in the act. In Alabama the emphatic declaration is made that, " The Courts shall pronounce void every special, private or local law which the Journals do not affirmatively show was passed in accordance with the provisions of this section."

References:
Pa. Const. 1873, iii, 8.
Ark. Const. 1874, v, 26.
Ala. Const. 1875, iv, 24; 1901, 106, 107.
Mo. Const. 1875, iv, 54.
Ga. Const. 1877, iii, 7, par. 16.
N. J. Am. 1875, iv, 7, par. 9.
Tex. Const. 1876, iii, 57.
La. Const. 1879, 48; 1898, 50.
Fla. Const. 1885, iii, 21.
Okla. Const. 1907, v, 32.

only other provision is one which may be considered an extension of this—the requirement of special committee procedure after introduction. This latter requirement has since been independently imposed in the contiguous State of Alabama, and in Virginia.[1]

(c) *Extension of the general bill rule of 1851*

The less stringent character of the Indiana, as contrasted with the Ohio, rule in regard to corporations, was not due to any distrust of the principle of checking special legislation by constitutional enactment. So far from this being the case, Indiana was the first State to make, in this same instrument of 1851, that long list of enumerated topics, concerning which special legislation is forbidden, which is now so familiar a feature of State Constitutions.[2] To this list it appended—the point which particularly concerns us here—the requirement that, " In all other cases where a general law can be made applicable, all laws shall be general, and of uniform operation throughout the State ". Similar provisions were adopted by Iowa and Kansas before the War, and since then this provision has become very widely diffused, so that something of the sort can now be found in thirty-three instruments.[3] The importance of the movement, it must be said, is not at all proportionate to its geographical extension. In several States the language clearly shows that the propriety of special legislation is a question for the

---

[1] In Georgia (Const. 1877, iii, 7, par. 15) a standing committee of the lower house, in which such legislation must originate, is organized. In Mississippi (Const. 1890, 89), committees of each house. In Virginia (Const. 1902, 51), a joint committee of the two houses.

[2] Ind. Const. 1851, iv, * 22.

[3] To the eleven States already cited (*vide* p. 23, note 1, *supra*) in which no provision affecting special legislation appears, add four more States on the borders of the Union: Wisconsin, Oregon, Louisiana. and (since 1885) Florida. All others have the provision.

Legislature itself to decide,[1] and this has also been the rule of construction adopted by the Courts in the doubtful instances. It is only in Missouri since 1875, in Minnesota since 1892, in Alabama since 1901, in Kansas since 1906, and in Michigan since 1908, that the question is expressly declared to be one for the Courts to determine.

Apart from this highly important addition to the rule, only two points need be considered in connection with this provision.

One is the fact that a few States, following Maryland in 1864, instead of forbidding special legislation where a general law can be made applicable, forbid special legislation where a general law already exists.[2]

[1] Texas (until 1876), New York, New Jersey, Maine, Mississippi, Virginia.

[2] Some confusion has been caused by this. The Maryland provision runs: "And the General Assembly shall pass no special law for any case for which provision has been made by an existing general law;" to which was added, both in 1864, and in 1867, a rather absurd provision requiring the passage of such laws at the first session after the adoption of the instrument. Georgia follows Maryland's major provision, with only verbal changes. Meanwhile Virginia (Const. 1850, iv, 35; 1870, v, 20), followed by Pennsylvania (Am. 1864, xi, 9), had developed a rule, appropriate to private legislation, in regard to the grant of powers and privileges; in 1872 West Virginia, followed the next year by Pennsylvania, fused this with the usual provision in language which, in the latter State, took the following form: "Nor shall any law be passed granting powers or privileges in any case where the granting of such powers and privileges shall have been provided for by general law, nor where the Courts have jurisdiction to grant the same or give the relief asked for"; and in 1890 this was adopted by Kentucky, *in addition* to the usual provision. Meanwhile, in 1875, Alabama, apparently under the Pennsylvania influence, provided that, "No special or local law shall be enacted for the benefit of individuals or corporations in cases which *are or can be* provided for by a general law, or where the relief sought can be given by any Court of this State"; and in 1890 Mississippi adopted this *in addition* to the usual provision. Finally, in 1901, Alabama changed this to the requirement that, "No special, private or local law, except a law fixing the time

The other is that the particular requirement for such laws that they shall be " of uniform operation throughout the State ", appears only in the three early instances of Indiana, Iowa, and Nevada, in Minnesota (north of Iowa), and (with the qualification which seems to rob it of all force) in South Carolina.[1]

of holding courts, shall be enacted in any case which *is* provided for by a general law, or where the relief sought, *etc."*

[1] The requirement of uniformity for *all* general laws appears, however, among these States, in California, Kansas, Florida (until 1885), Georgia, North Dakota, Wyoming, Utah and Oklahoma.

References:

Ind. Const. 1851, iv, 23.
Iowa Const. 1857, iii, 30.
Kans. Const. 1859, ii, 17; * Am. 1906.
Nev. Const. 1864, iv, 21.
Md. Const. 1864, iii, 32; 1867, iii, 33.
Mo. Const. 1865, iv, 27; 1875, iv, 53.
Fla. Const. 1868, v, 18 (until 1885).
Ill. Const. 1870, iv, 22.
W. Va. Const. 1872, vi, 39.
Tex. Am. * 1874, Const. 1876, iii, 56.
Pa. Const. 1873, iii, 7.
N. Y. Am. 1874, Const. 1894, iii, 18.
Ark. Const. 1874, v, 25.
Neb. Const. 1875, iii, 15.
N. J. Am. 1875, iv, 7, par. 11.
Maine Am. 1876.
Colo. Const. 1876, v, 25.
Ga. Const. 1877, i, 4, par. 1.
Cal. Const. 1879, iv, 25.
Mont. Const. 1889, v, 26.
N. D. Const. 1889, 70.
S. D. Const. 1889, iii, 23.
Wyom. Const. 1889, iii, 27.
Ky. Const. 1890, 59, 60.
Miss. Const. 1890, 87.
Minn. Am. * 1892, iv. 33.
S. C. Const. 1895, iii, 34.
Utah Const. 1895, vi, 26.
Ala. Const. 1901, 105, 110.

(d) *Extension of the interpreting rule of 1873*

We have seen that while in several States an already developed rule, requiring the uniform operation of general laws throughout the State, was seized upon as a convenient means of defining just what was meant by the insistence upon " general laws " for certain topics, in Pennsylvania and Missouri, on the other hand, a special, and quite different, rule of interpretation was made applicable, at the beginning, only to enumerated topics. This rule became later extended in an interesting manner.

The original provision, it will be recalled, consisted of two parts: a restriction; and a saving clause. When the restriction, providing that general laws might not be partially repealed, in such a way as indirectly to enact "such" special law, was adopted by Missouri, North Dakota, and Alabama, its position in the instrument was changed in such a way as to make it applicable, logically enough, to all proper subjects of general legislation, under the blanket provision just discussed. This is the first phase of the extension, and requires no comment.[2] When, however, Louisiana, in 1879,

Va. Const. 1902, 64.

Okla. Const. 1907, v, 59.

* Mich. Const. 1908, v, 30.

* N. Mex. Const. 1911, iv, 24.

* Ariz. Const. 1911, iv, 2, 19, par. 20.

[1] *Vide* sec. 1 (c), p. 30, *supra*.

[2] Local divisions are affected as follows:

Pennsylvania (Const. 1873, iii, 7), incorporations in general, lines of townships and boroughs in general, changing the lines of school districts, designation of places of voting.

Missouri (Const. 1875, iv, 53), the same, without reference to boroughs.

North Dakota (Const. 1889, 69, 70), incorporating or changing the charters of cities, towns and villages; designation of places of voting.

Alabama (Const. 1901, 105), only as they fall within the (peculiar) blanket provision.

adopting the same provision, omitted the word " such ", its character became entirely changed. In lieu of a mere safeguard against evasion, applicable only to certain subjects, it became an absolute rule of procedure, applicable, like the rule of notice, to all subjects. Kentucky, in 1890, added another link in the chain of development by prohibiting the Legislature also from " exempting from the operation of a general act any city, town, district or county "; Alabama, in 1901, provided independently that " No bill introduced as a general law shall be so amended on its passage as to become a special, private or local law "; finally, Virginia, the year following, provided that " the amendment or partial repeal [of a general law] shall not operate directly or indirectly to enact, and shall not have the effect of the enactment, of a special, private or local law "[1] Thus, by a curiously roundabout route, we reach Southern rules of general procedure very closely resembling, if not identical with, the Western rule of uniform operation.

Similarly with the saving clause, " but laws repealing local or special acts may be passed ". In Missouri and North Dakota this has become applicable at least to the blanket provision;[2] in Louisiana and Kentucky it has a general application, for what it is worth;[3] while in Minnesota

[1] Some such rule is desirable, of course, to protect the "notice" or "committee" rule from evasion. This excuse for its existence does not exist, however, in Kentucky.

References:

La. Const. 1879, 47 ; 1898, 49.

Ky. Const. 1890, 60.

Ala. Const. 1901, 111.

Va. Const. 1902, 64.

[2] Mo. Const. 1875, iv, 53.

N .D. Const. 1889, 70.

[3] La. Const. 1879, 47 ; 1898, 49.

Ky. Const. 1890, 60.

and Alabama it has received a special development of its own. Minnesota was so anxious to emphasize the fact that the license to repeal special acts is not to be construed as a license to amend them, that—inadvertently perhaps—it dropped, in 1892, the words " relating to the foregoing subdivisions," and thus stumbled upon a brand-new definition of a type of special legislation which is forbidden: " The Legislature may repeal any existing special or local law, but shall not amend, extend or modify *any of the same* ".[1] Alabama, on the other hand, has introduced the refinement that *special legislation repealing or modifying special legislation* is permissible only under the prescribed rules for notice. [2]

These absurd quibbles simply illustrate the inadequacy of this entire treatment of the administrative problem.

(e) *Extension of the Referendum rule of 1889*

The logical extreme of the tendency to demand Referenda, in particular types of districts, upon particular topics of legislative action, would be to require that the Legislature shall enact no law whatsoever, specially affecting any locality of any sort, without submitting it to the voters of the locality in question. This extreme step has been taken, very recently, by Michigan.[3] In Ohio, on the other hand, the extension of the Referendum is perhaps forbidden in the following words: " Nor shall any act, except such as relate to public schools, be passed, to take effect upon the approval of any other authority than the General Assembly, except as otherwise provided in the Constitution of this

---

[1] Minn. Am. * 1892, iv, 33.

[2] Ala. Const. 1901, 107.

[3] * Mich. Const. 1908, v, 30.

State." [1]   Oregon, however, adopting this provision in
1857, added to it this significant proviso: " Provided, That
laws . . . submitting town and city corporate acts and
other local and special laws may take effect or not, upon a
vote of the electors interested." [2]   In the other States the
Ohio provision does not occur, so that there can be no
doubt as to the competency of the Legislature to introduce
local Referenda whenever it pleases; while even in Ohio
it is certainly free to ascertain the sense of the community
before passing the measure.

Furthermore, in the general movement for more direct
popular government which has latterly swept over several
Western States, and of which the old-fashioned Referendum
provisions may be considered as the premonitory symptom,
there has developed, as is well known, an Initiative-Referendum privilege of the whole State as against the Legislature, the essence of which is, first, that a Referendum may
be demanded upon any measure, by a petition signed by a
certain per cent of the voters; and second, that by a similar
petition measures may be directly framed, and submitted
over the head, so to speak, of the Legislature.   By an easy
analogy, this device has come to be applied in a few States
to all local divisions, against their own local authorities at
least; and sometimes even against the Legislature.   As would
naturally be expected of a scheme the immediate origin of
which is not so much the negative one, of checking the Legislature, as the positive one, of putting all possible power
in the hands of the people, this device is thus in some ways
less extreme, in other ways more extreme, than the old-
fashioned obligatory Referendum, pushed, as in Michigan, to

[1] Ohio Const. 1851, ii, 26. Section 30 imposes a Referendum upon
changes of county lines (*vide* ch. iii, 1(b), 2(b), *infra*). Query: Is a
popular electorate an " authority"?

[2] Oreg. Const. 1857, i, 22.

its logical conclusion. It is less extreme, in that in the absence of a petition no Referendum occurs. It is more extreme, in that it provides a means whereby the authority against which it is directed may be not only checked, but superseded. As with some of the provisions already discussed, the bearing of all this, upon the exterior boundaries of districts, is somewhat remote. To possible subdivision of these districts, however, whether by the local authorities or by the Legislature, these provisions apply directly.

Six States have adopted provisions of this sort: Utah, for " any legal subdivision of the State "; Oregon, for " every municipality and district "; Oklahoma, for " every municipal corporation," and " every county and district "; Maine, for municipalities; Arkansas, for " each municipality," and " each county "; Colorado, for " every city, town and municipality ". Utah voters, " or such fractional part thereof as may be provided by law ", exercise their powers " under such conditions, and in such manner, and within such time as may be provided by law ", and no legal provision has in fact been made. In Maine the establishment of a uniform method is optional with the Legislature. In the four other instances the Legislature is required to pass general laws upon the subject, or details are placed within the competence of other organs, or are defined outright in the Constitution. In Oregon, Arkansas and Colorado the privilege seems to be accorded even against the Legislature.[1]

---

[1] The Oregon and Colorado reservation of powers to the people applies to " all local, special and municipal legislation, *of every character,* in and for their respective municipalities and districts." In Arkansas, the people of the localities are empowered to act " as independent of the legislative assembly." For details as to per cent. of voters, *etc., vide* ch. iv, sec. i, 6, pp. 87-8, *infra.*

References:

Utah Am. 1900, vi, I, par. 2.

Oregon. Am. 1906, iv, 1a.

Finally, in strong contrast with the preceding, New Mexico not only does not extend its Referendum provision to the people of the localities, but excludes from the operation of its general Referendum local or special laws—a very suggestive distinction.[1]

(f) *The Tennessee authorization of judicial control*

While in the Far West the tendency is to develop popular and local checks upon the Legislature, to the point even of displacing legislative control over localities, in Tennessee, on the other hand—the original home of the county Referendum—no such development has occurred. Instead, a peculiar provision survives from the period when the Judiciary was considered the natural arbiter of local affairs, and State Legislatures had not begun that policy of minute administrative control which has called forth elaborate checks and restrictions. As early as 1798 Georgia had required the Legislature to vest control over certain enumerated topics in the Courts. Since 1834, Tennessee, extending this idea, has broadly authorized its Legislature to " vest such powers in the courts of justice, with regard to private or local affairs, as may be deemed expedient ".[2]

3. SUMMARY

The preceding provisions are the unfortunate outcome of an interesting chain of events. The notion that the Legislature shall confine itself to acts of general application is a not unnatural one in itself, and receives an additional stimu-

---

Okla. Const. 1907, v, 5; xviii, 4.

* Me. Am. 1908, iv, part iii, 21.

* Ark. Am. 1910, v, 1.

* Colo. Am. 1910, v, 1.

1 * N. Mex. Const. 1911, iv, 1.

2 Tenn. Const. 1834, xi, 8; 1870, xi, 9. *Cf.* Ga. Const. 1798, i, 26; 1868, iii, 6, par. 5; 1877, iii, 7, par. 18.

lus from the theory of the separation of powers. The application of governmental powers to particular instances, however, is of the very essence of government, and has to be performed by somebody. In the English system of government these powers, so far as not absorbed by an encroaching Parliament, were exercised by the Crown. At the time of the Revolution, the prejudice against the Colonial Governor led to the reduction of the Executive into an officer of enumerated powers. In addition to the few special functions —such as the granting of pardons—which he might perform, and to the functions of the Courts in applying the civil and criminal law, there remained a broad field of administrative activity for which no constitutional organ was provided. The Legislature, therefore, as the organ of residuary powers, was obliged either to complete the work of the Convention, and provide such organ or organs, or to exercise these powers itself. It chose the latter as the simpler and more congenial course.

Now, a Legislature is not apt to perform acts of injustice as between man and man. But as a nursery of special privilege, or injustice as between an individual and the rest of the State, nothing better could have been devised than free Legislative action. The private interest, which is benefited much, influences its local representative directly; the rest of the citizens do not receive any remarkable injury, and have no one upon whom to bring pressure, even if they do remark it. Two representatives, each with a grateful constituent to please, indulge, between themselves, in the friendly game of " log-rolling ", which seems to benefit everybody, including themselves, and to hurt no one. In other words, the lack of any administrative organization worked so badly that in time the public woke up to the evils of the situation. Instead, however, of providing, through the Constitution, for an organization to take the place of the Legislature, attempts were made to utilize this body still, either by compelling it to pass special acts only under special restrictions; or, more commonly, by forbidding it to make special applications itself, but authorizing or requiring it to devise an organization which might make them. This task of completing the political structure, by the creation of multitudinous " Boards ", the Legislature has zealously pursued, and is still pursuing. To some extent, of late, these Boards have been placed upon a Constitutional basis, but the limited extent to which this has been done is a clear case of abdication, by the Convention, of its normal functions, and is a measure of our laggardness in conceiving, as a whole, the important problem of administrative organization.

Criticism of the Legislature's own contributions to the solution of this problem does not belong here. It may be said, however, that the attitude taken by the Courts in construing the meaning of the term " special legislation " has resulted in making this class of provisions perhaps the least satisfactory in the whole field of Constitutional law; and that their general phrasing, in terms which, on their face, require a general law for the rectification even of a local boundary, has no justification in common sense, but is a mere incident of ill-considered drafting.

CHAPTER III

The County

THE county has been all but universal in the States. Introduced at an early date into almost all the Colonies, and into almost all the United States territories from which later States were formed, it has been more uniformly utilized, at least as a judicial area, than any other territorial division. In Massachusetts, Connecticut and Rhode Island it rested upon only a statutory basis until the surviving Charters of these States were superseded by formal Constitutions.[1] In South Carolina, before the Civil War, the ancient county divisions seem to have been utilized chiefly as a means of identifying parishes lying within the same;[2] " Judicial districts ", however, are mentioned in an amendment of 1828, and in 1868 the title of these was formally changed to " counties ".[3] In Louisiana, counties appear under this name only until 1845; the size and general treatment, however, of " parishes " since, justifying us in considering these as being, from the beginning, equivalent to counties. Since 1875, the larger Missouri cities may have the functions, without the name, of counties. California, finally, contained no counties prior to their mandatory establishment by the

---

[1] Passing references to the county may be found in the Massachusetts Charter of 1691. (Thorpe, pp. 1875, 1878.)

[2] Cf. S. C. Const. 1776, 11; 1778, 13; 1790, i, 3, 7. In 1778, however, (Const. 1778, 39), the whole State was required to be divided into counties and districts, and county courts established.

[3] S. C. Const. 1868, ii, 3.

Legislature. The only other exceptions to the uniform rule of the county has been in connection with the problem of providing for territory too sparsely settled to support county organizations.[1]

Express restrictions upon Legislative control over county lines first appeared in Tennessee in 1796. As late as 1820 they were found in the instruments of only half a dozen Western States. Since then, they have been somewhat slowly introduced into old States as well as new, until now they exist in thirty-seven States in all, the exceptions being the six New England States, New Jersey, Delaware, North Carolina, Nevada and Arizona.[2]

I. CREATION OF NEW COUNTIES

Restrictions upon the creation of new counties were the first to develop. These may be classified into three broad groups: First, direct limitations upon the result to be attained in the creation of new counties, including prescriptions in regard to the area, population, or amount of taxable property to be included. Second, rules as to the manner in which the power to create new counties is to be exercised, including particularly the requirement of an extraordinary majority in the Legislature, or of a local Initiative or Referendum. Third, absolute prohibition upon the creation of new counties.

(a) *Direct limitations*

Beginning with Tennessee in 1796, a minimum area was mentioned in all new States before the War except Maine, Florida, Wisconsin and California; and in six of the States admitted subsequently. Michigan dropped the restriction in 1850, but since then, it has been extended also to Virginia,

---

[1] *Vide* ch. v, sec. ii, pp. 101 *et seq., infra.*

[2] Indirectly, the number of counties in New Jersey is limited to 60 (N. J. Const. 1844, iv, 3).

to the three States to the north and west of this, and to
South Carolina.¹ The restriction has usually applied both
to the new county, and to the reduced county or counties
thereby resulting; not, however, in several States which
first adopted the provision between 1816 and 1850.² The

¹ Not introduced into Illinois until 1848; in Iowa until 1857; in
Nebraska until 1875. Not introduced into Louisiana until 1845, nor revived after the War until 1879.

References:

Tenn. Const. 1796, ix, 4; 1834, x, 4; 1870, x, 4.

Ohio Const. 1802, vii, 3; 1851, ii, 30.

Ind. Const. 1816, xi, 12; 1851, xv, 7.

Miss. Const. 1817, vi, 19; 1832, vii, 17; 1868, iv, 37; 1890, 260.

Ala. Const. 1819, vi, 16, 17; 1867, ii, 2; 1875, ii, 2; 1901, 39.

Mo. Const. 1820, iii, 34; Am. 1849, iii; Am. 1861; Const. 1865, iv,
31; 1875, ix, 3, 15, 23.

Mich. Const. 1835, xii, 7 (until 1850).

Ark. Const. 1836, iv, 29; Am. 1850; Am. 1859; Const. 1868, xv, 12;
1874, xiii, 1.

Tex. Const. 1845, vii, 34; 1868, xii, 24; 1876, ix, 1.

La. Const. 1845, 8; 1852, 8; 1879, 249; 1898, 277.

Ill. Const. 1848, vii, 1; 1870, x, 1.

Va. Const. 1850, iv, 34; 1870, v, 19; 1902, 61.

Pa. Am. 1857, xii; Const. 1873, xiii.

Iowa Const. 1857, xi, 2.

Minn. Const. 1857, xi, 1, 2.

Or. Const. 1857, xv, 6.

Kans. Const. 1859, ix, 1.

W. Va. Const. 1862, vii, 12; 1872, ix, 8.

Md. Const. 1864, x, 1; 1867, xiii, 1.

S. C. Const. 1868, ii, 3; 1895, vii.

Neb. Const. 1875, x, 1.

N. D. Const. 1889, 167.

S. D. Const. 1889, ix, 1.

Idaho Const. 1889, xviii, 4.

Ky. Const. 1890, 63.

Okla. Const. 1907, xvii, 4.

² In Missouri, Arkansas and in Texas since 1876, only to the new
county, and to counties established prior to the adoption of the instrument. In Michigan (until 1850) only to this last type of county. In
Indiana the requirement has consistently been applied only to the parent

most usual figure has been 400 square miles, running larger in the South, especially in the early years.[1] Exceptions to the general rule occur in several States,[2] and in two cases a maximum area is also mentioned.[3]

A later requirement, originating in New York in 1821, was that of a minimum population. In 1834 it was adopted

county. In Texas, until 1876, and in Pennsylvania until 1873, only to the new county.

In the case of old counties, the language is that they may not be reduced below the minimum. Indiana, since 1851, and West Virginia, until 1872, are the only States in which it is clearly stated that counties already below the minimum may not be further reduced.

[1] 400 square miles in Pennsylvania, Maryland, West Virginia, Kentucky, Ohio, Indiana, Illinois, Michigan, Minnesota, Nebraska, Idaho, Oklahoma and Oregon.

432 sq. m. in Iowa and Kansas.

600 sq. m. in Virginia.

625 sq. m. in Louisiana.

400 sq. m. in Missouri until 1849; 400 for old and 500 for new until 1865; then 500 for both until 1875; then 410.

576 sq. m. in Mississippi before the War; since, 400.

625 sq. m. in Tennessee until 1834; then 625 for old, and 350 for new until 1870; then 500 for old and 275 for new.

625 sq. m. in South Carolina, 1868-95; then 500 for old and 400 for new.

24 "Congressional Townships" (864 sq. m.) in the Dakotas.

900 sq. m. in Alabama and Arkansas before the War; then 600.

900 sq. m. in Texas until 1876; then 700 usually, the old figure being retained, however, for counties to be formed in territory not already organized.

[2] The most important exceptions are in Ohio, 1851 (rule not applicable in the division of counties containing over 100,000 inhabitants), and in Minnesota, 1857, and Missouri, 1875 (rule not applicable in the erection of cities into counties). In Texas, since 1876, border counties may be erected under size. Special cases excepted in Tenn. since 1834; Ark. 1836-50, and cf. Am. 1859; Va. since 1850; Iowa since 1857; Mo. 1861-65, and since 1875 (City of St. Louis); Ala. since 1901.

[3] Mississippi, 1868-90, min. 400, max. 625, for both old and new counties. Texas since 1876, min. 700, max. 900, for new counties, in territory already organized.

by Tennessee, and since then has spread pretty generally
through the South and Far West, and to Pennsylvania—
usually in combination with the area provision.[1]   In the
middle West it has appeared only as a special provision for
densely-populated sections, in the absence of, or as an exception to, the general rule for area.[2]   Louisiana, Arkansas and
Ohio present the only instances before the War of the application of the rule to both the new and the parent county;

---

[1] The only States in which a general limitation of population has been
imposed, without the limitation af area, are New York, Florida, California, Washington and Wyoming.

The requirement was not revived in Florida after the War; nor in
Arkansas until 1874; nor in Louisiana until 1879.   It appeared in Texas
only between 1868 and 1876.

References:

N. Y. Const. 1821, i, 7; 1846, iii, 5; 1894, iii, 5.
Tenn. Const. 1834, x, 4; 1870, x, 4.
Ark. Const. 1836, iv. 29; 1874, xiii, 1.
Fla. Const. 1838, ix, 4 (until the War).
La. Const. 1845, 8; 1852, 8; 1879, 249; 1898, 277.
Mo. Am. 1849, iii; Const. 1865, iv, 31; 1875, ix, 3.
Va. Const. 1850, iv, 34; 1870, v. 19; 1902, 61.
Oreg. Const. 1857, xv, 6.
W. Va. Const. 1862, vii, 12; 1872, ix, 8.
Ala. Const. 1867, ii, 2; 1875, ii, 2; 1901, 39.
Tex. Const. 1868, xii, 24, 45 (until 1876).
Pa. Const. 1873, xiii.
Cal. Const. 1879, xi, 3.
N. D. Const. 1889, 167.
Wash. Const. 1889, xi, 3.
Wyom. Const. 1889, xii, 2.
Ky. Const. 1890, 64.
S. C. Const. 1895, vii, 3, 4.
Okla. Const. 1907, xvii, 4.

[2] Cities containing a minimum population may be erected into separate
counties in Michigan (Const. 1850, x, 2; * 1908, viii, 2) and Minnesota
(Const. 1857, xi, 2).

Counties containing 100,000 inhabitants may be divided, each part
to contain a minimum population, in Ohio (Const. 1851, ii, 30).

States newly adopting it since the War all apply it thus.[1] The original requirement, and the one most usually imposed before 1850, was that the county, to which the rule was applied, should not contain a number of inhabitants, or of electors, below that which would entitle it to one representative in the lower house. Tennessee and Texas required an absolute number of electors. The modern rule is an absolute number of inhabitants, ranging from 20,000 in Pennsylvania and the Middle West, to 1,000 in North Dakota.[2]

[1] In New York, Tennessee and Oregon, the requirement has consistently been applied only to the new counties; so also in Michigan and Minnesota (city-county). In Florida (until the War), in Missouri, 1849-65 and since 1875, and in Virginia, it has been applied only to the parent county. In Arkansas, and in Missouri, 1865-75, only to the new county, and to parent counties established prior to the adoption of the instrument.

West Virginia, until 1872, is the only case in which it is clearly stated that parent counties, already below the minimum, may not be reduced further.

Rule not applicable to special cases in Tennessee since 1834, in Virginia since 1850, and in Missouri, 1861-65.

[2] Ratio of representation in New York, Missouri and Alabama; in Florida, Arkansas and Louisiana, before the War; and in South Carolina for new counties.

350 electors in Tennessee, 1834-70; since then, 700. 150 electors in Texas, 1868-76.

20,000 inhabitants in Pennsylvania, and (under the special provisions in Michigan, Ohio and Minnesota. In 1908, however, the figure for Michigan city-counties was raised to 100,000.

15,000 in Oklahoma, and, for old counties, in South Carolina.

12,000 in Kentucky.

7,000 in Louisiana.

4,000 whites in Virginia, 1850, until the War, and counties containing less could be reduced one-fifth; 1870-1902, same, but 8,000 inhabitants; since 1902, 8,000 inhabitants only. 4,000 whites in West Virginia, 1862-72; since then, 6,000 inhabitants.

8,000 inhabitants for old counties, and 5,000 for new, in California.

5,000 in Arkansas.

2,000 in Washington.

Of other rules governing the location of county lines, the
most prevalent has been the requirement that the boundary of the new county shall not pass within a certain number of miles—most often ten—of an already established
county seat. Originating in Tennessee, in 1834, this requirement was copied by Illinois in 1848, and then not again
until Pennsylvania adopted it in 1873, since when it has
been taken up by eight Southern States, including California and Oklahoma. It has usually appeared in combination with both the preceding provisions.[1] In a few instances,
also, attempts have been made to secure square counties,[2] or
the recognition of already existing administrative or natural
boundaries.[3]

1,500 in Wyoming.
1,200 in Oregon.
1,000 in North Dakota.

[1] In Illinois and Texas, only in connection with the area provision.
In California, only in connection with the population provision.
   References:
Tenn. Const. 1834, x, 4 (twelve miles); 1870, x, 4 (eleven).
Ill. Const. 1848, vii, 1; 1870, x, 1 (ten miles).
Pa. Const. 1873, xiii (ten).
Ark. Const. 1874, xiii, 4 (ten).
Mo. Const. 1875, ix, 3 (ten).
Tex. Const. 1876, ix, 1 (twelve).
Cal. Const. 1879, xi, 3 (five).
Ky. Const. 1890, 63 (ten).
S. C. Const. 1895, vii, 5 (eight).
Ala. Const. 1901, 40 (seven).
Okla. Const. 1907, xvii, 4 (ten).
Special exceptions in Tennessee, Arkansas and Alabama.

[2] By Mo. Const. 1820, iii, 34, the minimum size for old counties was
"20 miles square". By an amendment adopted in 1849, "20 miles
square" or 500 square miles. This requirement lapsed in Missouri in
1865, but since 1876 new Texan counties, in territory not already ar-
ganized, must be square, except on the State borders (Tex. Const.
1876, ix, 1).

[3] Cities and towns may not be divided in those Ohio counties to
which the area restrictions do not apply (Const. 1851, ii, 30) nor in

Finally, most modern of all these direct limitations is a Wyoming provision, in 1889, supplementing the requirement of a minimum population, with that of a minimum amount of taxable property, in both the new and the reduced counties. The contiguous State of Idaho has since supplemented its area provision in this way; and South Carolina and Oklahoma have imposed this, in addition to all three other restrictions.[1]

(b) *Indirect limitations*

The rules affecting the manner in which the power to create new counties is to be exercised include several types of provisions with which we have already become acquainted —the requirement of a Referendum—of an extraordinary legislative majority—of general legislation—and also a few additional rules, of which the most important is an obligatory division of the debts of the old county.

The earliest and most widely diffused rule is the requirement of local action, in the shape either of an Initiative petition, a Referendum, or both. The original Tennessee instrument of 1796 contained, in addition to the requirement of a minimum area, the proviso that no new county should be formed except upon the petition of 200 free male inhabi-

---

any South Carolina county (Const. 1895, vii, 14). The population provisions of Michigan and Minnesota apply only to the erection of cities into counties. In South Dakota (Const. 1889, ix, 1) townships may not be divided; it is not clear whether the words " as near as may be " qualify this rule, or the stated minimum area. In North Dakota (Const. 1889, 167) natural boundaries are to be observed, " as nearly as may be ".

[1] Wyom. Const. 1889, xi, 3, $2,000,000 for new, $3,000,000 for old counties.

Idaho Am. * 1898, xviii, 4, $1,000,000 for both.

S. C. Const. 1895, vii, 3, 4, $1,500,000 for new, $2,000,000 for old counties.

Okla. Const. 1907, xvii, 4, $2,500,000 for both.

tants within the proposed boundaries. In 1834 this was
changed to the requirement of a majority Referendum in
that part of any old county proposed to be taken, to form
part or whole of a new county. For more than half a century Tennessee found no imitators. In 1848, however,
as an incident in the extreme democratic movement of the
time, Illinois required a majority of the *part,* and in addition
a majority Referendum of the entire old county. Since
then the movement has assumed three general forms. The
latter half of the Illinois idea—protection only to the old
county—spread rapidly throughout contiguous States to the
north and west—through Michigan and Ohio, to Pennsylvania, for a time—and, after the War, even to Louisiana.[1]
A Referendum only of the segregated section of the old
county, on the other hand, instead of a Referendum of the
entire old county, survived in Tennessee, and was established
after the War in several other Southern States, and in a few
Far Western.[2] And the full Illinois idea of a double protec-

---

[1] In Wisconsin, the provision applies, rather oddly, only to counties
actually containing an area of 900 square miles or less; in Michigan,
only to a reduction to less than sixteen surveyed townships (576 sq.
m.), or, until 1908, in case a city was to be set off as a separate county.
In Pennsylvania it applied only in case over one-tenth of the population was to be cut off.

References:
Wisc. Const. 1848, xiii, 7.
Mich. Const. 1850, x, 2; * 1908, viii, 2.
Ohio Const. 1851, ii, 30.
Pa. Am. 1857, xii (until 1873).
Minn. Const. 1857, xi, 1, 2.
Iowa Const. 1857, iii, 30.
Mo. Const. 1875, ix, 3, 20, 23.
La. Const. 1879, 250; 1898, 278.
N. D. Const. 1889, 168.
S. D. Const. 1889, ix, 1.

[2] Maryland, as early as 1851, *guaranteed* to a special district of one
county the privilege of becoming a separate county, after attaining a

tion—neither the advantages of union to be lost, nor the burdens of independence to be assumed, except by consent of the electors interested—has been imitated in a few scattered instances.[1] In occasional late instances more than a simple majority is required.[2] In almost every case this check is in

certain population, through a majority petition followed by a majority Referendum. This gave way, in 1864, to a general Referendum. So West Virginia, Arkansas, Wyoming, Utah and Oklahoma. Washington and Kentucky require the Initiative petition instead; South Carolina, both petition and Referendum.

In case parts of two or more counties are combined in forming a new one a Referendum is usually demanded in each part, as in Tennessee. In West Virginia, however, a Referendum only of the proposed new county is demanded. Maryland demands the consent of a majority of the voters in the whole of the new county *as well as* in each part; so also Wyoming, by virtue of the provision regarding municipal corporations, if this be held applicable; doubtless, however, affirmative majorities secured in all the parts would be construed as satisfying the general requirement, without the requirement of a second election.

References:

Tenn. Const. 1796, ix, 4; 1834, x, 4; 1870, x, 4.
Md. Const. 1851, viii; 1864, x, 1; 1867, xiii, 1.
W. Va. Const. 1872, ix, 8.
Ark. Const. 1874, xiii, 2.
Wash. Const. 1889, xi, 3.
Wyom. Const. 1889, xii, 2.
Ky. Const. 1890, 65.
Utah Const. 1895, xi, 3.
S. C. Const. 1895, vii, 1, 2.
Okla. Const. 1907, xvii, 4.

[1] Nebraska (Const. 1875, x, 2, 3) follows Illinois (Const. 1848, vii, 2, 4; 1870, x, 2, 3) in requiring a petition of the section and a Referendum of the entire old county. In Ohio (Const. 1851, ii, 30), where in general the county Referendum prevails, counties containing 100,000 inhabitants may be divided only after a Referendum in *both sections*. In Mississippi (Const. 1890, 260) the same requirement is imposed in the case of all counties, and in Michigan, of late, in case of the separation of a city-county (* Const. 1908, viii, 2).

[2] Two-thirds majority in Tennessee, since 1870, and in Louisiana

addition to one or more of the direct limitations already noted. [1]

The requirement of an extraordinary Legislative majority has been much less common. It originated in an Alabama provision of 1819, whereby county lines, in territory secured from the Indians, or by cession, should not, after having once been established, be later changed, except by a two-thirds vote of the Legislature. In 1867 the provision was given a general application in this State, and in the year following was adopted by the adjacent States of Georgia and Florida, but only until their next general Constitutional revision. Meanwhile, however, another Gulf State—Texas —had entered with a peculiar provision in regard to area: the prescribed minimum of 900 square miles applied absolutely only to the old county; a two-thirds Legislative majority was, however, required to create new counties below this figure. In 1876 this developed into a general requirement of a two-thirds majority, in addition, as in Alabama, to the direct limitations; by a curious reversal, however, of the original Alabama provision, it does *not* apply to territory that was not, in 1876, already organized into counties. [2]

The next restriction that developed was one designed to remedy the injustice of the common-law rule that, where the

since 1898. 60 per cent in Oklahoma. Two-thirds, following a petition of one-third, in South Carolina.

It should be noted also that the majority of legal voters required in Washington and Kentucky, for the Initiative petition, represents a larger figure, as well as a more difficult process, than the simple majority of those voting which is required in a Referendum.

[1] Wisconsin and Utah are the only exceptions.

[2] Ala. Const. 1819, vi, 17; 1867, ii, 2; 1875, ii, 2; 1901, 39.
Ga. Const. 1868, iii, 5 (until 1877).
Fla. Const. xiv (until 1885).
Tex. Const. 1845, vii, 34; 1868, xii, 24; 1876, ix, 1.

Legislature makes no regulation, " the old corporation owns all the public property within her new limits, and is responsible for all debts contracted by her before the act of separation was passed ". This movement originated, like most of these county rules, in Tennessee and Illinois, the former State requiring in 1870 that the segregated sections should " continue liable for their pro rata of all debts contracted by their respective counties prior to the separation, and be entitled to their proportion of any stocks or credits belonging to such old counties "; while Illinois, in the same year, provided that they should be liable for their " proportion of the indebtedness ", merely. A similar requirement as to debts has since been adopted by fifteen other Western or Southern States (including two doubtful cases [1]), of which Louisiana and Oklahoma are the only ones to provide also for a division of assets. Most of these, beginning with Missouri in 1875, have preferred to impose the liability upon the new county (which may be composed of sections of several old ones),[2] and two of the later States have defined the rule of apportionment with precision.[3]

[1] North Dakota and Idaho.

[2] Nebraska, Texas, Idaho and Kentucky are the only States to follow the original rule in this respect.

[3] Nebraska, Texas and Kentucky follow Illinois in providing that the section shall assume " its proportion of the indebtedness ". Missouri, Colorado and Idaho speak of a " ratable proportion ". California, Louisiana and South Carolina use the term " just "; Wyoming and North Dakota, " equitable ".

Florida provides that " Every newly established county shall be held liable for its proportion of the existing liabilities of the county or counties from which it shall be formed, rated upon the basis of the assessed value of the property, both real and personal, subject to taxation within the territory taken from any county or counties."

Washington, to the requirement of a " just proportion ", adds the words: " Provided, That in such accounting neither county shall be charged with any debt or liability then existing, incurred in the purchase of any county property or in the purchase or construction of any

A provision looking toward generality of action in the
erection of new counties was first adopted for counties by
Pennsylvania in 1873, and since then in Minnesota and several Far Western States. This provision has usually been
identical with, or included in the terms of, a provision in the
same State affecting corporations or municipal corporations.
Fresh matter is included in the Oklahoma provision, however, and in several States the location of the two provisions,
as well as the circumstances that in California the one relating to counties was inserted by special amendment a quarter

county buildings then in use or under construction, which shall fall
within and be retained by the county; Provided further, That this shall
not be construed to affect the rights of creditors."

Montana provides that the new county "shall be held to pay its
ratable proportion of all then existing liabilities of the county or counties from which it is formed, less the ratable proportion of the value
of the county buildings and property of the county or counties from
which it is formed."

Oklahoma does not in terms impose a liability, but requires the
Legislature to provide for "the equitable division of assets and liabilities."

References:
Tenn. Const. 1870, x, 4.
Ill. Const. 1870, x, 3.
Neb. Const. 1875, x, 3.
Mo. Const. 1875, ix, 3.
Colo. Const. 1876, xiv, 4.
Tex. Const. 1876, ix, 1.
Cal. Const. 1879, xi, 3.
La. Const. 1879, 252; 1898, 280.
Fla. Const. 1885, viii, 3.
Wyom. Const. 1889, xii, 2.
Wash. Const. 1889, xi, 3.
N. D. Const. 1889, 168.
Mont. Const. 1889, xvi, 3.
Idaho Const. 1889, xviii, 3.
Ky. Const. 1890, 65.
S. C. Const. 1895, vii, 6.
Okla. Const 1907, xvii, 4.

of a century after that relating to municipalities, throws doubt upon the applicability to counties of the more general provision. [1] In Pennsylvania the provision replaced a previously required Referendum. In California also, the Referendum provision does not occur. In the other States, however, both are present. [2]

Quite recently, two fresh developments have occurred, both in connection with the Referendum. South Carolina, in 1895, provided that elections upon the question of forming the same proposed new county should not be held oftener than once in four years; this idea was directly suggested by the provision regarding the location of county seats, about to be discussed, but finds its ultimate origin in provisions limiting the frequency of Legislative apportion-

[1] On the other hand, it will be recalled that Louisiana (Const. 1879, 46; 1898, 48) takes care expressly to exclude the organization of parishes from the operation of its corporation provision.

[2] In Pennsylvania, Minnesota and Utah, special legislation is forbidden, fortified, in Pennsylvania, by the prohibition of partial repeal of a general law, and in Minnesota, by the obligation to pass general laws. In the Dakotas, Wyoming and Oklahoma there is an obligation to pass general laws, without express prohibition of special legislation as well; in California, only an authorization to pass general laws. The Utah prohibition applies in terms only to the separation of territory from an already organized county. The Oklahoma requirement of general action covers not merely the creation of new counties but "the equitable division of assets and liabilities and the original location of county seats in such new counties"—the intent doubtless being that a single act shall embrace all these topics.

References:

Pa. Const. 1873, iii, 7.

N. D. Const. 1889, 167.

S. D. Const. 1889, ix, 1.

Wyom. Const. 1889, xii, 2.

Minn. * Am. 1892, iv, 33.

Cal. Am. 1894, xi, 3.

Utah Const. 1895, xi, 3.

Okla. Const. 1907, xvii, 4.

ment or Constitutional revision.[1] And both South Carolina and Oklahoma provide that the Referendum shall be taken upon more than the single question of boundary.[2]

In another, less direct way, also, did several of the preceding types of provisions become involved with the location of county lines. It will be recalled that in several States the new county line was not permitted to be drawn within a certain number of miles of an established county seat. What, however, was to prevent the Legislature from removing the court house of the old county? Tennessee, in 1834, met this situation by requiring a two-thirds majority of the Legislature to effect such a removal. Illinois next, in 1848, required instead a simple Referendum on the part of the county. Tennessee, then, in 1870, adopted a two-thirds Referendum, in addition to its original provision, this being the only instance in which local action and extraordinary Legislative majority are coupled in connection with county lines; while Illinois, in the same year, supplemented its Referendum requirement by provisions limiting the frequency of elections, and forbidding special legislation! Pennsylvania, three years later, contented itself with the " special " provision. All later States in which the location of the county seat affects the determination of county lines demand a Referendum for its removal, including even Texas and Alabama, where the extraordinary Legislative

[1] S. C. Const. 1895, vii, 2.

[2] In South Carolina, the question of county seat and name; in Oklahoma, " every question " (whatever this means—at least, questions of county seat and division of assets and liabilities).

It is worth noting that although the same majority is required for these questions as for the separation of territory—two-thirds, in South Carolina, and 60 per cent in Oklahoma—this majority needs to be attained only in the proposed county as a whole—not in each section separated from an old county. (S. C. Const. 1895, vii, 1, 2. Okla. Const. 1907, xvii, 4.)

majority would be more consistent with the general policy
in regard to counties. Most of the States demand a two-
thirds vote in the Referendum.[1] Most limit the frequency
of elections.[2] Most forbid special legislation,[3] and a few
positively demand general legislation as well.[4] In Oklahoma, where the required general legislation is written into
the Constitution, an Initiative petition of 25 per cent of the
voters calls the election, and a petition of 300 voters places
the name of a town, city or place upon the official ballot.[5]

[1] Simple majority in Illinois, Arkansas and Alabama, except that in
Illinois, since 1870, a three-fifths vote is required to remove the county
seat away from the center. Simple majority in Texas to remove it
from a point more than five miles from the center as " determined
by a certificate from the commissioner of the central land office ", to
a point within this radius. Two-thirds vote required in Texas to remove it if already within this radius, and in the other six States in
all cases.

Oklahoma provides a repeated election between the two highest, in
case no place receives two-thirds.

[2] Not oftener than once in ten years in Illinois, since 1870, and in
Oklahoma; five years in Missouri and South Carolina; four years in
California and Alabama; no limitation in Tennessee, Kentucky, Arkan-
sas and Texas.

[3] All except Tennessee, Arkansas and South Carolina.

[4] Missouri, Texas, Alabama and Oklahoma.

[5] Permanent special exceptions occur in Tennessee only.

References (not including States where similar provisions, by fixing
one spot in each county, affect, very distantly, legislative control over
county boundaries) :

Tenn. Const. 1834, x, 4; 1870, x, 4.

Ill. Const. 1848, vii, 5; 1870, iv, 22; x, 4.

Pa. Const. 1873, iii, 7.

Ark. Const. 1874, xiii, 3.

Mo. Const. 1875, v, 53; ix, 2.

Tex. Const. 1876, iii, 56; ix, 2.

Cal. Const. 1879, iv, 25; xi, 2.

Ky. Const. 1890, 59, 64.

S. C. Const. 1895, vii, 8.

Ala. Const. 1901, 41, 104.

Okla. Const. 1907, v, 46; xvii, 6.

(c) *Prohibition*

We have already seen that the Alabama-Texas rule, requiring, in place of a Referendum, an extraordinary Legislative majority for the creation of new counties, existed for a time in Florida and Georgia. In Florida the provision was abolished, leaving no restriction upon counties other than the carefully-drawn rule in regard to division of liabilities. In Georgia a development in the opposite direction occurred, the Constitution of 1877 providing that, " No new county shall be created." In 1904, however, this was changed to a prescription of a maximum number of counties.[1]

2. CHANGES OF BOUNDARY BETWEEN EXISTING COUNTIES

In New York, Michigan and West Virginia county provisions are applicable only in the process of creating new counties. In the remaining thirty-three States in which such provisions exist, the general tendency, since the middle of the century, has been to extend their application, with such modifications as the case demanded, also to changes of boundary between existing counties. As early as 1819, Alabama's requirement of an extraordinary Legislative majority (in territory subsequently to be acquired) referred to alterations of boundary, in general. Then in 1838 the framers of the instrument under which Florida, seven years later, was admitted, phrased their population provision in language which can be construed to refer to any reduction of an existing county. Iowa, in 1846, adopted an area provision which, in terms, applies only to mere changes of boundary. Finally, beginning with a generalization of the Referendum by Illinois, in 1848, and of the area provisions by Indiana and Ohio in 1851, the tendency to treat the two

---

[1] 146 counties (Ga. Const. 1877, xi, 1 par. 2; * Am. 1904).

Between 1846 and 1857 a similar provision existed—perhaps through careless drafting—in Iowa. (Const. 1846, xi, 2).

subjects together becomes strongly marked. So unequally, however, has it operated, that only in fifteen States to-day are the requirements substantially the same for the two types of change.[1] In the remaining eighteen, as in the three already mentioned, differing policies have been pursued in regard to the two topics. Thus, we find three States in which only one comparatively unimportant provision applies to mere changes of boundary, as well as to the erection of new counties.[2] We have eight States in which one or more important provisions are thus extended, while one is not.[3] We have a group of seven, finally, in which—whatever be the situation in other respects—we have provisions referring to mere county change and not to county creation.[4]

It will be convenient to take up the provisions in the same order as before.

[1] A block of eight contiguous States: Wisconsin, Minnesota, the Dakotas, Iowa, Missouri, Kansas, Oklahoma; with Utah to the west, Louisiana to the south, Indiana, Ohio and Maryland to the east, Florida and South Carolina to the southeast.

It is only, however, in Wisconsin, Iowa, Kansas, Indiana, Maryland and Florida that the requirements are identically the same for the two cases.

[2] The debt provision in Tennessee and California; the provision prohibiting special legislation in Pennsylvania.

[3] Including such unaccountable contrasts as those between Mississippi, in which the area provision is extended, and the Referendum not, and Nebraska and Illinois, where the reverse is true; between Oregon, where the area provision is extended and the population provision not, and Virginia, where the reverse is true; between Arkansas, where the area and population provision are extended, and the Referendum not; Wyoming, where the Referendum and population provisions are extended, the property provision not; Alabama, where the area and Legislative majority provision are extended, the population provision not.

[4] The Referendum in Texas, Idaho and Colorado, and (supplementing an extended Initiative petition) in Kentucky; prohibition of special legislation in Georgia, Washington and New Mexico.

(a) *Direct limitations*

Iowa's innovation in 1846 was to simplify the already
common area provision, by the use of the following language: " No new county shall be laid off hereafter, nor old
county reduced to less contents than 432 square miles." [1]
Similar language, so changed as not to prohibit, in terms,
as this appears to do, the creation of new counties, has been
employed since by about half of the States which have newly
adopted the provision, while ten other States, including
Iowa, have come over to this prevailing form. At present
the following solid block of States: Minnesota, the Dakotas,
Iowa, Missouri, Kansas, Oklahoma, Texas, Arkansas,
Louisiana, Mississippi, Alabama, with Oregon to the West,
Indiana, Ohio, Maryland and South Carolina to the East,
seventeen in all, have the provision with extended application; while Illinois, Kentucky, Tennessee and the two Vir-
ginias, with Pennsylvania to the east, Nebraska and Idaho
to the west, eight in all, limit it to the process of creating
new counties. [2] Oklahoma has also introduced a new restriction of area, in addition to the preceding, in the shape
of a prohibition against a transfer which will leave the reduced county smaller than the one augmented. [3]

The population provision, when used in connection with
the creation of new counties before the War, applied to the
parent county in six States. In three of these its application was from the beginning extended to cover any change
in county lines, [4] and the other three States came in after the
War. [5] On the other hand, in only four States in which the

---

[1] Iowa Const. 1846, xi, 2 (until 1857).

[2] For details and references, *vide* sec. 1 (a), pp. 48-50, *supra*.

[3] Okla. Const. 1907, xvii, 4.

[4] In Florida, Virginia and Ohio. In Florida and Ohio, however, the
language is ambiguous.

[5] Missouri, Arkansas and Louisiana.

provision has been newly introduced, in connection with county creations, has this extension been made, so that the general application now appears in only nine out of twenty cases. As with the extension or non-extension of the area provision, it is difficult to assign any reason for the varying practice since the War, other than that the first model to hand has usually been slavishly imitated, without any attempt to analyze its meaning.[1]

The county seat provision has been extended only in its three last appearances;[2] the requirement of a definite shape not at all; the recognition of administrative or natural boundaries in four States,[3] and the property provision in two,[4] where the tendency to generalize is strong.

(b) *Indirect limitations*

The Referendum has been very freely extended, in all of

[1] References:
Ratio provision in:
Fla. Const. 1838, ix, 4 (until the War).
Mo. Const. 1865, iv, 31; 1875, ix, 3.
Population provision (for details, *vide* sec. 1 (a), pp. 50-52, *supra*):
Va. Const. 1850, iv, 34; 1870, v, 19; 1902, 61.
Ohio Const. 1851, ii, 30.
Ark. Const. 1874, xiii.
La. Const. 1879, 249; 1898, 277.
N. D. Const. 1889, 167.
Wyom. Const. 1889, xii, 2.
S. C. Const. 1895, vii, 4, 7.
Okla. Const. 1907, xvii, 4.
[2] S. C. Const. 1895, vii, 5, 7.
Ala. Const. 1901, 40.
Okla. Const. 1907, xvii, 4.
[3] Ohio Const. 1851, ii, 30 (under a possible interpretation).
N. D. Const. 1889, 167.
S. D. Const. 1889, ix, 1.
Okla. Const. 1895, xvii, 4.
[4] S. C. Const. 1895, vii.
Okla. Const. 1907, xvii, 4, 7.

its three forms. Tennessee, its originator, never took this step, and a similar conservatism has been displayed by Tennessee's neighbors, Arkansas and Mississippi, by West Virginia, and by Michigan. All the other States, however, since its real vogue began in 1848, have given it a general form,[1] and three States, beginning with Texas and Colorado in 1876, have applied it to a mere change of boundaries while *not* applying it to the creation of new counties;[2] and Kentucky, having already the requirement of a petition from the segregated section, for both processes, goes back, for mere changes of boundary, to the double provision of its neighbor Illinois.[3]

In another way, also, the Referendum has received a very natural development. If the voters of the old county, or of the segregated section, or of both, are to have a voice in the matter, why not also the voters of the county asked to accept fresh territory? Illinois and Nebraska, accordingly, add, to their double requirement, a Referendum of the accepting county—three petitions or Referenda, in all, before any transfer can be made; Missouri and Texas supplement their Referenda of the old county—Utah and Oklahoma, their Referenda of the section—in the same manner. The same effect seems also to be attained by a phraseology originating with Ohio in 1851, and imitated by four States since: " all laws creating new counties, changing county lines, or removing county seats, shall, before taking effect, be submitted to the electors *of the several counties to be affected*

---

[1] In South Carolina, only the two-thirds Referendum—*not* the antecedent Initiative petition) is extended. Elsewhere the details are unchanged. For these details and references, *vide* I (b), pp. 54-56, *supra*.

[2] Texas (Const. 1876, ix) and Colorado (Const. 1876, xiv, 3) a Referendum of the county; Idaho (Const. 1889, xviii, 3) a Referendum of the segregated section.

[3] Ky. Const. 1890, 64, 65.

thereby, at the next general election after the passage thereof, and be adopted by a majority of all the electors vot· ing at such election, in each of said counties." [1]

We have seen that Alabama's original requirement of an extraordinary Legislative majority was the earliest provision, so far as it went, affecting mere changes of boundary. The Texan requirement was not originally so extended, nor. while it lasted, was that of Georgia. Alabama, however, clung to the extended application after the War; Florida's provision, while it continued in force, also applied generally, and finally, in 1876, Texas came over. [2]

The debt provision is a little different from the preceding in that it started by being applicable to transfers of territory as well as to the creation of new counties; indeed, in two States it is doubtful whether it is not applicable to transfers only, and it is only in two late instances (Wyoming and Montana) that it is not applied to transfers. In two States,

[1] Two-thirds majority is required in Louisiana for this, as for other purposes; elsewhere only a simple majority, even in Oklahoma. In Minnesota, Missouri and Texas the language is such that it is not clear whether a majority of the two counties voting together would not suffice.

References:
Ill. Const. 1848, vii, 4; 1870, x, 3.
Neb. Const. 1875, x, 3.
Mo. Const. 1875, ix, 4.
Tex. Const. 1876, ix, 1.
Utah Const. 1895, xi, 3.
Okla. Const. 1907, xvii, 4.

Ohio Const. 1851, ii, 30.
Minn. Const. 1857, xi, 1.
La. Const. 1879, 250; 1898, 278.
N. D. Const. 1889, 168.
S. D. Const. 1889, ix, 1.

[2] Ala. Const. 1819, vi, 17; 1867, ii, 2; 1875, ii, 2; 1901, 39.
Fla. Const. 1868, xiv (until 1885).
Tex. Const. 1876, ix, 1.

however, a curious distinction is made. Missouri, the first State to make the new county liable, instead of the segregated section, retained the original plan in case of transfer, and this example was followed the next year by Colorado.[1]

Similarly, the provisions looking towards generality of action are all extended to include mere changes in boundary, except in the late instance of California.[1] Georgia, Washington and New Mexico prohibit special legislation *only* in regard to mere change of boundary.[2]

The provisions limiting the frequency of Referendum elections, on the other hand, or requiring the simultaneous submission of other questions to the people, have not as yet been extended to other matters than the creation of new counties.

(c) *Prohibition*

Finally, that absolute prohibition which, in Georgia, in 1877, was applied to the creation of new counties, was provided in South Carolina, from 1868 to 1885, as to *other* changes of boundary.[3]

3. ABOLITION OF COUNTIES

The consolidation of counties with their neighbors has been treated as distinct from a mere change of boundary in six Southern States.[4] Of these, West Virginia, from

---

[1] For details and references, *vide* I (b), pp. 57-60, *supra.*

[2] Ga. Const. 1877, xi, I.
Wash. Const. 1889, ii, 28.
* N. Mex. Const. 1911, iv, 24.

[3] S. C. Const. 1868, ii, 3 (until 1895).
So in a special case in Missouri, for ten years (Am. 1855, x, until 1865). The use of the term "constitutional county" differentiates this from other provisional definitions of counties in the Constitutions.

[4] Note in this connection the Florida provision already cited, p. 26, *supra,* safeguarding the rights of creditors in the case of the abolition of *any* municipality.

1862 till 1872, and Kentucky and South Carolina, recently, seem to have regarded such consolidations as, within certain limits, rather desirable; Georgia, Louisiana and Mississippi, on the other hand, as at best a disagreeable necessity.

West Virginia had a saving clause, as against all provisions, permitting the Legislature to merge with its neighbor any county having a population of less than 4,000 whites. Kentucky has a saving clause, as against its area and county seat provisions only, permitting a merger of any county. South Carolina, which normally demands a two-thirds Referendum in the section proposed to be annexed, requires, in case of complete merger, a majority Referendum in both the annexed and in the absorbing county.[1]

Georgia, on the other hand, with no Referendum requirement in general, demanded one, in 1868, in a county proposed to be merged, and also extended its requirement of a two-thirds Legislative majority to cover this case; in 1877, the extraordinary majority in the Legislature was dropped, but a two-thirds Referendum demanded in the county. Similarly, Louisiana, since 1879, has supplemented its already generous Referenda requirements by demanding in the case of a parish proposed to be totally merged with another, a two-thirds majority of its voters; rather curiously, however, when in 1898 this figure was demanded for Referenda in general, a simple majority was retained for the parish absorbing a complete old parish. Finally, Mississippi has latterly imposed a majority Referendum requirement for the creation and for the merger of counties (not for mere changes of boundary); and in the case of merger has im-

[1] W. Va. Const. 1862, vii, 12 (until 1872).
Ky. Const. 1890, 63.
S. C. Const. 1895, vii, 10.

posed it upon both counties proposed to be consolidated; whether voting separately or together, is not clear.[1]

When one is tempted to revile the framers of Constitutional instruments for the blind way in which they incorporate ready-made provisions, one turns to provisions such as the above, and wonders how much these States have gained by their attempts at originality. *Can* conditions in these six States be so widely different, as to demand such wide variety of treatment?[2]

4. SUMMARY

These varying requirements show how difficult has been the problem, in growing communities, of adjusting the county to its double function as judicial division, and as unit of representation in the Legislature. The line between the control that the Legislature must retain, in order that the system may be sufficiently elastic, and the control of which it must be deprived, lest it taint the fountain of its own being, has been exceedingly difficult to draw in practice. The absence of any New England provisions is due to the limited use there made of the county for representative purposes. For reasons which will appear more clearly later, the writer believes that the best thing to do with county lines to-day is to fix them, as they now are, in the Constitutions. If they must be changed, Constitutional amendment is a very proper process. Our territory is now so widely settled, however, and these little divisions, in these days of improved

---

[1] Ga. Const. 1868, iii, 5; 1877, xi, 1.

La. Const. 1879, 251; 1898, 279.

Miss. Const. 1890, 271.

[2] The use of the county as a unit of representation in a legislative house of limited size (*cf.* chs. vii and viii, *infra*) often affects the possible total number of counties. So particularly by Del. Const. 1776, 4; Conn. Am. 1828, i, ii; 1901, xxxi; Md. Am. 1837, 2, 3; Ga. Am. 1843, i, 3, 7; Iowa Am. 1904, iii, 35.

means of communication, are at best so badly adapted to the prime needs of administrative organization, that few changes would seem to be called for. We already virtually regard the gridironed division of the State into counties as the conventional "pattern" of a cloth which we then cut to fit. In order to meet the growth of the body politic, we have frequently to patch and piece, but it is confusion worse confounded if the pattern also is shifting.

CHAPTER IV

Urban Districts

I. THE URBAN DISTRICT AS A WHOLE

THE urban district may be termed the natural enemy of the county. Pretty clearly and pretty uniformly the ideal has been kept in view of making county divisions the basis of all the rest—the unit to be compounded in making larger, to be subdivided in making smaller, equally uniform divisions. Orderly development along these lines has, however, been sadly interfered with by the necessity of making special provision for cities, towns, villages or boroughs—products of a population which refuses to distribute itself evenly over the surface of the State, heaping itself up, instead, into local centers. These congested spots do not lend themselves to uniform treatment even among themselves, and, exercising a social pressure too strong to be withstood, play ducks and drakes with any attempt to maintain State-wide symmetry of organization. Where the social unit has most nearly conquered the county, the greatest degree of symmetry has been attained. The New England town, stronger by reason of its greater antiquity than the county there, extended its jurisdiction over outlying territory until it met its neighbor town, and rural-urban areas were formed which, in New England and adjacent States, were for a time the units of which counties were merely an aggregate; transplanted as " townships " by the surveying instruments of the Federal land office, they became in numerous Western States uniform political subdivisions of counties. But alike in " town " and " township ", and in States where neither existed, strictly urban districts have continued to emerge. We have seen how few have been the Constitutional provisions requiring even that they shall not be intersected by county lines; similarly no consistent policy has been followed in regard to the adjustment of urban lines to those of the proper subdivisions of counties. While this question of the adjustment of urban to other boundaries is perhaps wisely left to the good sense of Legislatures to meet, the mere fact that these constantly-expanding urban areas are superimposed upon a scheme of division originally designed by rural representatives for a predominantly rural population, is a striking instance of how far our system of political organization lags behind the real needs of the present.

A few steps in the direction of removing cities from their unnatural inclusion in counties have indeed been taken. New York City, although not by Constitutional provision, has always been organized as one or more complete counties, except for a brief period after consolidation in 1897. The Michigan and Minnesota provisions of the 50's, authorizing the erection of cities of a certain size into separate counties have already been mentioned as exceptions to the general rules for area in these States. Missouri, in 1875, adopted a similar rule for cities of 100,000 inhabitants (dropping even the name of county). California, in 1879, authorized the complete merger, under a single charter, of any city and county. Colorado, in 1902, effected by Constitutional process such a merger for Denver. And in several other States the absence of area provisions, or (in Ohio) its modification, permits a similar degree of urban independence.[1] It cannot be said even of these pro-

[1] Mich. Const 1850. x, 2.
Ohio Const. 1851, ii, 30.
Minn. Const. 1857, xi, 2.
Mo. Const. 1875, ix, 15, 20-23.
Cal. Const. 1879, xi, 7.
Colo. Am. 1902.

visions, however, wise and significant though from some
points of view they are, that they contribute at all to the
much-needed simplification of our system of local divisions.

It was not until 1897, following the supersession of a
long antiquated Delaware instrument, that cities, as such,
were mentioned in the Constitutions of every State. The
real turning-point was the Mexican War. Prior to the War
of 1812, cities were mentioned, as general phenomena, only
in Virginia and Pennsylvania, and in the Vermont instrument, closely modeled upon the latter.[1] In the interval from
this to the Mexican War, they made their appearance in
Georgia, and the four States due west, in New York and
New Jersey, Maine, Massachusetts and Rhode Island, and
in Michigan,[2] but were still unmentioned in a majority of
the instruments. Beginning with Wisconsin and Illinois,
however, in 1848, they are mentioned in the original instruments of all newly-admitted States, and in the first complete new instrument adopted by the others. Reconstruction
facilitated this change in the South, and Connecticut and
New Hampshire amendments in 1876 and 1877 made the
recognition universal outside of Delaware. In something
over half the States other urban districts—village, borough,[3]
hamlet, or strictly urban " town "—have been mentioned at
the same time with cities. In a dozen instances, however,
principally where the rural " town " is strongest, they have

[1] Particular cities (New York City and Albany, N. Y., Annapolis,
Md., and New Orleans, La.) were mentioned in three other States.
The surviving charters of Connecticut and Rhode Island also author-
ized the representation of " towns, cities or places."

[2] Miss. 1817; Ga. 1818; Ala. 1819; La. 1845; Tex. 1845; N. Y. and
Mass. 1821; Me. 1834; R. I. 1842; N. J. 1844; Mich. 1835.

[3] The " borough " is here treated, for convenience' sake, as a strictly
urban district. This is not uniformly the case.

been mentioned later, or not at all;[1] while in seven States admitted prior to the Mexican War, "towns" are mentioned earlier than cities; doubtless with a general meaning.[2]

[1] In New York, first in 1846; in Connecticut in 1877; in the other New England States (except Vermont, under the Pennsylvania influence) and in New Jersey, Delaware and Maryland, not at all.

In Georgia first in 1868; in Minnesota, in * 1881.

[2] Ky. 1799; Ohio 1802; Ind. 1816; Ill. 1818; Tenn. 1834; Ark. 1836; Fla. 1838.

Particular towns (Baltimore, Md., six small towns in N. C., Charleston, S. C., Savannah and Sunbury, Ga.) are also mentioned in earlier instruments of four States.

Virginia (Const. 1902, 116) is the only State to distinguish sharply, on the basis of a population greater or less than 5,000, between "cities" and "towns". Cf. also Mass. Am. 1821, ii; Ky. Const. 1890, 156.

The term "town" was more commonly employed before the Mexican War than any other. Indiana, Kentucky, Tennessee, Mississippi, Louisiana and Florida still use no other term to describe urban districts other than cities; so the later instances of Oregon, Georgia. Iowa and Montana. Pennsylvania always had (in addition to townships) "towns" and "boroughs"; Virginia, boroughs alone until 1830; then boroughs and towns until 1850; then towns alone until the War; since 1870, towns and villages; the Pennsylvania borough was copied by Vermont; this may help to account for the use of this term by Connecticut, a hundred years later.

The first appearance of "village" is in Illinois, 1818, in connection with "town". New York, having rural "towns", used "village" in 1846 to characterize strictly urban districts, and Michigan, four years later, changed from "town" to "village". Much more usual, however, since the Mexican War, has been the continuous use of both "town" and "village" (so Wisc., Kans., Nev., the Carolinas, Colo., and all the States newly admitted since), or the addition of "village" where "town" alone was originally mentioned (so Ohio, Ala., Ark., Tex., Va., W. Va., Mo.), or even of "town" where "village" was originally mentioned (so Nebraska). California starting with "town" and "village" reverted in 1879 to "town" only, while Minnesota, starting in the same way, reverted in 1892 to "village".

Illinois, from 1818 till 1870, spoke of "hamlets" in addition to "towns" and "villages"; this term was revived in an Ohio amendment of 1905.

1. *Direct limitations*

The only direct limitation upon the result to be attained in the formation of urban districts is a provision which existed for ten years in Missouri, forbidding any city to be incorporated with less than 5,000 permanent inhabitants.[1]

2. *Extraordinary Legislative majority. Deferred action.*

Virginia, recently, has revived the extraordinary Legislative majority,[2] and New York has introduced a rule, requiring the submission of special city acts to local authorities, which may be considered a modification of the deferred action rule elsewhere applied to corporations or to all special legislation.[3]

3. *General legislation*

Of provisions encouraging general treatment of urban districts, there has been a great mass, the discussion of

[1] Mo. Const. 1865, viii, 5 (until 1875).

In Rhode Island (Const. 1842, v, 1) the combined number of towns and cities may not exceed 72.

Provisions in Massachusetts (Am. 1821, ii) and Pennsylvania (Const. 1873, xv, 1), permitting city governments to be organized in towns or boroughs of a certain population, would appear to have no relation to questions of boundary.

[2] Two-thirds of the members elected to each house are required for special legislation in regard to the organization or government of cities and towns (in addition to the committee procedure required for all special legislation). Va. Const. 1902, 117. *Cf.* ch. ii, sec. 1 (a), p. 25, *supra.*

[3] Three classes of cities are defined, by population. A bill relating to the property, affairs or government, (since 1907, "affairs *of* government") or the several departments, of less than all the cities of a class, must be given a public hearing in every city to which it relates, and must also be submitted to the mayor and legislative body—or, in cities of the first class, unless the Legislature otherwise provides, to the mayor only. Lacking local approval within fifteen days, it must then be passed a second time by the Legislature, before going to the Governor. N. Y. Const. 1894, xii, 2; * Am. 1907.

Cf. ch. ii, secs. 1 (b), 2 (b), pp. 25, 35, *supra.*

which presents considerable difficulties, owing, in part, to the presence in one and the same instrument of provisions relating to " municipal corporations," as well as to urban districts expressly; and, in part, to the difficulty in determining whether provisions relating in some way to urban districts relate in particular to their boundaries. We may introduce partial order into this chaos by assembling, first, the few cases in which the application of corporation provisions to urban districts has been expressly limited. Then, bearing in mind that our purpose is to trace tendencies and technical development, rather than to provide a working manual for the corporation lawyer, we shall consider separately the three broad classes into which the States, from the point of view of municipal corporations as such, are divided : States, that is to say, in which no generalizing provision exists; States in which there is only an authorization or an obligation to pass general municipal corporation laws; States in which special legislation affecting municipal incorporation is positively forbidden.[1] Within each of these classes we shall see what express provision has been made for urban districts; provision which, if it exists, and if it makes any change at all, always makes the " municipal " or unqualified " corporation " rule somewhat more stringent.

(a) *Express exceptions to existing incorporation provisions*

Only five such have been found. Missouri, for ten years, excepted cities from its prohibition of special incorporation, providing population and Referendum requirements instead. Wisconsin, for twenty years, and Minnesota, for about ten, excepted cities, providing no substitute. Louisiana, for about twenty years, excepted New Orleans, this exception being merged, after 1898, into a general exception of all

[1] *Vide* ch. ii, sec. 1 (c), pp. 26-29, *supra.*

municipal corporations having a certain population. Alabama, in 1901, very sensibly provided that the prohibition upon changing charters should not prevent the Legislature from " altering or rearranging the boundaries of any city, town or village ".[1]

(b) *No provision affecting municipal incorporations*

In four out of the fifteen States in which no effort has been made to promote a generalized treatment of municipal incorporations, broadly, this effort has been made in the case of urban districts in particular.

Virginia, in 1870, required the passage of general laws for the organization of cities, with the timid addition (copied from New York's private corporation rule) that no special act should be passed " except in cases where, in the judgment of the General Assembly, the object of such act cannot be attained by general laws ". This prohibition was changed in 1902 by being extended to towns; by being made absolute, so far as regards " the extension and the contraction, from time to time, of the corporate limits of cities and towns "; and by being made absolute, as against an ordinary Legislative majority, in all cases.[2] Texas, in 1874, adopted a carelessly-phrased provision which, two years later, became a prohibition upon special legislation incorporating cities, towns or villages or changing their charters; cities having a population of 10,000 or over, however, are excepted.[3] Colorado and Idaho merely require the

[1] Mo. Const. 1865, viii, 5 (until 1875).
Wisc. Am. * 1871, iv, 31 (until 1892).
La. Const. 1879, 46 (until 1898).
Minn. Am. * 1881, iv, 33 (until 1892).
Ala. Const. 1901, 104, par. 18.

[2] Va. Const. 1870, vi, 20; 1902, 117, 126. An extraordinary Legislative majority may, however, pass special laws *organizing* cities and towns.

[3] Tex. Am. * 1874; xii, 40; Const. 1876, iii, 56; xi, 4, 5.

Legislature to provide by general law for the organization (in the latter State also for the incorporation) of cities and towns, without, however, appearing actually to prohibit their special creation.[1]

(c) *Mere authorization or obligation to enact general municipal incorporation laws*

Of the eight States included under this head,[2] four—North Dakota, Wyoming, South Carolina and New Mexico— expressly prohibit special legislation incorporating or changing the charters of cities, towns or villages; and New York prohibits special legislation merely incorporating villages.[3]

(d) *Prohibition of special legislation incorporating municipalities*

In four of the numerous States in which municipalities may not be incorporated by special act, no similar provision affecting urban districts as such has been made.[4]   In seven of them (surviving cases), merely an obligation to provide for the organization of urban districts under general law has been added.[5]   In the remaining fourteen, the

---

[1] Colo, Const. 1876, xiv, 13.
Idaho Const. 1889, xii, 1.

[2] *Vide* p. 27, note 1, *supra*.

[3] S. C. Const. 1895, iii, 34.
N. D. Const. 1889, 69, par. 33.
Wyom. Const. 1889, iii, 27.
N. Y. Am. 1874, iii, 18; Const. 1894, iii, 18.
* N. Mex. Const. 1911, iv, 24.
Nevada, also (Const. 1864, viii, 8), supplements a mere authorization to enact general corporation laws, by an obligation to provide for the organization of cities and towns by general laws.

[4] Indiana, Tennessee, New Jersey, Louisiana.

[5] Mississippi has such an obligation, for municipal corporations in general; the other States have not.
California and Washington mention "incorporation" as well as "organization"; Michigan, "incorporation" only.   Mississippi, in-

prohibition has been expressly extended to urban districts. In these fourteen are included five States in which the " mild " general rule (not applicable to change of charter) prevails; in four of these, the more stringent rule has been adopted for urban districts.[1]

stead of either " organization " or " incorporation " mentions chartering and amending charters.

The districts affected are in Ohio, Nebraska (until 1875), and Arkansas (until 1874), " cities and incorporated villages "; in Kansas, " cities, towns and villages "; in Arkansas since 1874, " cities and incorporated towns "; in Missouri, California, Washington, Kentucky and Mississippi, " cities and towns ". In Michigan, there is to be a general law for " cities ", and another for " villages ".

References:

Ohio Const. 1851, xiii, 6.
Kans. Const. 1859, xii, 5.
Neb. Const. 1866, " Corp.", 4 (until 1875).
Ark. Const. 1868, v, 49; 1874, xii, 3.
Cal. Const. 1879, xi, 6, 7.
Ky. Const. 1890, 156.
Miss. Const. 1890, 88.
* Mich. Const. 1908, viii, 20.

[1] " Mild " rule repeated (" incorporation " forbidden) in Iowa; stringent rule newly imposed (incorporation or change of charter forbidden) in West Virginia, Utah, Oklahoma and Arizona.

In the remaining nine States, in which the stringent rule already exists for municipal corporations in general, " incorporating or changing the charters " of urban districts is usually forbidden. Alabama, however, forbids merely " incorporating " these districts; so Minnesota until 1892, since when, " incorporating, erecting, or changing the lines "; and Pennsylvania, for boroughs only, forbids erecting or changing limits.

The districts affected are, in Iowa, " cities and towns "; in Illinois, Missouri, Nebraska, South Dakota, Utah, Alabama, Oklahoma and Arizona, " cities, towns and villages "; in West Virginia, cities, towns and villages containing a population of less than 2,000; in Pennsylvania, " cities and villages ", and boroughs; in Washington, " towns and villages ". The Wisconsin and Minnesota provisions at first applied only to " towns and villages," cities being expressly excepted from the general rule; in 1892, however, Wisconsin cities were brought within the town and village rule, and the Minnesota provision was made to apply to " cities and villages."

Finally, for the sake of completeness, it may be added that the various interpreting rules, designed to prevent evasions of the preceding, have occasionally been made expressly applicable to urban districts. So the rule as to the uniform operation of the law,[1] and the Pennsylvania rule as to the partial repeal of a general law.[2] Classification provisions, originating as a license, applied to corporations in general, were developed into a safeguard, in connection with urban districts, before they were applied for this purpose to municipal corporations in general.[3]

References:
Iowa Const. 1857, iii, 30.
W. Va. Const. 1872, vi, 39.
Utah Const. 1895, vi, 26.
Okla. Const. 1907, v, 146.
* Ariz. Const. 1911, iv, 2, 19, par. 17.

Ill. Const. 1870, iv, 22.
Wisc. * Am. 1871, iv, 31; 1892, iv, 31.
Pa. Const. 1873, iii, 7.
Neb. Const. 1875, iii, 15.
Mo. Const. 1875, iv, 53; ix, 7.
Minn. * Am. 1881, iv, 33; Am. 1892, iv, 33.
Wash. Const. 1889, ii, 28, par. 8; xi, 10.
S. D. Const. 1889, iii, 23, par. 5.
Ala. Const. 1901, 104, par. 5.

[1] Wisc. * Am. 1871, iv, 31, 32; Am. 1892, iv, 31.
Minn. * Am. 1881, iv, 33, 34; Am. 1892, iv, 33.

[2] Expressly applicable to corporations and to urban districts in Pennsylvania (Const. 1873, iii, 7) and Missouri (Const. 1875, iv, 53); applicable to urban districts, though not, expressly, to corporations, in North Dakota (Const. 1889, 69, 70).

In Kentucky (Const. 1890, 60), among the States where this had developed into a general rule of legislative procedure (*vide* ch. ii, sec. 2 (d), pp. 39, 40, *supra*), cities and towns are among the types of districts which may not be exempted from the operation of a general act.

[3] In chronological order:

West Virginia (Const. 1872, xi, 1) requires the passage of general laws, "uniform as to the class to which they relate", for the organization of all corporations.

4. Simple Referendum upon organization

A majority Referendum, within the district proposed to
be incorporated into a city, was first temporarily imposed in
Missouri, between 1865 and 1875, in connection with its
peculiar population provision. Having then been required
in Wyoming, as we have seen, for the organization of any
municipal corporation, it has been required in South Carolina, since 1895, for the organization of cities and towns
only. In Illinois, since 1904, Chicago may be increased or
diminished only subject to a Referendum of the city, and of
the territory proposed to be annexed or disconnected.[1]

Arkansas (Const. 1874, xii, 3) requires the passage of general laws
" for the organization of cities (which may be classified) and incorporated towns ".

Missouri (Const. 1875, ix, 7) followed by Colorado (Const. 1876,
xiv, 13) require the classification by general law of cities and towns
into not more than four classes.

California (Const. 1879, xi, 6) followed by Washington (Const.
1889, xi, 10), Idaho (Const. 1889, xii, 1), Utah (Const. 1895, xi, 6),
Oklahoma (Const. 1907, xviii, 1), and Arizona (* Const. 1911, xiii, 1),
require the classification of cities and towns in proportion to population.

South Dakota (Const. 1889, x. 1) and Wyoming (Const. 1889, xiii,
1) require the classification of municipal corporations into not more
than four classes.

Kentucky (Const. 1890, 156) classifies cities and towns, in its instrument, on the basis of population, into six classes. So New York
(Const. 1894, xii, 2)—cities only—three classes; and Minnesota (Am.
* 1896, iv, 36)—cities only—three classes; (Am. * 1898, iv, 36)—cities
only—four classes.

South Carolina (Const. 1895, viii, 1) requires merely the classification, by general law, of municipal corporations.

Virginia (Const. 1902, 116) classifies urban districts in its instrument, on the basis of population, into two classes, known as " cities "
and " towns " respectively.

[1] Mo. Const. 1865, viii, 5 (until 1875).

Wyom. Const. 1889, xiii, 2.

S. C. Const. 1895, viii, 2.

Ill. * Am. 1904, iv, 36.

The Massachusetts and Pennsylvania population requirements (cf.
p. 77, note 1, supra), for a change from town or borough to city gov-

5. *Freedom from Legislative control over charter formation*

The provisions just discussed are a mere adaptation, to urban districts, of rules far more commonly applied to the formation of counties. Closely connected with them, historically, but with a shift of emphasis from boundary lines to governmental form, are the so-called Freeholders' Charter provisions, originated in 1875—as a substitute for the preceding—by Missouri, and now appearing in the instruments of nine Western States. The idea being here primarily to insure to the inhabitants of already established urban districts, at least of a certain size,[1] control over the formation of their own charters, the question of how these districts are to be delimited is almost totally ignored. Minnesota expressly requires a three-fifths vote to change established " patrol limits "; and Missouri made the separation from the county of St. Louis of an enlarged city to depend upon Referenda in both the county and the city. Otherwise, the provisions apply to the exterior boundaries of cities perhaps only to this extent, that they render impossible the old practice of defining their boundaries as a mere incident to legislative acts of incorporation.

Apart from the question, which we need not here consider, of what topics of government are or are not entrusted to the uncontrolled discretion of a locality which operates under this charter system,[2] these States may be divided, on the basis of control over the charter itself, into three classes.

ernment, are coupled with Initiative provisions. (Mass. Am. 1821, ii: Pa. Const. 1873, xv, 1).

Cf. also the recent Michigan rule, applicable to all local acts, p. 41, *supra.*

[1] In Missouri, cities containing over 100,000 inhabitants. In California, 100,000 until 1887; then 10,000 until * 1892; since then, 3,500. In Washington, 20,000. In Arizona, 3,500. In Oklahoma, 2,000. In Colorado, cities of the first and second class. In Minnesota and Michigan, any city *or village.* In Oregon, any city *or town.*

[2] In Missouri, California until 1905, Oklahoma and Arizona, the

In Missouri, the advance over the already existing simple Referendum consisted merely in replacing the Legislature, as the original framing body, by a Board, or Charter Convention, caused to be popularly elected by the City at any time, free to propose any scheme of government which should be consistent with the Constitution and laws of the State, and should include a mayor, and two houses of legislation, of which at least one to be chosen by general ticket—such charter, or such sections of the same as might be separately submitted, to go into force when ratified by popular vote and deposited in specified offices of record.

California and Minnesota do not go quite so far as Missouri. California replaces the charter outline prescribed in the Constitution (and, since 1905, the requirement also that the charter shall be consistent with the *laws* of the State) by the requirement that the instrument shall be submitted to the Legislature, for approval or rejection as a whole, by a majority of the members elected to each house. Minnesota, again, retains the Missouri requirements as a whole, and in addition provides that the Legislature, before incorporation, shall prescribe the general limits within which the charter shall be framed; the original Board, moreover, is to be chosen, not by the city, but by the District Judges, at the call of the Legislature.

The other four States, on the other hand, go even farther than Missouri. All drop the Constitutional outline of city government, and all semblance of legislative control, though Washington, Oklahoma and Arizona retain the requirement of consistency with the Constitution and the laws, and the

charter government is expressly subject to the laws of the State; in Washington and Michigan, to its general laws; in Minnesota, to general laws, under a system of classification, and to criminal laws; in Oregon, to its criminal laws. Colorado, and California since 1905, express no reservation.

two latter States, by a device borrowed from the President's power in the admission of new States, give the Governor the determining power as to whether this condition has been complied with. Oklahoma provides also for an Initiative petition and Referendum on the question of whether a Charter Convention shall be held, in case the legislative authority of the city does not call one of its own volition. Colorado drops the requirement that the charter must be consistent with the Constitution and the laws, and deprives the Legislature of concurrent power to form a charter. Oregon deprives the Legislature of this power, and, in place of other details, merely provides that " the legal voters of every city and town are hereby granted power to enact and amend their municipal charter." Michigan merely provides that under the general incorporation laws, " the electors of each city and village shall have power and authority to frame, adopt and amend its charter."

Provisions similar to the above, for amending the charter, also appear in all nine States.[1]

[1] Amendments are submitted to the Referendum of the urban district by its own legislative authority in Missouri and Washington, in California until * 1902 and in Arizona; by its legislative authority, or by Initiative petition, in California since 1902 and in Oklahoma; by Initiative petition only, it would seem, in Colorado; by Initiative petition, at least, in Oregon. The Minnesota Legislature is authorized to prescribe the duties of the judicially appointed Board relative to submitting amendments; and, since 1898, the Legislature must provide that the Board shall act ministerially in submitting Initiative petition amendments. Michigan does not state how " the electors " act. New Charter Conventions are clearly permissible only in California since 1905, in Colorado and in Arizona; in the two latter states they may be called by Initiative petition and Referendum. California charters may not be amended oftener than once in two years; *special* elections on one and the same question may not be held oftener in Colorado.

The submission of charters or of amendments in sections is expressly authorized, except in Oregon, Oklahoma and Michigan; except, also, for the original charter, in Colorado, where, instead, a system of repeated Charter Conventions is provided.

6. *Local Initiative-Referenda provisions*

Three broad types of local Initiative-Referenda have recently developed, quite distinct from one another in theory, but so inextricably intertwined in practice, and in that confusion of thought which our defective political terminology breeds, that they must necessarily be considered together.

The first type of such provision is a power given to the electorate to check, or to supersede, the actions of its local authorities, in the discharge of their ordinary governmental functions. Provisions of this type, applicable to urban districts, were adopted by Utah, first, in 1900, and since then by Colorado, Oklahoma, Maine and Arizona, and have of course no relation whatsoever to the exterior boundaries of these districts.[1]

The figure for Referenda is uniformly a simple majority, except in Missouri and Minnesota (four-sevenths for the charter, three-fifths for amendments) and in California (three-fifths for amendments, until * 1902). For Initiative petition the figure varies from 5 per cent of the preceding gubernatorial vote, or 10 per cent for ordering a special election, in Colorado, to 5 per cent of the legal voters in Minnesota; 15 per cent of the qualified voters, in California; not more than this amount, in Oregon; 25 per cent of the vote cast at the last election, in Oklahoma and Arizona.

Washington provides no means of recording the charter.

For extension of these provisions to all municipalities, *cf.* ch. ii, sec. 1 (e), p. 31, *supra*.

References:

Mo. Const. 1875, ix, 16, 17, 20-25; Am. 1902.

Cal. Const. 1879, * xi, 8; Am. * 1887; * 1892; 1902; 1905.

Wash. Const. 1889, xi. 10.

Minn. * Am. 1896, iv, 36; Am. 1898.

Colo. Am. 1902, xx, 4-6.

Oreg. Am. 1906, xi, 2. *Cf.* iv. 1a.

Okla. Const. 1907, xviii, 2, 3, 4.

* Mich. Const. 1908, viii, 21.

* Ariz. Const. 1911, xiii, 2.

[1] The Colorado provision, superseded in 1910, applies only to cities of the first and second class; the Arizona provision to incorporated

A second type of provision confers a similar power in the case of Charter Conventions or charter amendments, under some of the Freeholders' systems just described. This perfection of the original plan, under which only the local legislative authority (or, in Minnesota, the judicially appointed Board) could initiate changes, was made by Minnesota in 1898, and since then by Colorado, California, Oregon, Oklahoma and Arizona, and affects exterior boundaries most remotely, if at all.[1]

Finally, Oregon, in 1906, followed by Colorado and Arkansas in 1910, appear to give the local electorate control, not only over the acts of its own authorities, but also over such acts even of the State Legislature as specially affect it. This power, if it is upheld by the courts, affects the determination of exterior boundaries directly.[2]

cities and towns (not to villages); the others, to all urban districts. For application of all except the Colorado provision to other than urban districts, *vide* ch. ii, sec. 2 (e), *supra*.

Utah (Am. 1900, vi, 1, par. 2) leaves all details to the Legislature.

Colorado (Am. 1902, xx, 5, 6) requires 5% of the preceding gubernatorial vote (or 10% for a special election) for an Initiative petition proposing measures; other details to be determined by the charter.

Oklahoma (Const. 1907, xviii, 4) requires 25% of the vote cast at the preceding election for petitions either proposing measures or invoking the Referendum.

In Maine (* Am .1908, iv, part 3, 21) the system may be optionally introduced by any city council, subject to a Referendum upon its adoption. The Legislature however may at any time introduce a uniform method. No further details.

Arizona (* Const. 1911, iv, 1, 8) requires 15% of the qualified electors for proposing measures, 10% for invoking the Referendum; and, until provided by general law, the localities may prescribe the basis upon which these percentages are to be computed.

[1] For details, *vide* p. 86, note 1, *supra*.

[2] All three provisions apply to all urban districts, and to other districts as well. *Vide* ch. ii, sec. 2 (e), p. 43, *supra*.

In Oregon (Am. 1906, iv, 1a) and Colorado (* Am. 1910, v, i) *not more than* 15% of the legal voters may be required for petitions

II. URBAN SUBDIVISIONS

The extent to which urban subdivisions have come to be mentioned in the Constitutions affords a fair measure of the increasing importance of urban districts. Wards are first mentioned in the original Pennsylvania instrument, expiring in 1790;[1] then, revived again in New York's second instrument in 1821, they spread pretty generally before the War through the North Atlantic States, including Maryland and Virginia, and through the Middle West, including Kansas; since the War also to several other Southern States, Nebraska, Colorado, Washington and Oklahoma. Even divisions of wards have come to be mentioned, under a special appellation, in Maryland.[2] " Districts ", as an alternative for wards, appear in Kentucky;[3] districts for police magistrates coordinate with those for justices of the peace in rural territory, appear in Illinois and Nebraska;[4] district court justices in New York;[5] sewerage districts, coordinate with rural drainage districts, in Louisiana;[6] subdivisions of cities, towns and villages are mentioned in gen-

proposing measures, nor more than 10% for invoking the Referendum, and the localities determine details in connection with municipal measures proper.

Arkansas (* Am. 1910, v, 1) requires not more than 8% of the legal voters for the Initiative, or 5% for the Referendum petition.

[1] Pa. Const. 1776, 30 (until 1790).

[2] N. Y. 1821; Me. 1834; Pa. 1838; Mich. 1839; R. I. 1842; N. J. 1844; Wisc. 1848; Ky. 1850; Va. 1850 (not mentioned after the War until 1902); Md. 1851 (and precincts of Baltimore wards in 1864); Ohio 1851; Ind. 1851; Mass. 1855; Kans. 1859; Neb. 1866; Ark. 1874; Ala. 1875; Mo. 1875; Tex. 1876; Colo. 1876; N. H. 1877; La. 1879; Wash. 1889; Minn. 1892; Del. 1897; N. C. 1900; Okla. 1907.

[3] Ky. Const. 1890, 160.

[4] Ill. Const. 1870, vi, 21.
Neb. Const. 1875, vi, 18.

[5] N. Y. Const. 1894, vi, 17.

[6] La. Am. 1904, 281.

eral, in connection with a guarantee of election of local officers, in Wisconsin and Virginia;[1] in connection with a limitation of indebtedness, in Utah.[2] The divisions of the city of New Orleans are most prominent. As early as 1845, it had " municipalities ", appearing again in 1898 as " municipal districts " (distinct from wards). Between 1868 and 1879 it was specially divided into coroner's districts. In 1879 separate city, police and magistrate's courts are mentioned; by a process of development to which we shall have occasion to refer again, these gave birth in 1898 to city court, city criminal court, and recorder's court districts, defined as such in the Constitution.[3]

Before the War, the only provision affecting the formation or maintenance of these subdivisions, in terms, was a Virginia requirement of 1850, that cities and towns containing more than 5,000 white inhabitants should be laid off into wards for voting purposes.[4] Since the War, several of the New Orleans districts have come to be completely defined in the instrument;[5] New Hampshire wards may not be altered in such a way as to lump fractions of the representative quota;[6] wards in Minnesota may not be erected nor

---

[1] Wisc. Const. 1848, xiii, 9.
Va. Const. 1870, vi, 20 (until 1902).

[2] Utah Const. 1895, xiv, 3.

[3] La. Const. 1845, 8; 1868, 93; 1879, 135, 136; 1898, 140, 141, 143, 147, 309; Am. 1906, 140.

[4] Va. Const. 1850, iii, 2.

[5] The two coroner's districts are defined in terms of streets (La. Const. 1868, 93) until 1879. City courts, originally limited in number to not less than three nor more than eight, have developed into two city court districts, defined in terms of " municipalities ". (La. Const. 1879, *135; Am. 1884; 1898, 143, 147). Police magistrate's courts, originally unrestricted in number, have developed into two city criminal court districts, defined in the same terms, but not identical with, the preceding (Const. 1879, 136; 1898, 140).

[6] N. H. Am. 1877, ii, 9.

changed, and in Kentucky and Alabama may not be
changed, by special act;[1] Virginia city councils have a constitutional right " in a manner prescribed by law ", to
change the number or boundaries of wards.[2] Elsewhere,
these subdivisions may be defined in the charter, or by legislative act not in charter form, or by the local authorities
under the charter. In the former cases, the provisions affecting urban districts in general, of course apply. In the
latter case, any provision which affects the form of local
government may be said to be germane. Such are the
Freeholders' Charter and Initiative-Referenda provisions,
of somewhat doubtful relevance to exterior boundaries.
Such, finally, is a charter outline prescribed in one State—
Virginia—which has remained untouched by the Western
populistic movement.

III. SUMMARY

Most of the provisions discussed in the preceding pages
bear only remotely upon the subject of urban boundaries.
In general they may be said to have the negative effect of
destroying the power originally possessed by the Legislature
to alter urban lines, exterior and interior, at will, without
any regard to its method of procedure. To determine what
control they have substituted for this would demand a special study of its own, based upon the constructions which
the several State Courts have placed upon their respective
Constitutional provisions. It is fortunate that we have Courts
which can interpret this chaos. It is fortunate that in their
interpretations they have kept the necessary organizing
power of the State from being hopelessly enmeshed in a

[1] Minn. * Am. 1892, iv, 33.
  Ky. Const. 1890, 59, par. 20.
  Ala. Const. 1901, 104, par. 29.
[2] Va. Const. 1902, 121.

tangle of technicalities. But it would be much more fortunate if the people, speaking through their Constitutions, had analyzed the urban problem with a little more care, and so been able to formulate self-interpreting provisions.

What seems to me to have been the main trouble with us in the past—I criticize, not our policy, but our technical procedure—is that in our zeal for local self-government, we have neglected to define our terms. We have sought Home Rule, without making clear what our homes were to be. We have directly deprived the Legislature of some of its control over cities. We have made the exercise of that control which it retains more difficult. We have vested fuller control over local affairs in the city itself. We have admitted the people of the city to a more direct participation in its local government. But we have not, except in the rarest instances, even faced the problem of who shall decide what the boundaries of a constantly-growing city shall be. If this question is to some extent answered in the general provisions we have discussed, the answer may fairly be said to have been inadvertent.

This is a very small technical point, it may be said, this question of urban boundaries. It is true that the more important question facing Constitutional framers to-day is how the line between urban and State functions is to be drawn; and that it is only because of its connection with this large and difficult problem that the definition of areas needs to be considered. But can the larger question be answered unless we answer the smaller one as well? When we contrast the negative results which this chapter has afforded with the completely elaborated Referendum checks which so many States have imposed upon Legislative control of local boundaries, I think the underlying reason for the distinction suggests itself. Every representative, in Legislature or Convention, lives in some county, and hence is equally

interested in finishing up the county job in a workmanlike—
we may say even in an absurdly overdone—manner. But
it is only a small minority of delegates who represent urban
districts in any especial sense. While these have secured
some concessions to their demands for local Home Rule—
concessions, in most cases, of form rather than of substance—they have not secured a broad consideration of the
entire problem, with all the elements involved. When this
problem comes to receive the attention which, in the opinion
of the average city-dweller, at least, it deserves, the first
logical step will be to define, in terms too clear to require
reference to the Courts, how the boundary between urban
and rural territory is to be determined.

CHAPTER V

DISTRICTS FOR GENERAL OR JUDICIAL PURPOSES OTHER THAN COUNTY AND URBAN

I. MINOR DIVISIONS

IN every State rural districts smaller than the county have been found necessary. The original English "hundred" still survives in Delaware, where it has been mentioned in the Constitution since 1792. The use of the ecclesiastical "parish" for civil purposes—also in accordance with English tradition—was more common during the Colonial period, and is reflected in the early instruments of four States: Georgia, where in 1777 it was used as the term in which the newly-created counties were (provisionally) defined; South Carolina, where parishes are recognized under this name, side by side with "districts", in both 1776 and 1778;[1] New Hampshire, where "parishes with town privileges" appear both in 1784 and in the still surviving instrument of 1792; and Louisiana, where the parish, appearing in 1812 as a subdivision of the county, has since 1845 usurped the latter's functions.

After the transformation of South Carolina's parishes and districts, in 1790, into a uniform system of legislative districts ("election districts," so-called) these latter came to be used until the War as the general areas of local government.[2] Militia districts were similarly made use of

[1] Particular parishes survived until the War. *Cf.* S. C. Const. 1790, i, 7; 1865, i, 3.

[2] First mentioned as thus used in S. C. Am. 1828, v, 4.

for judicial purposes in Tennessee, until 1834, and continuously since 1798 in Georgia;[1] and "election districts" (polling precincts) have been impressed for service in Maryland.[2] "Plantations and places unincorporated" also survive in the antique instruments of Massachusetts, New Hampshire and Maine, as reminders of the fact that even in New England the uniform division of the State into urban-rural towns has been a slowly-realized ideal.[3]

Apart from these few anomalies, of which only Delaware hundreds, Maryland election districts, and Georgia militia districts are of importance to-day, the principal disagreement between the States has been as to the greater or less use which should be made of the "township". This term, which, in its original and most accurate use, describes the territory occupied by the juristic personality, the "town", was first applied to areas surveyed ahead of population, under the system of township planting in New England and in the Wyoming Valley of Pennsylvania, and later, under the operation of the National Land Office, to the rectangular tracts laid out in the Western territory. To this fact, reinforced by the traditions of town government brought with them by New England settlers, is to be ascribed the appearance of the "town" or "township", throughout the North and West, as the characteristic area

---

[1] "Captain's Company" in Tennessee (Const. 1796, v, 12—until 1834).
"Captain's district" before the War, and "Militia district" since, in Georgia (Const. 1798, iii, 5; 1868, v, 6; 1877, vi, 7).

[2] First mentioned as thus used in Md. Const. 1851, iv, 19.

[3] In Massachusetts these anomalies came to be described as "districts" in 1821 and 1836, and in 1840 we hear no more of them. (Mass. Am. 1821, iii; 1836, xii; 1840, xiii). "Districts" are also mentioned in Rhode Island (Am. 1864, iv).

The broad topic of what local districts actually survived, without being mentioned in the Constitutions (*e. g.* parishes and manorial districts in New York) is of course not here treated.

of local government. It is not the exclusive area, however, in all of these States, even; while in the original Southern States, or in the Southwestern territory where " congressional townships " (as they came to be called) were less frequently surveyed, it does not appear at all before the War. Attempts made during the Reconstruction period to introduce the township into eight Southern States, have left permanent results only in four.[1] As a general result of this township movement we may distinguish between three classes of States to-day:[2]

First, those in which the " town " or " township "[3] is the only county subdivision mentioned, for purposes either of local government in general or of minor judicial administration. Twenty-two States in all come under this head: virtually all north of the Ohio River and the Red River of the South, running as far west as North Dakota, Kansas and Oklahoma, but not including Illinois, Nebraska and South Dakota; and, in addition to these, California and Nevada beyond the Rockies.[4]

Second, Illinois and the Northwestern States not included in the above, and, since the War, West Virginia, Ala-

[1] The temporary appearances are: Maryland, 1864-67; Florida, 1868-85; Mississippi, 1868-90; Virginia, 1870-74.

The case for the township is stated in its extreme form. It is not always possible to determine from the instrument whether the district mentioned under this name is in actual use either for general or for judicial purposes. In Missouri, prior to 1875, and in Alabama, since 1867, it would look as though the townships were used only for school purposes. Their mention in West Virginia, since 1872, is probably an inadvertence.

[2] The occasional appearance of the " borough " as a rural district (*cf.* p. 75, note 3, *supra*) is not considered in this classification.

[3] " Town " only in New England, New York, Wisconsin, and (until 1862) California.

[4] Towns were not actually mentioned in New Hampshire until 1784, owing to the brevity of the Revolutionary instrument.

bama and the Carolinas. In these fourteen States we have evidence that, side by side with townships, other districts may or must be used for local judicial purposes: " districts " in Illinois and West Virginia; " districts " or " precincts " in Nebraska; " precincts " in North Carolina, Alabama and the Far West; " beats " in South Carolina from 1868 to 1895, since then, " magistrate's districts ".[1]

Third, nine remaining Southern States: Virginia, Kentucky, Tennessee, Mississippi, Louisiana, Texas, Florida, New Mexico and Arizona. In these, as in the three anomalous States of Maryland, Delaware and Georgia, there is now no mention of townships at all, but other local districts under various names, or no names at all, appear, as optional or obligatory divisions of counties for judicial purposes.[2]

Actual rules in regard to the formation of these local districts do not appear in the Northeast at all, and not emphatically in the West. Wisconsin, it is true, followed by California until 1879, provided that the system of town and county government should be as nearly uniform as practicable; and Nevada adopted the same provision without

[1] In Pennsylvania also, until 1838, districts (apparently identical with those established for voting purposes) were named as judicial units, side by side with townships.

In Illinois neither type of district is mentioned until 1848; in South Carolina until 1868. In Nebraska, " districts " are mentioned from the beginning, townships as well in 1875. In North Carolina, townships are first mentioned in 1868, " precincts " as well in 1876; in West Virginia, townships in 1862, " districts " as well in 1872; in Alabama, townships (other than Congressional), first in 1867, " precincts ", only, in 1875; both, since 1901.

[2] First in Mississippi, since 1832. In Tennessee, following the original use of militia districts for this purpose, in 1834. In Texas from the beginning, in 1845. In Virginia since 1850 (converted for a time after the War into townships). In Kentucky since 1850. In Louisiana, from 1852 till the War, and revived since 1879. In Florida since 1885, following the use of townships.

qualification; Idaho and Utah require a uniform system of *county* government, and general laws providing for township or precinct (in Utah township *and* precinct) organization. Illinois, again, in the same year as Wisconsin, provided, instead, that the Legislature should provide for township organization by general law, under which any county might organize by majority vote of its electors; and has been followed by Wyoming. California, since 1879, has tacked this provision on to the requirement of a uniform system of county government, and Washington has followed suit; while Illinois itself, since 1870, followed by Nebraska, Missouri and North Dakota, has added, instead, a permission to the county to dispense with a township organization, already formed, by a like vote of the electors. Just what effect any of these provisions have, however, upon the mere division of counties into townships, as distinguished from the structure of government erected therein, must be a matter of judicial interpretation.[1] More certainly applicable is a Michigan provision permitting County Boards of Supervisors to organize—or, since 1908, to organize and consolidate—townships, under such restrictions and limitations as shall be prescribed by law;[2] provisons in

---

[1] In some of the Referendum provisions, a majority of those voting, instead of a majority of the electors, is required.

References:

Wisc. Const. 1848, iv, 23.

Ill. Const. 1848, vii, 6; 1870, x, 5.

Cal. Const. 1849, xi, 4; 1879, xi, 4.

Nev. Const. 1864, iv, 25.

Neb. Const. 1875, x, 5.

Mo. Const. 1875, ix, 8, 9; Am. 1902.

Idaho Const. 1889, xviii, 5.

Wash. Const. 1889, xi, 4.

N. D. Const. 1889, 170, 171.

Wyom. Const. 1889, xii, 4.

Utah Const. 1895, xi, 4.

[2] Mich. Const. 1850, x, 11; * 1908, viii, 15.

two contiguous Western States designed to protect the original rectangular shape;[1] and prohibtions of special legislation erecting new townships or changing township lines, in Pennsylvania, Missouri and Minnesota.[2]

In the South, on the other hand, the provisions, though not always complete, are usually explicit, at least to the point of requiring that such districts shall exist.[3] Eleven varying rules may best be presented chronologically by States:

Mississippi, until 1890, required merely that "districts" (once referred to also as "beats") should exist; since then there are to be five districts in each county, not to be created by special legislation, and with a two-thirds county Referendum for change in boundaries, elections to be held not oftener than once in four years.

Tennessee requires "districts", not more than 25 in a county, or 4 for every 100 square miles.

Virginia required first "districts" as nearly equal as might be in area and population. In 1870, townships were required, compactly located, at least three in each county, and none additional containing less than 30 square miles. In 1874 the same rule was prescribed for "magistrate's districts". In 1902 the minimum area for additional districts was preserved, but other restrictions abolished.

---

[1] Minnesota (Const. 1857, xi, 3), by implication, forbids civil townships to differ from "congressional townships" except when these are divided by county lines, or contain under 100 inhabitants, in which case adjacent units may be combined.

South Dakota (Const. 1889, ix, 4) requires the organization of counties, by general law, into townships, identical with congressional townships, "so far as natural boundaries and population admit".

[2] Pa. Const. 1873, iii, 7.

Mo. Const. 1875, v, 53.

Minn. * Am. 1892, iv, 33.

[3] They are optional in Texas before the War (Const. 1845, iv, 13) and in Louisiana (Const. 1852, 78; 1879, 125; 1898, 126).

Kentucky, until 1890, required merely that " districts " should exist; since then, that there shall be three to eight in each county, and that their boundaries shall not be changed by special legislation, except when new counties are created.

West Virginia required at first three to ten townships, as compact as possible with reference to natural boundaries, and containing as nearly as possible an equal white population and not less than 400 inhabitants; boundaries to be controlled by the County Board of Supervisors, with Referenda of the townships affected. Since 1872, " districts " are to be three to ten in number, as nearly equal as possible in area and population, and the County Court controls.

Maryland, between 1864 and 1867, required merely that the Legislature should provide " townships or permanent municipal corporations " by general law, in place of the existing election districts.

North Carolina, in 1868, provided for the first establishment of townships by the joint action of the first elected County Commissioners, and the Legislature, but made no provision for future control. Since 1876 the Legislature is unfettered, even as to the continuance of the system.

Florida's Reconstruction instrument contained only the Nevada provision for a uniform system of county and township government. Since 1885, at least two " justice districts " are to be formed in each county by the County Commissioners.

Texas required at first, indirectly, five " justices precincts "; since 1876, four to eight, with control in the Commissioners Court of the county.

Alabama, since 1875, seems merely to require that " precincts " shall exist, and, since 1901, that their boundaries shall not be changed by special legislation, except when county lines are changed.

South Carolina requires that townships, established prior to 1895, and not expressly abolished in 1903, shall continue to exist as bodies corporate, but expressly authorizes the Legislature to change their lines or to organize new townships.

No rule for " precincts or districts " in New Mexico or for " precincts " in Arizona.[1]

II. JUDICIAL SUBSTITUTES FOR THE COUNTY

Next in order of size is the county itself. Everywhere, except in South Carolina during its early years, this has been the normal jurisdictional area for the lowest Courts of Record, supplemented, but not supplanted, except optionally in Nevada, by systems of minor and of major judicial divisions.

The uniform extension of the county system over the entire State, however, and the uniform maintenance of each county with all its characteristic functions unimpaired, have not been so universal.

1. *Territory outside of the county system*

The gridironing of the entire State area into counties

[1] References:

Miss. Const. 1832, iv, 23; 1868, vi, 23; xii, 6; 1890, 90, 170, 171, 260.

Tenn. Const. 1834, vi, 15; 1870, vi, 15.

Va. Const. 1850, vi, 27; 1870; vii, 2; Am. 1874; 1902, 111.

Ky. Const. 1850, iv, 34; 1890, 59, par. 20, 142.

W. Va. Const. 1862, vii, 1, 13; 1872, viii, 27.

Md. Const. 1864, x, 2 (until 1867).

N. C. Const. 1868, vii, 3, 4; 1876, vii, 14.

Fla. Const. 1868, v, 21; 1885, v, 21.

Tex. Const. 1868, v. 19; 1876, v. 18.

Ala. Const. 1875, vi, 26; 1901, 104, par. 29, 168.

S. C. Const. 1868, iv, 21; 1895, v, 23; vii, 2.

* N. M. Const. 1911, vi, 26.

* Ariz. Const. 1911, vi, 9.

has waited, in many States, upon the settlement of unoc-
cupied lands. One method of treating such territory is to
organize it into " districts ", bearing somewhat the same
relation to counties that the Federal territories do to the
States of the Union. Districts of this nature are mentioned in the original instrument of Virginia [1] and the second instrument of Kentucky.[2] South Carolina, also, in an
early and unsuccessful attempt to introduce the county system, provided for complementing it in this manner.[3]

2. *Augmented counties*

An advance upon the preceding system is the attachment
of territory to a particular county for all judicial purposes.
Such attachment is mentioned, as a general phenomenon, in
Michigan, in four recent Far Western States, and, since
the War, in Texas. The reference in Michigan is to " country " or " territory ", which apparently may be attached at
will. In Colorado it would look as though *any county* might
be attached to another for judicial purposes. The first
Texas rule was that, upon the certification of the District
Judge that Courts could not properly be held in any county,
the Governor must attach the same to that county whose
county seat was nearest that of the county in question; in
1876 this was changed to a permission to divide unorganized
territory into counties in advance of population, and attach
the same to convenient organized counties. Finally, three
States admitted in 1889 make the distinction between
" unorganized " and " organized " counties most clear by

[1] " District of West Augusta."   Va. Const. 1776, Thorpe, p. 3816
(until 1830).

[2] " Districts, counties or towns."   Ky. Const. 1799, vi, 11 (until 1850).

[3] " The whole State shall be divided into districts and counties, and
county courts established."   S. C. Const. 1778, 39 (until 1790).

providing that the Legislature shall make provision for attaching the one to the other for judicial purposes.[1]

Two other Western States mentioned in their "Schedules" the existence of similar attachments, made during the Territorial period;[2] and five expressly permit specified attachments or combinations of counties, until otherwise ordered by the Legislature.[3]

3. *Divided counties*

Nevada is peculiar in expressly permitting the division of counties into districts, to serve as the judicial unit; and Arkansas, since 1874, accords this permission in one special instance.[4]

4. *Differentiated districts* [5]

In still other States, a differentiation of judicial organi-

---

[1] This distinction is first drawn in the New York instrument of 1821, and is recognized to some extent in all of these States, except prior to 1876 in Texas.

References:

Mich. Const. 1835, Sched. 12; 1850, iv, 3; * 1908, v, 3.
Tex. Const. 1868, xii, 24; 1876, ix, 1.
Colo. Const. 1876, vi, 17.
N. D. Const. 1889, 115.
S. D. Const. 1889, v, 27.
Wyom. Const. 1889, v, 24.

[2] Iowa Const. 1846, xii, 7.
Kans. Const. 1859, Sched. 19.

[3] *Three* such special groupings in Wisconsin (Const. 1848, vii, 5). *One* in Oregon (Const. 1857, xviii, 11), Nevada (Const. 1864, vi, 5), and California (Const. 1879, vi, 6). *Nine* in Washington (Const. 1889, iv, 5).

In Illinois, also, for a time (Const. 1848, vii, 3—until 1870), territory stricken off from a county, but not actually organized within the period prescribed, was to remain a part of the parent county, for all purposes, until otherwise ordered.

[4] Nev. Const. 1864, vi, 5.
Ark. Const. 1874, xiii, 5.

[5] Note also the Alabama chancery districts, sec. iii, 4, p. 121, *infra*.

zation has occurred, which has resulted in the displacement of the county, not for all, but for some, of its characteristic uses. Thus, as early as 1792, the New Hampshire Legislature was empowered, subject to a majority petition, to divide any county into two districts for the registry of deeds.[1] Probate or inferior Court districts, in addition to counties, are, or have been, mentioned in five States.[2] Prosecuting Attorneys, whose jurisdiction is sometimes coterminous with the county, sometimes with the circuit group of counties, are in two States expressly permitted to be honored with county groups of their own.[3] Illinois since 1870, has permitted groups of counties to be formed for " County Court " purposes only; and Virginia and West Virginia, for a time, made such unions compulsory, under certain circumstances, upon the Legislature.[4] Finally, Oklahoma has a remarkable provision whereby any county, containing taxable property of less than $2,500,000, shall, upon petition of one-fourth of the electors and a majority Referendum, be attached to the adjoining county containing the least taxable property; the combination then has the characteristics of a single county in all except two respects: the

[1] N. H. Const. 1792, 72 (amended numbering, 71).

[2] Conn. Am. 1850, ix.
Vt. Am. 1850, xvii.
Ala. Am. 1850, v, 12; Const. 1867, vi, 11 (until 1875).
Tenn. Am. 1853, vi, 3, 5; Const. 1870, vi, 4.
Neb. Const. 1866, " Judiciary," 5 (until 1875).

[3] Oreg. Const. 1857, vii, 17.
Ala. Const. 1901, 167.

[4] Ill. Const. 1870, vi, 18.
Va. Const. 1870, vi, 13 (until 1902). Counties containing less than 8,000 inhabitants must be attached, for this purpose, to adjoining counties.
W. Va. Const. 1872, viii, 34 (until 1879). Counties must be joined for this purpose, upon their own initiative and after a majority Referendum in each.

County Court must circulate between the two county seats; and the attached portion may regain its independence by repeating the original procedure.[1]

III. MAJOR JUDICIAL DISTRICTS

The effort to economize official material in a sparsely-settled territory, and at the same time to make access to justice easy, naturally leads to an itinerant judiciary. The arrested development of regions within which, or of points at which, sessions of the highest Court are to be held, into constitutionally-defined districts of appellate jurisdiction—the far commoner and fully-perfected development of " circuits " (crooked lines) into similar Lower Court districts—provide an interesting subject for examination in all except the two small States of Delaware and New Jersey, and conservative New England.

1. *Highest Court districts*

The requirement that the highest Court shall move, as a whole, appeared in Maryland's original instrument, under which, and until as late as 1851, the sessions were to be held in each of its two well-defined " Shores ".[2] Then South Carolina, in 1790, required annual sessions at each of two places.[3] Next Ohio, from 1802 until 1851, required annual sessions in each county, adding, however, a peculiar permission to the Judges to form two " circuits ", within each of which half their number might act for the whole.[4] Finally Louisiana, in 1812, required sessions to be held during

---

[1] Okla. Const. 1907, xvii, 5.
[2] Md. Const. 1776, 56 (until 1851).
[3] S. C. Const. 1790, x, 3 (until 1816).
[4] Ohio Const. 1802, iii, 2, 10 (until 1851).

nine months of each year at New Orleans, with appellate jurisdiction over a specified group of counties; during the rest of the year at such place as the Legislature (at intervals of five years) might determine, with jurisdiction over the remaining counties.[1]

This represents the extreme stage reached in the development of independent areas of jurisdiction for the highest Court. In five States higher up the Mississippi River, and in Virginia, weakened provisions of a similar nature were introduced after the War of 1812, and still survive in Tennessee, Illinois, Minnesota and Virginia.[2] A mere authorization to the Legislature to require sessions at more than one place replaced the original South Carolina provision in 1816, the original Louisiana provision in 1845, and since then has been introduced into several other States.[3] In general, the

[1] La. Const. 1812, iv, 3 (until 1845).

[2] Mo. Const. 1820, v. 5; 1865, vi, 5 (until 1875). Mere authorization of not more than four full appellate districts.

Tenn. Const. 1834, vi, 2. Requirement that sessions shall be held within each of three " Grand Divisions." Changed by Const. 1870, vi, 2, to requirement that they shall be held at each of three specified places.

Ill. Const. 1848, v, 3. Requirement of sessions within each of three " Grand Divisions ", to be formed " as nearly equal as may be ". By Const. 1870, vi, 4, the Legislature is authorized to change their number or boundaries.

Ky. Const. 1850, iv, 9 (until 1890). Mere authorization of sessions within one or more of the districts within which the Judges were to be elected (*vide* ch. ix, sec. 2, *infra*).

Minn. Const. 1857, vi, 2. As the preceding, but requiring a two-thirds Legislative majority.

Va. Const. 1870, vi, 7; 1902, 93. Requirement of sessions at "two or more places".

[3] At such places as the Legislature prescribes. S. C. Am. 1816, x, 3 (until the War); Fla. Const. 1838, v, 4 (until the War); Cal. Const. 1849, vi, 10 (until 1879); Mich. Const. 1850, vi, 4; * 1908, vii, 3; W. Va.

notion of an itinerant highest Court lingers to some extent, but has not resulted in the Constitutional definition of jurisdictional areas for the same.

2. *Circuits and their equivalents*

The ancient custom of sending individual Judges on circuit through the shires or counties almost of necessity leads to the development of habitual routes of travel, determined by the judges themselves or by the Legislature. A further very natural development is the transference of the term " circuit ", from the path traversed, to the group of counties which are thus habitually combined under the jurisdiction of a single judge on his travels. Constitutional treatment of these circuits has everywhere been accompanied by the creation, for circuit purposes, of a special class of judges, with

---

Const. 1872, viii, 9; N. C. Const. 1876, iv, 7; N. D. Const. 1889, 88; Idaho Const. 1889, v, 8; Okla. Const. 1907, viii, 9.

At such *place* as the Legislature prescribes. Iowa Const, 1846, v, 3; 1857, v, 3.

At New Orleans during a specified part of the year, during the balance at the discretion of the Legislature. La. Const. 1845, 66; 1852, 68; 1868, 76; 1879, 84 (until 1898).

At the seat of government and not more than two other places. Tex. Const. 1845, iv, 3. Changed to the seat of government, only, in 1868 (Const. 1868, v, 4); then to the seat of government and two other places (Am. * 1874); then to the original provision (Const. 1876, v. 3). Finally, by an amendment of 1891 (Am. 1891, v, 3, 5), sessions of the highest civil court are to be held at the seat of government only; those of the highest criminal court, as before.

At the seat of government, and elsewhere at the discretion of the Legislature. Wisc. Const. 1848, vii, 11; Ohio Const. 1851, iv, 2; Oreg. Const. 1857, vii, 7; Kans. Const. 1859, iii, 3; S. C. Const. 1868, iv, 5; 1895, v, 5; Oreg. * Am. 1910, vii, 4.

At the seat of government, and, at the discretion of the Legislature, at three other places. Ark. Const. 1868, vii, 3 (until 1874).

In the other States the location of sessions is either not treated, or is fixed at one place, usually at the seat of government; in Louisiana, however, since 1898, at New Orleans.

jurisdiction limited to particular districts.[1]   This movement,
beginning in Pennsylvania in 1790, extended, during the
next generation, into Maryland and New York, and into
Ohio, Indiana, Mississippi, Alabama and Missouri.   Since
the advent of the Jacksonian Democracy, every new State
has started with this system, which also came to be mentioned in 1835 in Georgia, between 1845 and 1853 in the
instruments of Louisiana,[2] Illinois, Virginia, Kentucky and
Tennessee, after the War also in the Carolinas.   The idea
has survived wherever established,[3] but, in the course of
this progression through forty States, the relation of the
judge to his district has experienced some modification,
roughly represented by a growing preference for the term
" Judicial district " in place of " Circuit ".[4]   That is to say,
as the population, and hence the volume of judicial busi-

---

[1] This was the case even in New York, where, owing to the existence
of a higher Court, the local functions of Supreme Court Judges have
always been the more prominent.   Since the abolition of Circuit
Judges in 1846, however, the Supreme Court Judges, though obliged
to reside in separate districts, retain a measure of their former State-
wide jurisdiction.   In Oregon, districts were established at once—
special Circuit Judges only *in futuro*.   In the other States provisions
authorizing an exchange of districts between the Judges are common,
but no lower Judge has, as a rule, jurisdiction, at one and the same
time, over more than one district.

[2] Not mentioned in Louisiana between 1852 and 1868.

[3] Indistinct allusions to " districts " of this nature appear also in
Massachusetts (Am. 1855, xix) and Connecticut (Am. 1876, xx).

[4] " Circuits " in Pennsylvania until 1838, Ohio until 1851, New York
until 1846; consistently in Indiana, Alabama, Missouri, Arkansas,
Florida, Wisconsin, Virginia, West Virginia, South Carolina, and
South Dakota; also in Maryland since 1851, Georgia since the War,
and Illinois since 1870.
" Circuits " in Michigan, but one special large " Judicial District "
until 1908.   " Circuits or Districts " in Tennessee.   " Common Pleas
Districts " in Ohio.   " Appellate Districts " in California (but *cf.* p.
118, note 1).
In all other cases, " Judicial Districts ".

ness, has increased, justification has been found for increasing the number of Judges in the State, either by diminishing the size, and hence increasing the number, of the districts themselves, or by increasing the number of Judges provided for each district. In Washington and Arizona, for instance, the district has disappeared, having been reduced to the (here quite large) county. In New York, on the other hand, there has been an increase in the number of Judges for each comparatively large district. Thus both on the Pacific slope and in New York, as well as in several other States where the evidence is not so clear, fixed Courts are now so abundant as to facilitate judicial relief without judicial locomotion.

The numerous direct limitations upon the result to be obtained, in the formation of these districts, will be treated, as usual, in the order of their first appearance.

(a) *Restrictions upon the number of counties composing a district*

The original Pennsylvania plan was to assign an upward limit of six and a downward limit of three to the number of counties which might be included within one circuit. This model was followed by Alabama, and, for a time, by Mississippi and Arkansas. Abolished in the two last States, it has developed in the first two named somewhat differently. In the industrial State of Pennsylvania, with its large volume of judicial proceedings, small districts are encouraged; the upward limit has been lowered first to five and then to four; the downward limit was abolished in 1838, while since 1873 counties containing 40,000 inhabitants must constitute separate districts. In Alabama, on the other hand, the upward limit was first raised to eight, then to twelve, and finally, in 1901, removed altogether; while the downward limit has remained unchanged except that, since this last-named year, a county containing 20,000 inhabitants, and taxable property of $3,500,000, may be constituted separately, or combined with one other county.[1]

(b) *Restrictions upon the number of districts in the State*

The preceding definition of the district in terms of counties is not well adapted to a State in which the number of counties is rapidly increasing. Ohio, accordingly, the next State after Pennsylvania, preferred to set a downward limit (three) upon the number of the *districts*. This example, with much variation in the figure, has since been quite commonly followed, and though, in most of the earlier instances, it has been abandoned, a minimum figure still appears in seven Western States and in Kentucky, Louisiana and Florida.[2] Experience seems to have demonstrated that

[1] The upward limit in Mississippi was raised to 12 in 1832. The Arkansas figures were 5 and 7.

Pa. Const. 1790, v, 4; 1838, v, 3; 1873, v, 4, 5.

Miss. Const. 1817, v. 3; 1832, iv, 13 (until the War).

Ala. Const. 1819, v, 5; 1867, vi, 4; 1875, vi, 4; 1901, 139, 147.

Ark. Const. 1836, vi, 4 (until 1848).

[2] *Three* in Wyoming (Const. 1889, v. 19, 20, 21); also in Ohio (Const. 1802, iii, 3) until 1851, Indiana (Const 1816, v, 3) until 1851, Nebraska (Const. 1866, " Judiciary", 2, 8) until 1875.

Four in Oregon (Const. 1857, vii, 2); also in New York (Const. 1821, v, 5) until 1846, Florida (Const. 1838, v, 5) until the War, Iowa (Const. 1846, v, 4) until 1857, and Colorado (Const. 1876, vi, 13, 14) until * 1886.

Five in Wisconsin (Const. 1848, vii, 5, 6) and Kansas (Const. 1859, iii, 5, 14).

Six in Nebraska since 1875 (Const. 1875, vi, 10, 11) and North Dakota (Const. 1889, 104, 106).

Eight in South Dakota (Const. 1889, v, 16, 17) and Florida (* Am. 1902, v, 8; 1910, v, 35).

Nine (apparently) in Michigan (Const. vi, 6, 7; xix, 4); changed by an amendment of 1905 to the number then existing; and since 1908 no restriction. Nine also in Illinois (Const. 1848, v. 7) until 1870, and (apparently) in West Virginia from 1872 (Const. 1872, viii, 10, 14, 15) until 1879.

Twelve in Louisiana (Const. 1845, 75; 1868, 83) until 1879, except for

Legislatures are more apt to form too many districts than too few. The downward limit has been accompanied by an upward limit in six States, in four of which, Oregon, Kentucky, Louisiana and Wyoming, this double limitation still survives. In the other two, both limitations disappeared together, but in one of these, New York, the upward limit was subsequently reëstablished for a time; and in Illinois, since 1870, an upward limit has taken the place of the previously established minimal figure.[1]

a break from 1852 till the War, when districts were not mentioned; and in Kentucky (Const. 1850, iv, 19, 24) until 1890.

Twenty in Virginia (Const. 1850, vi, 2-5) until the War.

Twenty-one in Louisiana since 1879 Const. 1879, 107, 108; 1898, 107).

Number established by Legislature at first session after adoption of instrument, in Kentucky since 1890 (Const. 128, 132).

[1] *Eight* in New York (Const. 1821, v, 5) until 1846. Between 1869 (Am. vi, 5) and 1894, also, the existing number of districts (actually eight) might not be increased.

Twenty in Louisiana (Const. 1845, 75) until 1852, and from 1868 (Const. 1868, 83) until 1879; then *thirty-one* (Const. 1879, 107, 108) until 1898; since then (Const. 1898, 107) *thirty*.

Sixteen in Kentucky (Const. 1850, iv, 24) until the population of the State should exceed 1,500,000. This figure was reached by the Census of 1880, and in 1890 a new sliding limitation was copied from Illinois.

Seven in Oregon (Const. 1857, vii, 2). In imitation of Kentucky it was also provided that, until the white population should amount to 100,000 the number of districts should not exceed five. Here, also the population figure was reached in 1880.

Four in Wyoming (Const. 1889, v, 21) until the taxable property in the State shall exceed $100,000,000.

One district for every 100,000 inhabitants of the State, plus such districts as may be formed in counties containing over 100,000, and plus the Cook county district, in Illinois (Const. 1870, vi, 13, 15, 23).

One district for every 55,000 inhabitants, in West Virginia, from 1872 (Const. 1872, viii, 15) until 1879.

One district for every 60,000 inhabitants of the State, plus one for each county having 150,000 inhabitants, in Kentucky since 1890 (Const. 1890, 132, 137).

Vide also p. 117, *infra* for the peculiar provision existing in Alabama for a time, in connection with the requirement of an extraordinary Legislative majority.

Finally, in Georgia until the War, in Florida and in North Carolina for a time since the War, and in California to-day, the number of districts has been precisely determined.[1]

(c) *Constitutional definition, in terms of counties*

It is doubtless because the Susquehanna River and Chesapeake Bay, dividing Maryland into two sharply-distinguished geographical sections, familiarized this State with fixed political divisions, that districts here have from the very beginning been expressly defined as groups of specified counties.[2]   New Mexico, with less apparent justification, does the same.[3]   Florida, also, has occasionally emphasized her precise determination of the number of districts by defining the county contents of each;[4] and the recent Washington-Arizona plan of identifying the Superior Court district with the county may be considered as an instance of the same distrust of the Legislature.   Beginning, moreover, with New York in 1846 special districts—usually for urban territory—have been separately constituted in seven States.[5]

---

[1] *Three* in California (* Am. 1904, vi, 4).

Five in Georgia from 1835 (Am. 1835, iii, 1) until the War.

Seven in Florida from 1868 (Const. 1868, vii, 7; xvii, 3) until 1870; then *five* (Am. 1870, iii; Am. 1875, v) until 1885; then *seven* again (Const. 1885, v, 8, 10) until 1902; then *eight* (* Am. 1902, v, 8) until 1910.

Twelve in North Carolina (Const. 1868, iv, 12, 13) until 1876.

[2] *Six* groups (Am. 1805, ix) until 1851; then *eight* (Const. 1851, iv, 8) until 1864; then *thirteen* (Const. 1864, iv, 24) until 1867; since then (Const. 1867, iv, 19) *eight* again.

[3] *Eight* groups, new counties to be attached to any contiguous district (* Const. 1911, vi, 25).

[4] Fla. Const. 1868, vii, 7; xvii, 3 (until 1870); Am. 1875, v (until 1885).

[5] In New York (Const. 1846, vi, 4, 16—until 1869), the city (and county) of New York.

In Michigan (Const. 1850, xix, 1—until * 1908), the Upper Peninsula counties and islands.

(d) *Requirements of contiguous territory or contiguous counties*

Thirteen Western States, beginning with Arkansas in 1836, provide—usually in connection with some other restriction—that the districts shall consist of contiguous counties.[1] These, with Kentucky and South Carolina, are the only States expressly to provide that counties may not be divided.[2]

(e) *Rules as to the population to be included*

The first clear suggestion that population is an index of the volume of judicial business, and hence a fit measure of the judicial district, appeared in New York, where, from

In Ohio (Const. 1851, iv, 3), Hamilton county.

In Missouri (Const. 1865, vi, 14), the county of St. Louis; since 1875 (Const. 1875, vi, 27; ix, 24) the language is not clear, but apparently the county of St. Louis, as it existed before division, is perpetuated as one circuit.

In Illinois (Const. 1870, vi, 23), Cook county.

In Louisiana (Const. 1879, 107, 130; 1898, 107, 132), the parish of Orleans.

In Colorado (Am. 1902, xx, 1), the city and county of Denver.

[1] Ark. Const. 1836, vi, 4 (until the War) ; Const. 1874, vii, 13.
Wisc. Const. 1848, vii, 6.
Ohio Const. 1851, iv, 3.
Kans. Const. 1859, iii, 14.
Ill. Const. 1870, vi, 13.
Minn. Am. 1875, vi, 4.
Mo. Const. 1875, vi, 24.
Neb. Const. 1875, vi, 11.
Colo. Const. 1876, vi, 14.
N. D. Const. 1889, 106.
S. D. Const. 1889, v, 17.
Mont. Const. 1889, viii, 14.
Cal. * Am. 1904, vi, 4.
So also N. Y. Const. 1846, vi, 4, 16 (until 1869).

[2] Ky. Const. 1850, iv, 19; 1890, 128, 132 (not expressly applicable to other than the initial division).
S. C. Const. 1895, vii, 13.

1846 until 1869, it was provided that, if the districts were changed, they should be made, at their first rearrangement, " equal in population, as nearly as may be ".[1] Illinois and Minnesota later gave weaker expression to this attractive but absolutely unattainable ideal of a population symmetrically divided for judicial purposes.[2]

The Constitutional definitions, already mentioned, of special urban districts, side by side with a limited number of rural districts, is a more practical, though less ambitious, attempt to secure something like an equal volume of business among the several districts; and in a few States, including Illinois, since the Civil War, generalized provisions have been adopted encouraging, or insuring, this degree of uniformity. The Illinois provision is highly involved, but appears to mean that counties containing under 50,000 inhabitants, and counties containing over 50,000 but whose business does not occupy nine months of the year, may not be established as separate districts; other counties may be, subject to the upward limitation of number (not more than one circuit, in addition to these, for every 100,000 inhabitants in the entire State) ; and whenever a county newly passes the 100,000 mark, the limit moves up one circuit.[3] Kentucky *requires* separate establishment for any county containing 150,000 inhabitants, and permits it (subject to the upward limit of not more than one district in addition to the preceding, for every 60,000 inhabitants in the entire

[1] N. Y. Const. 1846, vi, 4, 16 (until 1869).

[2] Ill. Const. 1870, vi, 13, 15. " As nearly equal as circumstances will permit, having due regard to business, territory and population."

Minn. Am. 1875, vi, 4. " Population as nearly equal as may be practicable."

In neither State is it clear that the provision refers to other than the initial division.

[3] Ill. Const. 1870, vi, 13, 15. *Cf.* p. 111, note 1, *supra.*

State) for counties containing 40,000 inhabitants which
include a city of 20,000.[1] The provisions requiring separate
establishments in Pennsylvania, and permitting them in
Alabama, have already been mentioned.

Virginia, in 1902, after a long interval during which no
restrictions upon Legislative control appeared, transferred.
the familiar rule of a minimum population, from the creation of new counties, to the creation of new judicial districts.[2]

Two general types of indirect limitations have also developed.

(f) *Retarding provisions*

The device, long familiar in connection with Legislative
apportionment, and which we have seen sparingly applied
to the formation of counties, of prescribing intervals during
which no change may occur, was applied first to judicial
districts by Louisiana in 1845, and subsequently by a dozen
States in all, in six of which it survives. In New York
and West Virginia it is now the only restriction.

Several varieties of this provision have developed. The
original Louisiana provision, while in force, permitted action
of any sort only every sixth year; and with some variation
as to figure, this was the rule in Virginia before the War,
and is the existing rule in Illinois, West Virginia and New
York.[3]

---

[1] Ky. Const. 1890, 132, 137, 138. *Cf.* p. 111, note 1, *supra.*

[2] Va. Const. 1902, 95. The new district not to contain less, nor an
old district to be thereby reduced to less, than 40,000 inhabitants.

[3] The six-year figure in Louisiana was the same as the length of the
Judge's term, but inasmuch as a system of partial renewal was in
force, the identity is of no significance. Virginia named eight years,
that being the Judge's term. In Illinois changes may be made only at
the session preceding the (sexennial) general election of Judges. So

For a time, New York, followed by Iowa, had a peculiar additional restriction, permitting the number of districts to be changed, at the periodical times, not more than one, in either direction; similarly Kentucky, with different periods for change in number and for change in boundary.[1] Kentucky has finally developed a rule permitting the number of districts to be increased, at any time, but permitting mere changes of boundary only at the first session after the (decennial) enumeration.[2] West Virginia and Missouri, for a time, had provisions curiously contrasting with the preceding.[3]

Finally, three Western States have adopted a rule permitting increase in the number of districts only at intervals

in West Virginia, where the term is for eight years. In New York, districts may be altered "once after every [decennial] enumeration."

La. Const. 1845, 75 (until 1852).

Va. Const. 1850, vi, 5 (until the War).

N. Y. Am. 1869, vi, 6; Const. 1894, vi, 1.

Ill. Const. 1870, vi, 13.

W. Va. Am. 1879, viii, 14.

[1] The original number of districts in New York was *eight*—changes at the first session after every (decennial) enumeration. In Iowa, *eleven* districts—changes every fourth year, that being the term of Judges. In Kentucky, *twelve* districts—changes in number (only to increase) every fourth year; other changes at the first session after the (octennial) enumeration.

N. Y. Const. 1846, vi, 16 (until 1869).

Ky. Const. 1850, iv, 24, 27 (until 1890).

Iowa Const. 1857, v, 10 (until 1884).

Since 1884, changes may be made in Iowa only at regular sessions.

[2] Ky. Const. 1890, 132, 134.

[3] In West Virginia (Const. 1862, vi, 3—until 1872), mere changes of boundary could be made at any time, but change in number only every tenth year.

In Missouri (Const. 1865, vi, 14—until 1870), changes of any sort could *not* be made at the session preceding the general election of six-year Judges.

which correspond to the length of the Judge's term; mere changes in boundary may apparently be made at any time.[1]

(g) *Extraordinary Legislative majority*

In Ohio, since 1851, and in California for a time, the requirement of two-thirds of the members elected to each house, for change of any sort, is the only restriction upon the formation of these districts. In five Western States a similar requirement is imposed in addition to the minimum number and contiguous territory rules—in three of these, in addition to the retarding provision as well—but only with reference to an increase in the number of districts. Alabama, for a time, in addition to its rule limiting the number of counties in a district, required a two-thirds majority to increase the number of *districts* above eight.[2]

Notwithstanding this heaping-up of provisions in a few Western States, the general tendency in the country as a whole, so far as any can be discerned, seems to be in the direction of leaving control of these districts entirely in the hands of the Legislature. Twenty-four instruments to-day contain only the slightest, if any, restrictions.[3]

---

[1] Four years in Nebraska (Const. 1875, vi, 11) and North Dakota (Const. 1889, 106). Six years in Colorado (Const. 1876, vi, 14) until * 1886.

It is often provided that changes shall not have the effect of depriving a judge of his office; but Nevada (Const. 1864, vi, 5), provides that the changes themselves shall not *take effect* until the Judge's office is regularly vacated.

[2] Two-thirds of the "members elected", in Ohio, California and Nebraska; elsewhere, two-thirds of the "members".

Ohio Const. 1851, iv, 15.

Kans. Const. 1859, iii, 14.

Cal. Am. 1862, vi, 5 (until 1879).

Ala. Const. 1875, vi, 4 (until 1901).

Neb. Const. 1875, vi, 11.

Colo. Const. 1876, vi, 14; * Am. 1886.

N. D. Const. 1889, 106.

S. D. Const. 1889, v, 27.

[3] New England, New Jersey and Delaware do not mention these

3. Intermediate districts and their offshoots

Since 1850, the desire to provide appellate opportunities has led, in seven States, to systems of appellate districts.[1]

The original Virginia plan, which did not survive the War, was to require precisely *five* such districts, each containing *at least* four circuits, subject to rearrangement, like the circuits themselves, only every eighth year. Missouri, in 1865, a little more liberal, required *at least five* districts, each to contain *at least* three circuits, all outside the county of St. Louis, which was a separate circuit and a separate appellate district in itself; no retarding provision appeared, nor indeed any mention of subsequent change at all, and five years later the entire system was abandoned. In 1875, however, a special appellate district was established, to consist of the City of St. Louis and four adjacent counties, and, in 1884, the entire State was freshly divided into two districts, with power to the Legislature to create a third, and to alter lines at will. Louisiana, too, in 1879, excepted the Parish of Orleans, requiring in the rest of the State merely *five* districts, the boundaries of which might at any

districts. Georgia and Tennessee mention them, without insisting that they exist. With temporary or unimportant exceptions South Carolina, Missouri, Texas, Minnesota, Nevada, Montana, Idaho, Utah and Oklahoma, from the beginning—Indiana since 1851, Mississippi and Arkansas since the War, North Carolina since 1876, and Iowa since 1884—contain no provision except the requirement that there shall be such districts. So also California until 1862, and Virginia, 1870-1902.

Note also the Pacific slope tendency to identify this type of district with the county.

[1] "Sections" above "Circuits" in Virginia; "Districts" above "Circuits" in Missouri and Illinois; "Circuits" above "Districts" in Louisiana, and above "Common Pleas Districts" in Ohio; "Supreme Judicial Districts" above "Districts" in Texas; "Departments" above "Districts" in New York. California "Appellate Districts" perhaps belong here, rather than with Circuits.

time be changed; and then, in 1898, adopted the Missouri plan of a special district consisting of Orleans and four other parishes only; since 1906, however, the rest of the State is again to be divided into *two* appellate districts, with complete freedom otherwise to the Legislature.

Illinois and Ohio are still more liberal, the former, since 1870, merely permitting, the latter, since 1883, requiring districts without any restriction.

Finally, Texas, since 1891, has established, for civil purposes only, appellate districts, limited to *two or three* in the first place, with authority given to the Legislature to increase them, but not to diminish. And New York, in 1894, required the establishment of *four* " departments ", of which the county of New York to be one, the others " to be. bounded by county lines and be compact and equal in population as nearly as may be "; changes may be made " once every ten years ", and the number of departments, in sharp contrast with Texas, may not be increased; it is impossible to discover from the language whether the other restrictions apply except to the first division. Neither here, nor in any of the other surviving provisions, is the attempt made to insure harmony of lines between these districts and the smaller circuits or districts.[1]

Within these districts appellate courts, composed either of already existing judges, or of judges specially created, hold Court. *Where* do they hold Court? As in the case of the Supreme Court, this question is variously answered.

---

[1] Va. Const. 1850, vi, 5 (until the War).

Mo. Const. 1865, vi, 12 (until 1870); Const. 1875, vi, 12; * Am. 1884, 1-3.

Ill. Const. 1870, vi, 11.

La. Const. 1879, 97, 98; 1898, 99, 100, 131; Am. 1906, 100.

Ohio Am. 1883, iv, 6.

Tex. Am. 1891, v, 6.

N. Y. Const. 1894, vi, 2.

In Ohio, and in Louisiana until 1898, the Court went on circuit through the several counties or parishes. In Missouri, Illinois, and in Louisiana since 1906, it meets at such places—in Texas at such *place*—as the Legislature determines; in New York, at such places as the Judges assigned to the Department determine. And in Virginia the Court was required to meet in each of the distinct "*districts*" into which, as well as into "circuits," the appellate "section" was to be divided.[1]

4. *Coördinate districts and their offshoots*

In four Southern States, the tendency to differentiate judicial organization, the manifestation of which, in the case of county business, we have already seen, has led to the establishment of equity or criminal districts, distinct from the regular civil circuits.

Alabama first, in 1867, required "chancery divisions", without restriction until 1875, when an upward limit of three as contrasted with eight for the civil circuits, was fixed, unless increased by a two-thirds vote of the Legislature; since 1901, the rule is the same as for the circuits. Alabama's neighbor, Mississippi, has also had "chancery districts" since 1868, at first to be composed of not more than four counties; but since 1876, in accordance with the provision regarding circuits, without restrictions. Tennessee, since 1870, has mentioned chancery districts. Texas, finally, in 1876, permitted the establishment of special criminal districts, containing cities of at least 30,000 inhabitants; in 1901 this was reduced to a permission to continue one such district already established.[2]

---

[1] At least two of these districts, to contain complete circuits, and to be wholly included in the section; the whole system subject to rearrangement only at intervals of eight years.

[2] Ala. Const. 1867, vi, 7, 8; 1875, vi, 7, 8; 1901, 145, 146, 147.

In Mississippi (and in Alabama at first) the chancery judges go on circuit through the counties. From the beginning, however, the subdivision of the Alabama divisions into " districts " has been required, and, since 1875, Court is to be held in each of these, instead of in each county.

IV. MAJOR DIVISIONS FOR GENERAL PURPOSES

The county,[1] with hardly an exception, is the largest division used for general governmental purposes. This, rather than the larger judicial division, corresponds to the French *département* as the territorial unit to the authorities of which the duty of administering the laws in general is assigned. The prevailingly smaller size of our districts, as compared with the French, as well as our preference for the local election of the authorities therein, measures our greater degree of " decentralization ". It is worth noting, however, that the East and West Shores of Maryland were utilized, prior to 1851, for other purposes than judicial;[2] and that South Carolina's requirement of sessions of its highest Court at two specified places, in which the germ of a division of the state into two districts may be discerned, received a similar extension.[3] The obsolete requirement that the Connecticut

---

Miss. Const. 1868, vi, 17; Am. 1876; Const. 1890, 152, 164.

Tenn. Const. 1870, vi, 4.

Tex. Const. 1876, v, 1; Am. 1891, v, 1.

Georgia, also, from 1868 (Const. v, 4) until 1877, permitted the use of Senatorial districts (*vide* ch. viii, *infra*) for criminal purposes, the Judge going on circuit through the counties.

[1] *Vide* ch. iii, *supra*.

[2] There was to be a Treasurer and a Register of the Land Office for each Shore. Md. Const. 1776, 13, 51 (until 1851).

[3] Distinct Treasurers for Charleston and Columbia; distinct *offices* for the Secretary of State and for the Surveyor General. When, in 1816, the location of judicial sessions was left to the Legislature, these administrative requirements were left unchanged. S. C. Const. 1790, x, 1, 2 (until the War).

and Rhode Island Legislatures should meet at different places may also be mentioned as a relic of historical divisions, originally quite independent of one another.[1]

V. SUMMARY

The net effect of all the tendencies and movements enumerated in this chapter has been, of course, to produce great dissimilarity between State and State, as regards their general system of political divisions. Ten States, it will be found, clearly recognize three, and only three, types of State-wide divisions, for general or judicial purposes: the county, one division smaller, and one larger.[2] With regard to none of the other existing instruments can this statement, with literal accuracy, be made; while the rules under which these districts may be created, abolished or changed, show even greater variety. Looking at the situation a little more broadly, however, we may say that these three tiers of divisions still constitute the standard American system, to which all divergencies of individual States may conveniently be referred—a minor division, representing the natural "neighborhood"; a major division, serving the administrative convenience of the State; and the intermediate county, too large for the one purpose, too small for the other, and for which only an historical justification now exists. No

---

[1] Alternate annual sessions of the Connecticut Legislature at Hartford and New Haven. Conn. Const. 1818, iii, 2—until 1872.

May sessions of the Rhode Island Legislature always at Newport, until 1900. October sessions, originally, once every two years at South Kingston, once every four years at Bristol, and once every four years at East Greenwich; adjournment from October session to Providence. In 1854 the October session was abandoned, and adjournments from the May session were to be at Providence. Since 1900, all sessions at Providence. R. I. Const. 1842, iv, 3; Am. 1854, iii; 1900, xi.

[2] These States are Pennsylvania, Maryland, Virginia, West Virginia, Kentucky, North Carolina, Florida, Indiana, Iowa and Kansas.

substitute for, or modification of, this system has secured
anything like general acceptance. And it is also pretty generally true that Legislative control over minor or major divisions is not restricted to any great extent, while over
counties it is; just how restricted, is a question variously
answered. On only one or two positive principles, in short,
does national experience thus far coincide. The rest remains to be worked out in the laboratory.

CHAPTER VI

DISTRICTS FOR SPECIAL ADMINISTRATIVE PURPOSES

I. MILITIA DISTRICTS

CONSTITUTIONAL recognition of military districts rings oddly on our modern ears, but is sufficiently explained by the frontier conditions in the eight contiguous States where, beginning with Georgia in 1777, this recognition was first accorded. Maryland, in 1851, was a belated imitator of these models. Though in several of these States the provisions were eventually dropped, they still survive in Georgia, where the militia district is still used as the minor civil division; in Tennessee, where it was similarly utilized, prior to the creation of the present justices district; in Kentucky, Ohio and Mississippi.

As a rule, there is only a recognition that districts, corresponding to one or more of the traditional service grades, exist. The original Georgia provision, however, in force until 1789, required counties containing less than 250 men, liable to bear arms, to be formed into independent " companies "; every larger county, into one or more "battalions"; and, since 1798, it has been clearly implied that Company districts are to be subdivisions of counties; before the War, also, that Battalion districts were to be either subdivisions of, or entire counties. In Tennessee, prior to 1834, the implication seems to be that counties shall constitute field officers' districts, for infantry, and captain's districts for cavalry, and shall be subdivided into captain's districts for infantry, and aggregated to form field officers' districts for cavalry. In Missouri, the River was named, for ten years after 1865, as the dividing line between two military districts, to be subdivided by the Governor. And in Mississippi, since 1868, Congressional districts have been constituted " Military Divisions ".[1]

[1] "Companies" and "Battalions" in Georgia, 1777-89, and in Kentucky, 1792-99.

"Captain's Companies" and field officers' di. tricts; also cavalry districts of corresponding grades, in Tennessee, 1796-1834.

"Captain's Districts," "Companies," or "Company Districts;" "Battalions," or "Battalion Districts;" "Fegiments," "Brigades" and "Divisions," in Georgia, 1798, till the War; Kentucky, 1799-1890; Indiana, 1816-51; Tennessee, since 1834; Florida, 1838 till the War; Maryland, 1851-64.

"Company Districts," only, in Ohio, 1802-51.

Company officers' and field officers' "Commands," in Missouri, 1820-61.

Unspecified districts, in Mississippi, 1832 till the War, and in Ohio since 1851.

"Military Districts" and subdistricts in Missouri, 1865-75.

"Militia Divisions" (under Brigadier-Generals) in Mississippi since 1868.

"Militia Districts" (corresponding to the original "Captain's Districts") in Georgia, since the War.

"Companies, Battalions, Regiments or other Commands," in Kentucky, since 1890.

Of these, the Georgia "Captain's Districts" or later "Militia Districts" have been Constitutionally impressed for civil purposes, since 1798; Georgia "Battalion Districts" also prior to the War; Tennessee "Captain's Companies," prior to 1834.

References:

Ga. Const. 1777, 35 (until 1789); 1798, i, 25; iii, 5; iv, 3; 1868, v, 6; 1877, vi, 7, 8.

Ky. Const. 1792, vi, 4; 1799, vi, 11; 1850, vii, 3; 1890, 222.

Tenn. Const. 1796, v, 11; vii, 1, 2, 6; 1834, viii, 1; 1870, viii, 1.

Ohio Const. 1802, v, 1; 1851, ix, 2.

Ind. Const. 1816, vii, 3, 4, 5; xii (until 1851). *Cf.* Const. 1851, xii, 5, permitting the division of the militia into "sedentary" and "active" classes.

Mo. Const. 1820, ix, 1 (until 1861; *cf.* Thorpe, pp. 2176, 2179); Const. Ordinance, 1865, Thorpe, p. 2220 (until 1875).

Miss. Const. 1832, v, "Militia," 2; 1868, ix, 6; 1890, 218.

Fla. Const. 1838, vii, 1 (until the War).

Md. Const. 1851, ix, 1 (until 1864).

2. VOTING DISTRICTS

Provisions looking towards the division of the smallest areas of popular election (counties, cities or towns) into still smaller districts, to serve the purely administrative purpose of collecting votes, appeared first in Pennsylvania, in 1776, and since then, in ten States in all, surviving in eight, on or near the Atlantic seaboard. Pennsylvania, also, in 1838, in the interval between abandoning its original rule, and taking over a new one, assumed the existence of such districts in a clause defining the residential qualifications of voters. The frequent subsequent adoption of similar clauses by other States indicates a widespread recognition of the advisability of small voting districts; small both in area and in voting population. The importance of such districts, as a means of facilitating the formal expression of the popular will, is indeed so great, that it is remarkable that explicit rules have not been more generally prescribed.

The original Pennsylvania plan, lasting only until 1790. was to permit the division of any county, " at its own choice ", into districts.[1] The next State to face the problem was Georgia, which, in 1798, provided an entirely different rule, placing control of its " precincts " (" election-precincts ", since the War) in the Courts, though requiring the Legislature to prescribe the manner in which these powers should be exercised.[2] This provision survives in Georgia to-day; and in 1873 Pennsylvania itself gave the county or city courts power to divide townships or wards. with the proviso that the districts must be compact, and that when over 250 votes had been cast in a district, it must be divided.[3]

---

[1] Pa. Const. 1776, 18 (until 1790). Like the Maryland districts, these seem to have been used also for judicial purposes.

[2] Ga. Const. 1798, i, 26; 1868, iii, 6; 1877, iii, 7, par. 18.

[3] Pa. Const. 1873, viii, 11.

Maryland, on the other hand, in 1799 required the Legislature to divide each county and Baltimore city into a specified number of districts. The number in two cases was subsequently changed by constitutional amendment, and finally, in 1837, all restrictions were removed. A prohibition upon special legislation, temporarily imposed in 1864, is the only limitation which has since been made in this State. It has already been pointed out that these " election districts " have come to be utilized as the regular minor judicial divisions.[1]

Kentucky, the same year as Maryland, was liberal from the beginning. It gave a clear authorization to the Legislature to divide counties at will, and was followed in this respect by Louisiana and Mississippi, as they entered. In 1845, Louisiana supplemented this by a permission to delegate this power to the county or municipal authorities; but neither here nor in Mississippi did the provision survive the War. Kentucky, in 1850, *required* the Legislature either to divide the counties, or to delegate the power to some county authority; and this continued in force until 1890, since when the only provision in this State is a prohibition upon change of boundaries by special legislation, except in the creation of new counties.[2]

The only other positive rule affecting these districts is a requirement in Connecticut, since 1876, that a newly-incorporated town, not privileged with separate representation, shall constitute a separate election district in the town from

---

[1] Md. * Am. 1799, vi, 1; 1803, viii; 1807, x; 1837, 12; Const. 1864, iii, 32 (until 1867).

[2] Ky. Const. 1799, ii, 5; 1850, ii, 5; 1890, 59. " Precincts " (voting districts) are expressly mentioned in addition to " districts " (minor judicial districts).

La. Const. 1812, ii, 5; 1845, ii, 7; 1852, ii, 7 (until the War).

Miss. Const. 1817, iii, 8; 1832, iii, 8 (until the War).

which the major part of its territory is taken.[1] And the only other provisions which directly affect these districts at all, are authorizations accorded since the War, to the Legislatures of three States, to make such divisions.[2] Prohibition upon special legislation designating *places* of voting is, however, beginning with Indiana in 1851, common.[3]

[1] Conn. Am. 1876, xviii.

Cf. also the obsolete Virginia provision requiring the division of the more populous urban districts into *wards* (Va. Const. 1850, iii, 2).

[2] In Maine (Am. 1869, xiv—Amended Const. ix, 16), only towns having over 4,000 inhabitants, or having voters residing upon an island, may be divided into " voting districts ".

In Massachusetts (Am. 1885, xxix) any town, and in South Carolina (Const. 1895, vii, 13) any county, may be divided.

[3] In twenty-three States to-day. California and Kentucky, however, permit special legislation when new counties are organized; Alabama, when county lines are changed.

Ind. Const. 1851, iv, * 22, 23.

Oreg. Const. 1857, iv, 23.

Md. Const. 1864, iii, 32 (until 1867).

Nev. Const. 1864, iv, 20.

Fla. Const. 1868, v, 17; 1885, iii, 20.

W. Va. Const. 1872, vi, 39.

Pa. Const. 1873, iii, 7.

N. Y. Am. 1874; Const. 1894, iii, 18.

Neb. Const. 1875, iii, 15.

Mo. Const. 1875, v, 53.

Tex. Const. 1876, iii, 56.

Colo. Const. 1876, v, 25.

Cal. Const. 1879, iv, 25.

La. Const. 1879, 46; 1898, 48.

Minn. Am. 1881, iv, 33.

Mont. Const. 1889, v, 26.

Ida. Const. 1889, iii, 19.

Wyom. Const. 1889, iii, 27.

Minn. * Am. 1892, iv, 33.

Ky. Const. 1890, 59.

Ala. Const. 1901, 104.

Va. Const. 1902, 64.

Okla. Const. 1907, v, 46.

* N. Mex. Const. 1911, iv, 24.

3. EDUCATIONAL DISTRICTS

" School districts," under this name, first appear in the Michigan and Texas instruments of 1835 and 1845; in six other Western States before the War; to-day, in thirty-seven States;[1] larger educational districts also, since the War, in Virginia, California, Idaho and Oklahoma.[2] Before the War, no restrictions upon the power of the Legislature to utilize other divisions for these purposes, or to make special divisions of its own, were imposed. The few provisions adopted since have been principally in the South.

For minor divisions, Alabama led off, in 1867, with a provision empowering its State Board of Education to make such districts, distinct from the township; after eight years, the dropping of this provision left the Legislature in full control; in 1901, however, the establishment of separate

It may be that under one or two of the older instruments, where no recognition of special voting districts was made, their formation was impossible. In the States where they are permissible, other minor divisions, notably judicial precincts and city wards, are frequently utilized for this purpose, resulting in the former case in much confusion of terminology. Broadly speaking, the term "election district" is in use in most of the States from Maryland north, in Illinois and a few States to the north and west of this, and in Mississippi. In most of the other States " precinct," " election precinct," or " polling precinct " is employed. In Maryland "precinct" is used to denote the subdivisons of Baltimore wards for voting purposes.

[1] Mich. 1835, Tex. 1845, Iowa 1846, Ill. and Wisc. 1848, Cal. 1849, Oreg. 1857, Kans. 1859, Nev. 1864, Mo. 1865, Ala. 1867 (omitted 1875-1901), N. C., S. C., Fla., Miss. and Ark. 1868, Ga. 1868 (omitted 1877—* 1904), Va. 1870, W. Va. 1872, Pa. 1873, Neb. 1875, Colo. 1876, and all States admitted since Colorado, from the beginning. Also, Conn. 1877, Minn. * 1886, Ky. 1890, Del. 1897, La. 1898.

The missing States are five in New England, New York, New Jersey, Maryland (mentioned 1864-67), Ohio, Indiana and Tennessee.

[2] Virginia, 1870-74 (no title) and again since 1902 (" School Divisions ").

California, since 1879; Idaho, since 1889; and Oklahoma, since 1907 (" Board of Education Districts ").

districts by special legislation was forbidden. North Carolina, since 1868, requires counties to be divided by county commissioners. South Carolina, since the same date, requires the Legislature to provide for the formation of school districts, without restrictions, at first; since 1895, these districts must be subdivisions of counties, " as compact in form as practicable having regard to natural boundaries ", and containing from 9 to 49 square miles except in cities of over 10,000 inhabitants; and incorporation by special act is forbidden. Virginia, from 1870 till 1902, required the division of townships, or of the " magisterial districts " into which these were changed, into compactly located school districts, containing not less than 100 inhabitants; since 1902, however, the formation of school districts, distinct from the magisterial district, is entirely at the discretion of the Legislature. In West Virginia, since 1872, no " independent free school district " is to be created, except by a majority Referendum in the school district or districts out of which it is to be created. Special legislation " changing school districts " was forbidden by Pennsylvania in 1873; changing their lines, by Missouri in 1875; erecting them or changing their lines by Minnesota in 1892 and by Delaware in 1897. Cities of the first and second class were constituted separate school districts in Utah in 1895, and the city and county of Denver was so constituted in 1902 in Colorado.[1]

[1] Ala. Const. 1867, xi, 6 (until 1875); 1901, 104, par. 22.
N. C. Const. 1868, ix, 3; 1876, ix, 3.
S. C. Const. 1868, x, 3; 1895, iii, 34, par. 5; xi, 5.
Va. Const. 1870, vii, 3; Am. 1874; 1902, 133.
W. Va. Const. 1872, xii, 10.
Pa. Const. 1873, iii, 7.
Mo. Const. 1875, v, 53.
Minn. * Am. 1892, iv, 33.
Del. Const. 1897, ii, 19.

For major educational divisions the use of the county has often been prescribed. Virginia, however, between 1870 and 1874, in imitation of its rule requiring the attachment of a county containing under 8,000 inhabitants, to a contiguous county, for certain judicial purposes, *permitted* attachment, under the same conditions, for the election of a Superintendent of Schools. So California, since 1879, has permitted the grouping of contiguous counties for this purpose. In 1902 Virginia also revived special treatment in more elaborate form; since this year, the State Board of Education is empowered to divide the State into " school divisions," comprising not less than one county or city each, no county or city to be divided.[1]

4. INTERNAL IMPROVEMENT DISTRICTS

" Highway districts " are mentioned in Michigan since 1850, as divisions of townships; since 1908, however, these may be replaced by road districts of any size. In West Virginia, for a time, " precinct " divisions of townships are mentioned, in connection with roads. In Virginia, townships, while they lasted, were required to be divided into " road districts ". These are mentioned in Washington as divisions of counties.[2]

One special levee district was mentioned in Louisiana in 1868; since then districts, the authorities of which may contract indebtedness or levy assessments or taxes, for various purposes of internal improvement, have appeared

Utah Am. 1900, x, 6.
Colo. Am. 1902, xx, 7.
[1] Va. Const. 1870, vii, 1 (until 1874) ; 1902, 132.
Cal. Const. 1879, ix, 3.
[2] Mich. Const. 1850, xi, 1 ; * 1908, viii, 18, 26.
W. Va. Const. 1862, vii, 2 (until 1872).
Va. Const. 1870, xii, 4 (until 1874).
Wash. Const. 1889, xi, 6.

in nine States in all. In most cases these districts are merely mentioned, in connection with a restriction upon their corporate powers, or there is a mere authorization to the Legislature to provide for them. In Louisiana, however, the power to organize levee districts is excepted from the prohibition of special legislation affecting corporations —includes the power to create, with the concurrence of an adjacent State or States, districts lying partly outside the State—and terminates when the Federal government shall assume permanent control over levees. In Mississippi only two specified levee districts seem to be authorized, and boundaries may not be changed without four weeks' notice of the bill, in the county containing the domicile of the levee commissioners, and reference to an appropriate committee in each house. South Dakota, finally, provides that no "county, municipal corporation or civil township"— since 1902, also no "district or other subdivision"—may be included in such special bonding district, except by majority Referendum.[1]

Two other States mention, or authorize, "drainage districts", without mention of financial powers.[2]

---

[1] Louisiana, "Levee districts", Const. 1868, 149; 1879, 46, 214-216; 1898, 48, 239-241. "Lrainage districts," Const. 1898, 281; Am. 1904, 1906.

Illinois, "Drainage districts" (including care of levees). Am. 1878, iv, 31.

Mississippi, "Levee districts," Const. 1890, 228, 234.

Kentucky, "Taxing districts," Const. 1890, 157 et seq.

South Dakota, Districts or subdivisions for providing water, Am. 1896, xiii, 4; for providing water and sewerage, Am. 1902.

California, "Irrigation and Reclamation Districts," Am. 1902, xiii, 13¾ [sic].

Texas, Districts for levee, irrigation, drainage, navigation, or road purposes, Am. 1904, iii, 52.

Oklahoma, "Improvement Districts," Const. 1907, xvi, 1.

Iowa, * Am. 1908, i, 18.

[2] S. D. * Am. 1906, * N. Mex. Const. 1911, xvi, 4.

5. MINOR ADMINISTRATIVE DISTRICTS

West Virginia's " Schedule ", in 1872, shows that " assessment districts," as divisions of counties, were in existence at that time; under the new instrument they were not expected to continue. Florida, however, in 1885, expressly required the Legislature to authorize the County Commissioners to divide counties into " taxation districts " of the same general nature.[1]

" Water districts," coördinate with counties and urban districts, are mentioned in Idaho.[2]

6. CONSERVATION DISTRICTS

California, in 1879, reserved tide-lands, within two miles of an incorporated city or town, from sale to private persons. Washington, ten years later, provided that commissioners should determine the boundaries of such lands, to be from 50 to 600 feet wide, and extend for one mile on each side of the city. Of somewhat similar nature is a requirement, also made in this State, that public lands lying in any incorporated city, or within two miles of its boundary, shall be sold only under specially provided regulations. Wyoming requires the State to be divided into four " water divisions " for the administration of the natural water supply of the State. And California, since 1902, authorizes the division of the State into " fish and game districts ".[3]

7. POLICE DISTRICTS

Special districts for the administration of the police

[1] W. Va. Const. 1872, Sched. 9.
Fla. Const. 1885, viii, 7.
[2] Idaho Const. 1889, xv, 2.
[3] Cal. Const. 1879, xv, 3; Am. 1902, iv, 25½ [*sic*].
Wash. Const. 1889, xv. 1; xvi, 4.
Wyom. Const. 1889, viii, 4.

power of the State are rarely found. In Texas, since 1891, the County Courts are authorized to divide counties into local-option districts. In Delaware, on the other hand, the city of Wilmington, the rest of Newcastle county, and each of the other two counties of the State, are specified as local-option districts.

Idaho mentions " organized mining districts ". Alabama forbids special legislation " establishing stock districts." Oklahoma requires the creation of mining districts for inspection purposes.[1]

8. SUMMARY

The significance of these special districts, resorted to with increasing frequency in late years, lies in the extent to which we are departing from our original system of administering State government by counties. After having developed elaborate schemes for restricting Legislative control of county lines, we now tend more and more to ignore these quasi-permanent divisions. We entrust the discharge of the more recently developed functions of government to central authorities, without any territorial division at all. Or we establish new divisions, usually as compounds or as subdivisions of the existing counties, but otherwise with few restrictions upon legislative control. The number of such districts which actually exist is of course far greater than the number which have received in some way constitutional recognition. From the point of view of artistic symmetry our present system of territorial divisions thus leaves much to be desired. District

---

[1] Tex. Am. 1891, xvi, 20.
Idaho Const. 1889, xv, 3.
Del. Const. 1897, xiii.
Ala. Const. 1901, 104, par. 23.
Okla. Const. 1907, vi, 25.

overlaps district in a manner as difficult for the voter to understand as it is for the student to expound. The operations of government are to this extent rendered more technical, and, like the rules of judicial procedure, thrown into the hands of an expert class. Only that being whom we all abuse and all utilize—the professional politician, who gives his whole life to the work—can carry a working conception in his head of the way in which all these divisions coördinate with one another in practice.

This state of affairs is undoubtedly unfortunate. Believers in the democratic theory of government must deplore any circumstance which tends in practice to destroy that equality of political influence which they would like to see belong to every voter. It is true that the American ideal—complete abolition of class government of every sort —is one which, like all high ideals, never can be reached. However highly the mass of the voters may be educated, there will always be a class, more highly educated along special lines than they, who will deserve, and obtain, political weight, out of all proportion to their actual numbers. The fact that an ideal cannot be reached, however, makes it none the less desirable to cherish and pursue. The expert's inherent advantage needs not to be enhanced by artificial means. Simplicity of operation is an end of value in itself, and rigging the ship of State with superfluous ropes makes us entirely too dependent upon those who "know them". At the same time, it must be admitted that the problem of simplifying our system of territorial divisions is not an easy one to solve. The county system is not well adapted to the discharge of our newer governmental needs. Yet the abolition of counties, long in use, for judicial purposes, would throw endless confusion into our system of records. Probably the best we can do is to see to it that the newer administrative units, large and small, are harmoniously related among themselves, however they stand with relation to counties. It should not be forgotten, too, that inequalities and overlappings contain at least this concrete good: by their very artificiality, they accustom voters to regard themselves primarily as citizens of the whole State, rather than of a self-centered locality.

CHAPTER VII

DISTRICTS OF REPRESENTATION IN THE LOWER HOUSE

THE term "apportionment", originally signifying the distribution of representatives among permanently-established administrative districts, has gradually been extended to include the definitions of temporary districts for this special purpose. The two phases of the topic cannot be satisfactorily separated in discussion.

During the Colonial period, outside of three New England Colonies, both the territorial unit and the number of representatives to which it was entitled were determined entirely by the active government itself. In practice, the New England unit was the town; elsewhere, the English system of a mixed county and borough basis usually prevailed. Over-represented minorities had naturally not been eager to surrender their provisions, so that nowhere, at the time the Revolution occurred, did the number of representatives which each district returned bear any uniform relation to the number of electors who returned them. Indeed, it may be said that the principle of proportionate representation of localities was only just beginning to develop at this time. As with the equal representation of the States in the Federal Senate to-day, it doubtless seemed to many that separate districts, rather than the entire population of the Colony, were being represented in the Colonial Assembly, and that the number of voters which each district might happen to contain had little to do with the question. With the subsidence of strong local feeling, this attitude, except as between town and country, has gradually disappeared, and in many cases we have gone to the opposite extreme, placing a decidedly exaggerated emphasis upon the importance of a mathematically accurate system.

Since the Revolution, the capital invention in the treatment of the problem has proved to be a Pennsylvania provision, adopted in September, 1776, requiring the Legislature to redistribute the representation, in accordance with the proportionate principle, at intervals of seven years, and depriving it of all control at other periods. It will be convenient to discuss, first, early systems which do not contain this feature of obligatory periodic reapportionment; second, those systems in which the main features of the Pennsylvania plan have been retained; third, later systems in which the plan has been modified or supplemented in important particulars. Under each head, a general chronological order will be followed.

I. EARLY SYSTEMS OF REPRESENTATION

Under the original Connecticut Charter, surviving until 1818, not more than two persons might be returned from each " place, Towne or Citty ". By the Constitution adopted in this year, "towns", used obviously in a sense which would include cities, were to return the same number " as at present practiced and allowed "—that is, either one or two. Since 1874, every town which contains, by the last United States census, a population of 5,000, is entitled to two representatives. Smaller towns are confirmed in their historic claim to either one or two, irrespective of their size. Newly incorporated towns constitute separate election districts of the town from which the major portion of their territory was taken, until each section contains 2,500 inhabitants. The gross discrimination against the larger urban districts requires no comment.[1]

[1] Conn. Charter, 1662, Thorpe, p. 531; Const. 1818, iii, 3; Am. 1874, xv; 1876, xviii.

Under the Rhode Island Charter, until 1842, the Legislature was expressly authorized to determine what "places, townes or cityes" should be represented, by not more than two persons each; Newport, however, was guaranteed the right of returning not more than six; Providence, Portsmouth and Warwick, not more than four persons each. Since the adoption of a State Constitution the Legislature has been authorized, but not required, to reapportion representation after any Census, State or Federal—that is to say, whenever it pleases—under the following rule: At least one member for each town or city; one additional member for every fraction of the " ratio " exceeding one-half; no town or city to have more than a sixth of the total number, limited to 72—or, since 1909, one-fourth of the total number, limited to 100; this, in spite of the fact that Providence now contains nearer one-half than one-third of the population. Towns and cities, originally, might not be divided; since 1909, however, each must be divided, at once, and may be divided, at any time, into single-member districts, " as nearly equal in population, and as compact in territory as possible." [1]

The next oldest provision, in force after the Revolution, was that of the Massachusetts Charter, revived by the Provincial Congress in 1775, under the advice of the Continental Congress, whereby the Legislature was authorized to determine what number each " County Towne and Place " should return.   Under this authority the Legislature introduced a system of proportional representation which, in 1780, was crystallized in the following Constitutional rule: Every town already incorporated to return at least one member, but no new town to be incorporated with the right of representation unless it contains at least 150 " ratable

[1] R. I. Charter, 1663, Thorpe, pp. 3214, 3215 ; Const. 1842, v, 1 : * 1909, xiii.

polls "; larger towns to return one additional member for every 225 polls over this number. This lasted until 1836, when it was replaced by a modified form of the Pennsylvania provision.[1]

New Hampshire, in its original crude instrument, of January, 1776, also left everything to the Legislature, which, in practice, also introduced a roughly proportional system. In 1784 the Massachusetts plan was adopted, with the following modifications: The unit was the " town, parish, or place entitled to town privileges "; the " mean increasing number " was 300 polls, instead of 225; the problem of undersized units (units containing less than 150 polls), new and old, was met by requiring the Legislature to " class " them into groups, returning one member, the elections to be held in each unit in annual succession, beginning with the largest; if the situation of an undersized unit, however, was such as to render this " very inconvenient ", the Legislature was authorized, upon the application of a majority of the voters, to accord it a separate representative. Finally, since 1877, city wards are substituted in the list of units for parishes; 600 inhabitants, under the last Census, State or Federal, are taken for the minimum, and 1,200 for the increasing number, with the proviso that towns are not to be divided, nor wards changed, in such a way as to increase representation. The " classifying " system remains, in general, as before, but for inconveniently situated units is elaborated somewhat. " Since they cannot send part of a person, all of the time, why not have them send all of a person, part of the time?" is a very natural query, considering the spirit of the provision; and

---

[1] Mass. Charter, 1691, Thorpe, p. 1878; Const. 1780, part II, ch. i, iii, 2 (until 1836).

this absurd practice, possible under the rule as originally framed, has accordingly now been made obligatory.[1]

Two months after New Hampshire's first instrument, that of South Carolina appeared, specifying twenty-eight parishes and (administrative) districts among which its representatives were distributed, in amounts ranging from 4 to 30. In a second instrument, adopted two years after this, one six-member parish was divided into districts returning three members each, and another into districts returning four and two, respectively; the voice of Pennsylvania is also heard in a provision requiring reapportionment " according to the particular and comparative strength and taxable property of the different parts " of the State, at the expiration of seven years, and every fourteen years thereafter. It should be noted, however, that neither of these instruments was adopted by a Convention elected for this purpose; they were therefore adjudged by the Courts to be merely declarations of policy, not binding upon the Legislature. Control over apportionment was first actually taken from this body, in most emphatic manner, by the Constitution of 1790, which specified forty-four " election districts " by name, among which representatives, from 2 to 15 in number, were permanently apportioned. This lasted until 1808, when the periodic requirement was again introduced, in a form, which, although very peculiar, may best be considered in connection with the general movement.[2]

Next, Virginia, in June, followed English precedent, with some modifications. Two representatives were accorded to each county, and to the district of West Augusta; one

---

[1] N. H. Const. 1776, Thorpe, p. 2453; 1786, Thorpe, p. 2461; 1792, part ii, 9, 10, 11; Am. 1877.

[2] S. C. Const. 1776, 11; 1778, 13, 15; 1790, i, 3 (until 1808).

each to Williamsburgh and Norfolk, and to other cities or boroughs to which the Legislature might allow particular representation; but if any city or borough should for seven years contain less than one-half the number of electors in some one county, then the right of representation should cease. This provision, which lasted until 1830, is interesting as being the first application of the traditional septennary period of the English Parliament to purposes of proportional representation.[1]

Next, New Jersey, in July, made a provisional apportionment of six members to each county, but authorized the Legislature to change the number or proportion at any time, " on the principle of more equal representation ". This provision, in force until 1844, contains the germ of that idea which Pennsylvania, two months later, was to develop fully.[2]

Delaware, in the same month as Pennsylvania, gave a flat representation of seven to each of its three counties. After 1792, the number could be increased by a two-thirds vote of the Legislature. This lasted, without change even in the number of counties, until 1897, by which time the county containing Wilmington was greatly under-represented as compared with the other two, while that portion of Newcastle county which lies outside of Wilmington was hopelessly submerged by the city. The change made was to establish thirty-five representative districts, each returning a single member: ten districts in each county, excluding Wilmington, and five in that city. The discrimination against Wilmington, which contains, like Providence, more nearly one-half than one-third of the entire population, is emphasized by the rule that the boundaries in general are

[1] Va. Const. 1776, Thorpe, p. 3815 (until 1830).
[2] N. J. Const. 1776, 3 (until 1844).

absolutely fixed in administrative and other lines " as the same are now established and located ", except in the case of the exterior boundaries of the Wilmington districts. These move out, as the city expands, the extension of the interior lines being blocked out beforehand. Thus under no circumstances can the city ever return more than one-seventh of the total number, while the diminished county districts, unless they are absolutely wiped out, will retain their separate representation.[1]

Maryland, two months later, preferred, to the Pennsylvania plan, that of its neighbor to the south, with slight modifications. The representation of each county was fixed at four, instead of two, as in Virginia; only two specified urban districts, Annapolis city and Baltimore town, were accorded representation, with two members each; the loss of the right to return this number, in case of a diminished voting population lasting for seven years, was made applicable to Baltimore only; and the right would attach again, in case the population should again equal one-half that of some county. This lasted until 1837.[2]

North Carolina, in December, and until 1835, allotted two members to each county, and one each to six specified towns.[3]

Georgia, the following spring, allotted two members to one town, four to another (Savannah), fourteen to one county, ten to each of five other specified counties. For two other specified counties, and for those subsequently laid out, a sliding scale was adopted: If 10 electors, one member; if 30, two; if 40, three; if 50, four; if 80, six; if 100, ten. In 1789, this was changed to a fixed representa-

[1] Del. Const. 1776, 3; 1792, ii, 2; 1831, ii, 2; 1897, ii, 2.
[2] Md. Decl. of Rights, 1776, 37; Const. 1776, 2, 4, 5 (until 1837).
[3] N. C. Const. 1776, 3 (until 1835).

tion, varying from two to five, for each of eleven specified counties; in 1795, twenty counties were named, to return two, three, or four members each; only three years later, however, this was abandoned for the periodic system.[1]

Two months after Georgia, New York, the last of the original thirteen States to establish a working system of government, followed Pennsylvania's lead, and so did every new State for the next eighty years, with the single exception of the first of them, Vermont. In spite of the fact that in most respects this State followed Pennsylvania very closely, the New England traditions as to town representation were too strong to be overcome. From its origin until the present day, every " inhabited town " in Vermont has been entitled to one member and no more, except during periods of seven years immediately after the adoption of the successive instruments, when towns containing eighty taxable inhabitants were entitled to two members.[2]

To conclude: During the period of the Jacksonian Democracy, the twenty-four States in the Union were divided, from the point of view of area, into two well-defined groups. Sixteen contained 30,000 square miles or over; the other eight, 12,000 or less. By the close of the year 1835—say at the end of the second generation after the outbreak of the Revolution—the larger States had all adopted some variant of the Pennsylvania plan; none of the smaller. Massachusetts and Maryland came over in the next two years; New Jersey, before ten years had elapsed; the remaining five small States, however—Connecticut, Rhode Island, New Hampshire, Vermont and Delaware, the combined area of which is less than the smallest of the other group—have clung till this day to antiquated systems which, in four cases

---

[1] Ga. Const. 1777, 4, 5; 1789, i, 6; Am. 1795, iii (until 1798).

[2] Vt. Const. 1777, ch. ii, 7, 16; 1786, 1793, ch. ii, 7, 8.

out of the five, are grossly unjust to the larger centers of population.   When we come to consider the upper house, moreover, we shall see how New Jersey and Maryland offend in this branch of the Legislative system.

The imperviousness of these little communities to the dominant theory of representation is good empirical proof of the importance of mere superficial area as a factor in the development of political institutions.   Whether the dominant theory is itself beyond criticism we need not here enquire.   To those who regard the " ignorant vote of the great cities " as a menace, it will not appeal; the fact that in a few crevices and crannies of the Union the rural population is so safely entrenched should be to these a cause of rejoicing.   A majority of the population—perhaps because of their ignorance—will rejoice, rather, that the crannies and crevices are so few.   To these, the attempt to enforce equal representation must seem a praiseworthy adherence to the Republican principle, as always understood.   They will recall with wonder the distrust once felt as to the possible permanence of Republics of large size, and will feel that in the very largeness of our other States has lain their comparative salvation.

Without entering into this controversy, this much, at least, may safely be said.   Between little States, and little faith in the equal capacity of all men for self-government, some inherent harmony seems to exist..   We shall see that discrimination against urban centers is by no means confined to these small States.   But broad belief in the people colors most vividly the institutions of those States which cover the broadest expanse of territory.

II. OBLIGATORY PERIODIC REAPPORTIONMENT

Everywhere except in the instances mentioned, and except in Idaho and Arizona, some provision looking toward a comprehensive periodic reapportionment has been made. The period, originally of seven years, was placed for a time as low as two years in Iowa, and as high as twenty years in North Carolina and Maryland; under the influence of the Federal Census provision it has finally settled down to ten years in twenty-five States. In a contiguous group of fourteen States—Wisconsin, Minnesota, Iowa, and all west of the Missouri River, north of the 37th parallel and California—the Federal period is broken into two parts, usually of five years each; and the period is at least five years, at most ten, in Maine, and is six years in Indiana. The ten-year period is usually, though not always, incidental to the use of the Federal Census as the official basis for the apportionment; so also almost invariably in the North-western group, where an intermediate State Enumeration is required in addition. In Maine and Indiana, however, as well as in five of the existing ten-year provisions, a State Enumeration is the only basis. Sometimes either Federal or State Census may be used, and in some of these cases no time-schedule for the State Census is prescribed; New Jersey, Maryland and Arkansas, that is to say, require a reapportionment after the Federal Census, but also permit one after a State Enumeration, which apparently may be made at any time.[1]

The tendency to rely upon the Federal Census is connected with a growing willingness to adopt aggregate population as the numerical basis, in place of special classes of the people, such as the Federal government could not be trusted to enumerate separately. The most logical basis for apportionment is, of course, the number of qualified electors; and although the practical difficulty of ascertaining this has led, in all except four States, to a general adoption of popu-

---

[1] For details regarding period and census, *vide* p. 151, note 1, *infra*.

lation, free from qualifications as to age or sex, as a sufficiently accurate measure, in several States the exceptions to
manhood suffrage are still sufficiently great to call for
similar exceptions in the enumeration of the inhabitants.
Six different ways of approaching the problem may accordingly be distinguished.

The original method, surviving in Tennessee, Indiana,
Massachusetts and Arkansas, was to base the apportionment upon the number of qualified electors, in terms, or
upon the number of persons possessing, in a general way,
suffrage qualifications.[1]

As early as 1778, however, South Carolina required that
both the number of white inhabitants, and the aggregate
amount of taxable property, in the various parts of the
State, should be considered; the details of this double standard, or "mixed basis", as it came to be called, with a
change from the aggregate property to the aggregate taxes
paid, were subsequently carefully worked out, and remained in force in this State until the War.[2]

---

[1] "Taxables" in Pennsylvania until 1873; "taxable inhabitants" in
Tennessee until 1834.

The New England "ratable polls" will be recalled. These survived in New Hampshire, until 1877, and in Massachusetts, for four
years after the introduction of the periodic system, until 1840.

"Free males over 21" in Kentucky, until 1850; "white males over
21" in Ohio and Indiana, until * 1881; "free white males over 21" in
Missouri, until 1849, and in Arkansas, until the War.

"Males over 21" or "adult males" in *Indiana* since * 1881, and in
Arkansas, since 1874.

Electors or legal voters in New York until 1821; Louisiana until
1852; *Tennessee* since 1834; Kentucky, 1850-90; *Massachusetts* since
1857; Mississippi, 1868-90. This was the basis also for the early sliding scales of representation provided for special cases, without the
periodic requirement, in Virginia, Maryland and Georgia.

Registered votes in Florida, 1868-85.

[2] The rule of 1808 prescribed, as one basis, the white population; as
the other, the average taxes raised by the Legislature, during the pre-

Then, beginning with Georgia in 1798, comes a group of States in which property considerations do not figure, but specified classes of the population, usually whites, are made the basis; this system was swept away between 1850 and 1870 everywhere except on the Pacific coast, where it survived in California until 1879, and is still the basis in Oregon.[1]

Meanwhile Maine, in 1819, adopted the wiser plan of naming the entire population, *except for certain* specified classes; this was quickly adopted by New York, as a substitute for its original electoral plan, and has come to be the system in ten States in all: these two, North Carolina, a contiguous group of four Northwestern States, and Nevada, California and Washington.[2]

ceding ten years, "whether direct or indirect, or of whatever species, paid in each [district], deducting therefrom all taxes paid on account of property held in any other district, and adding thereto all taxes elsewhere paid on account of property held in such district."

[1] "Free whites" in Georgia, Mississippi and Alabama, until the War. "Whites" in Illinois until 1870, Michigan until 1850, Iowa until 1868, California until 1879, *Oregon* from the beginning, West Virginia until 1872, Maryland, 1864-67. "Permanent free whites" in Missouri, 1849-65.

"Federal numbers" (three-fifths of slaves and of Indians not taxed) in North Carolina and Florida until the War, and in Maryland, 1837-51.

"Free population, excluding Indians not taxed, Africans, and descendants of Africans," in Texas until the War. The Enumeration was also to designate particularly the number of qualified electors.

Whites and civilized Indians in Michigan, 1850-70.

[2] The excluded classes are:

Aliens and Indians not taxed, in Maine from the beginning, and in North Carolina since the War.

Aliens, paupers, persons of color not taxed, in New York, 1821-46; aliens, and persons of color not taxed, 1846-74; aliens only, since 1874.

Indians not taxed, only (the Federal basis, since the adoption of the Fourteenth Amendment), in Minnesota from the beginning; Indians uncivilized or members of a tribe, in Michigan, 1870-1908.

From this it was, of course, an easy step, first taken by Massachusetts in 1840, to make simple population the basis; if we include Connecticut, Rhode Island and New Hampshire, where the population is considered in greater or less degree, although not under a periodic reapportionment plan, one more than half the States in the Union now have this system.[1]

Finally Virginia, in 1850, left the question of numerical basis to the Legislature, with the proviso that if, at the first stated period, it could not agree upon a basis, four alternative plans for both houses should be submitted to the voters by the Governor, with repeated election between the two plans receiving the highest vote, in case no majority should be secured; the basis thus determined to be utilized permanently thereafter.[2] This safeguarding provision was dropped after the War, but the basis has never been prescribed. There is also no actual prescription of numerical basis to-day in Mississippi, Kansas, or Idaho, for either house, nor for the lower house in North Dakota, though in all

" Persons not eligible to become citizens of the United States under the naturalization laws" (Chinese) in California since 1879.

Indians not taxed, soldiers and sailors of the United States Army and Navy, in Wisconsin, Nevada, Nebraska and South Dakota, and —with the addition of the words " in active service "—in Washington.

[1] New Jersey since 1844, Maryland 1851-64, and since 1867, Ohio since 1851, Louisiana 1852, Missouri 1865, Alabama 1867, Iowa and South Carolina 1868, Illinois 1870, West Virginia 1872, Pennsylvania 1873, Texas 1876, Georgia 1877, Florida 1885, Kentucky 1890, Michigan 1908, Colorado, Montana, Wyoming, Utah, Oklahoma and New Mexico, from the beginning. So also Massachusetts 1840-57, Arkansas 1868-74, and (not under the periodic plan) Rhode Island since 1842, Connecticut since 1874, New Hampshire since 1877.

[2] The four Virginia plans were: (1) Basis of number of voters for both houses; (2) The South Carolina " mixed basis " for both houses; (3) Voter basis for the lower house, taxation basis for the upper; (4) Voter basis for the lower, " mixed basis " for the upper.

these States, except the last, population is doubtless intended.[1]

The apportioning body has usually been the Legislature. In a few States, however, where the rules are stringent, the ministerial duty of applying them has been vested in other organs: In Massachusetts, from 1836 till 1857, the Governor and Council, since then, the Secretary of the Commonwealth; in Ohio, since 1851, the Governor, Auditor and Secretary of State. In Maryland, from 1837 till 1851, no apportioning body was mentioned, the number of delegates to which each unit was entitled being based upon its population, by a rule intended perhaps to be self-executing; for the next sixteen years the Legislature was in charge, but, since 1867, the Governor. Oklahoma provides that the successive determinations involved in its complicated process shall be presented, by bill, to the Governor for his approval.[2] In a few States, also, as we shall see, local bodies have come to participate in the process.

New York, in 1894, followed by Oklahoma, has given an important sanction to the apportionment rules by providing that the result is subject to review by the Supreme Court at the suit of any citizen, under such reasonable regulations as the Legislature may prescribe, such suits to be given precedence over all others, and the Court, if not in session, to convene promptly.[3]

Not all these forty-one States have, however, retained the essential feature of the Pennsylvania plan: a requirement of reapportionment at stated intervals, coupled with a prohibition upon reapportionment at other times. Among the

---

[1] The basis was also not actually prescribed in Texas, 1868-76, and Georgia, 1868-77.

[2] Okla. Const. 1907, v, 10, par. (i).

[3] N. Y. Const. 1894, iii, 5; Okla. Const. 1907, v, 10, par. (j). Oklahoma omits the word "reasonable".

States which have retained the original idea, in nearly its original rigidity, the most important development has been a departure from the original notion of permanent local districts, the varying political importance of which should be reflected in the varying number of representatives which each shall return to a central gathering. In place of this conception of the Legislature as primarily an aggregation of local representatives, we have come to regard it more as a plural organ, representing the voters of the State, as a whole, even though each seat in it is filled by only a local section of the voters. The successive steps by which, under the influence of this view, we have tended to abandon the permanent district, returning a variable number of members, and to substitute the variable district, returning always a single member, are of considerable interest.[1]

---

[1] The details affecting period and census may best be assembled without regard to other distinctions between the systems.

Omitting special reapportionments, required at shorter intervals during the early years of many States, a regular *seven-year* period, based upon a preceding State enumeration, was provided in Pennsylvania, 1776-1857, New York 1777-1821, Tennessee 1796-1834, Georgia 1798—the War; a *four-year* period in Kentucky 1792-1850, Ohio 1802-1851, Louisiana 1812-45, Missouri 1820-49, Arkansas 1836—the War; a *ten-year* period, similarly based, in New York since 1821, Tennessee since 1834, Massachusetts since 1836, Florida since 1838, Louisiana 1845-52, and 1868-98, Alabama 1850-75, Mississippi since 1868; a *ten-year* period, similarly based, in South Carolina, 1808-1886, New York since 1821, Tennessee since 1834, Massachusetts since 1836, Florida since 1838, Louisiana 1845-52, and 1868-98, Alabama 1850-75, Mississippi since 1868; a *five-year* period in Indiana 1816-51, Illinois 1818-48; a *six-year* period in Alabama 1819-50, Indiana since 1851; a period of *from three to five years* in Mississippi 1817-32, and of *from four to eight years,* 1832—the War; a period of *from five to ten years* in Maine since 1819; an *eight-year* period in Texas 1845—the War; a period of *at least ten years* in Louisiana 1852—the War. The enumeration was usually subject to legislative control, but in Georgia (Const. 1798, i, 25 —until the War), and recently in New York (Const. 1894, iii, 4), an independent administrative machinery has been provided; and in South

I. *The permanent district*

Entire administrative districts (or in one case permanent

Carolina (Am. 1808; Const. 1868, ii, 5—until 1886) the Governor was authorized to act in default of the Legislature. Originally no time limit was set within which the Legislature must make the apportionment; this is the rule to-day in *Maine* and *Tennessee*. As early as 1798, however, Georgia required action at the first session after receipt of the returns; *Indiana, Massachusetts* and *Mississippi* still retain this provision. Kentucky, first, in 1799, named the year within which the apportionment must be made; since 1885 this has been the rule in *Florida*. Louisiana, first, in 1845, named the first *regular* session, which since 1894 is the rule in *New York*. Until the War, Louisiana went so far as to prohibit all legislation, after an enumeration, until the apportionment had been made.

The *seven-year* period, without any reference to an enumeration or census, the successive apportionments being dated in years, was continued in Pennsylvania from 1857 till 1873; similarly for the *four-year* period in Missouri, from 1849 till 1865, and for the *ten-year* period in Virginia since 1830, and in Kentucky since 1890. The arrangement of dates in Virginia, except from 1850 till the War, clearly indicates that this State was the first to contemplate making use of the Federal census as a basis.

The Federal Census was mentioned nowhere by name, however, until 1835, when Michigan initiated the movement, which has been so widely followed, of utilizing not only this but an *intermediate State apportionment*. In addition to the fourteen Northwestern States in which this system survives, it appeared in Michigan 1835-1908, Illinois 1848-70, California 1849-79, Missouri 1865-75, Arkansas 1868-74. As a rule, the apportionment in these States is to be made at the first session after the Census or Enumeration; in Illinois, Iowa (since 1904), Nebraska (since 1875), and the Dakotas, at the first *regular* session; in Arkansas, by the first Legislature elected afterwards; in Missouri and Nevada, no time limit is set. In Kansas, apportionments are to be made at dated intervals of five years, on the basis of the Census or Enumeration of the preceding year," which must be taken by the State itself "at least once in ten years" (Kans. Const. 1859, ii, 26; x, 2). Everywhere an interval of precisely five years is the ideal, which, because of the prevalence of biennial sessions, can rarely be realized in practice.

Simultaneously with this action on the part of Michigan, North Carolina, also in 1835, took another step in the direction of complete dependence upon the Federal Census, by providing, until the War,

special Legislative districts), uncombined and undivided, were the original units of representation in eighteen States,

for an apportionment at dated intervals of *twenty years,* to be based either upon a State Enumeration or upon the Federal Census. Ohio. since 1851, has applied the same system to the *ten-year* period; and express authorization of either basis, with reapportionment at the first session after the returns (instead of at dated intervals) is the rule in North Carolina 1868-73, and in Alabama and Missouri, since 1875; this probably is also what South Carolina, since 1886, attempted to express in detective language. In New Jersey, since 1844, a slightly different arrangement is in force. The Legislature must reapportion at its first session after every Federal Census, but apparently may also order an enumeration of its own at any time; and, more clearly, this is the situation in Maryland since 1864 (the apportionment to be made " as soon as practicable " until 1867, " immediately " since then) and in Arkansas, since 1874 (at the first regular session). Alternative use of State or Federal Census, it will be recalled, may also be made in Rhode Island and New Hampshire, not under the periodic system.

Iowa had a peculiar rule, 1846-1904, under which reapportionments must be made at each (*biennial*) regular session; after 1857, a State Enumeration at intervals of *ten years* was also required. This State, in 1904, came over to the Northwestern system.

There remain the States in which the Federal Census, and this only, is to be used. Such was first Maryland, with a *twenty-year* period, 1837-51, and with a *ten-year* period, 1851-64; the latter has been the model, since the War, for the new State of West Virginia, for Georgia and Texas since 1868, Virginia 1870-76, Illinois since 1870, Pennsylvania since 1873, North Carolina since 1873, California since 1879, Louisiana since 1898, Michigan since 1908, and for Oklahoma and New Mexico. In Maryland, while the twenty-year period was in force, the new distribution of representatives would appear to occur automatically " from and after the promulgation of every second Census "; after 1851, however, and usually in the other States, the formal apportionment is made at the first session of the Legislature after the returns; in Louisiana, however, at the first regular session; in West Virginia, " as soon as possible after each census "; in Georgia, 1868-77, " after each Census "; in Illinois and Michigan, at dated intervals. In Connecticut, also, it will be recalled, the Federal Census alone is made use of.

For references, *vide* under the several systems of apportionment, *infra,* but note for North Carolina, * Am. 1873, ii, 5, and for South Carolina * Am. 1886, ii, 4, 5, referring solely to enumeration.

admitted prior to the Mexican War. In New Jersey, and in a half-dozen Southern States,[1] this sytem still survives, and has been revived in Ohio since 1903, and was introduced into Iowa in 1904. Although this is only a small minority of the total number of States, the diversification among the others is so great that this is actually the largest group which can be appropriately classified together. The unit in all the surviving instances is the county. Urban districts, however, at least of a certain size, continued to be represented in addition, in accordance with English and Colonial tradition, in Pennsylvania and Maryland, so long as the system of permanent districts survived, and, before the War, in Mississippi, Alabama and Texas; while in South Carolina, before the War, the peculiar " election district ", which later acquired administrative functions, was utilized.

These special South Carolina districts were strictly " permanent ". Administrative districts elsewhere were so only in the sense that they were to be permanently utilized as units of representation. In connection with the creation of new counties, a few modifications of the general principle were necessarily admitted.[2]

---

[1] The Carolinas, Georgia, Florida, Alabama and Arkansas.

[2] Under five instruments, no county, thereafter erected, was to be accorded separate representation until it should be so entitled by numbers. (Pa. Const. 1790, i, 4; 1838, i, 4; Ky. Const. 1792, i, 6; Mich. Const. 1835, iv, 4; Fla. Const. 1838, ix, 4; Mo. Am. 1849, iii.) Under four, more specifically, such counties were to be considered, meanwhile, for purposes of representation, as parts of the counties from which they were taken (Tenn. Const. 1796, ix, 4; Ohio Const. 1802, vii, 3; Ala. Const. 1819, vi, 16; Tex. Const. 1845, vii, 34).

In other States, it will be recalled, the purpose of these provisions —a safeguard against the creation of undersized units of representation—was attained by prohibiting the creation of such counties, even for administrative purposes. *Cf.* ch. iii, pp. 52, 65, 66, *supra.*

New York (Am. 1801, iv; Const. 1821, i, 27) and Arkansas (Const. 1836, iv, 34; 1874, viii, 1) insure separate representation only to counties already in existence when the instruments were drafted.

The original Pennsylvania rule for the distribution of members among the cities and counties was merely that the Legislature should " appoint a representation to each in proportion to the number of taxables ".[1] In 1790, a limitation upon the total number was set, and this was the simple rule usually provided in the North; so, to-day, in New Jersey and Alabama. In New York, however, between 1777 and 1801, generally in the South, and in the two recent Western instances, more or less complicated mathematical rules appear, in some cases—so in the Carolinas and Arkansas to-day—designed to further proportionate equality of representation, so far as that is possible under this plan; in other cases—in Georgia, Florida, Iowa and Ohio, to-day—clearly drafted by rural representatives in their own interest.[2]

The question of whether, if counties large enough to be entitled to separate representation are erected, they are to be accorded this privilege at once, without waiting for the regular apportionment, is touched upon only in Alabama (Const. 1867, viii, 2—until 1875), in South Carolina (Const. 1895, iii, 3), and in Florida (Const. 1885; vii, 4; * Am. 1900). Alabama permitted a reapportionment between the counties; the clause refers, however, in terms only to the first apportionment period. South Carolina appears to require it in all cases. Florida gives the new county a member at once; since 1900, this is " in excess of the limit prescribed in section 2 of this article"; i. e., the representation of the old county is not reduced.

[1] Pa. Const. 1776, 7, 17 (until 1790).

[2] Limitation of total number, and nothing more, except the requirement, more or less clearly expressed, that each county was to have at least one member, appeared in:

Pennsylvania, 1790-1857 (60 to 100).

Kentucky, 1792-99 (40 to 100).

Tennessee, 1796-1834 (22 to 26, until the number of taxables should exceed 40,000; then not more than 40).

New York, 1801-46 (100, and increasing at each reapportionment, at the rate of 2 per annum, until 150 should be reached; in 1821, however, a flat total of 128 was fixed).

2. *Unions of administrative districts*

Even where the more populous districts were not deliber-

Ohio, 1802-51 (24 to 36, until 22,000 white males over 21; then 36 to 72).

Indiana, 1816-51 (25 to 36, until the same condition was fulfilled; then 36 to 100).

Missouri, 1820-49 (not to exceed 100).

Michigan, 1835-50 (48 to 100).

Florida, 1838—the War (not to exceed 60).

New Jersey, since 1844 (not to exceed 60).

Texas, 1845—the War (45 to 90).

Alabama, since 1875 (originally, not to exceed 100; since 1901, not to exceed 105, plus one additional for each new county created).

In Pennsylvania, however, Philadelphia was treated as a county, and other cities, towns and boroughs, at least until 1838, might be accorded separate representation. In Texas the apportionment was to be among the several counties, cities or towns.

The earliest detailed rule appeared in New York, in 1777. Under this, the representation of each county was to be increased or diminished by 1 for every gain or loss of 1/70 of its electors, as established by the first Census, until a maximum of 300 should be reached, which was then merely to be apportioned in accordance with the proportionate principle. The rule was dropped in 1801, because absolutely unworkable under a system of changing county lines.

Georgia, in 1798, adopted the original Massachusetts plan, modified by being based upon a periodical enumeration, and in other important particulars. Counties containing under 3,000 of the enumerated population returned 1; under 7,000, 2; under 12,000, 3; all larger, 4. This discrimination against the larger counties was accentuated from 1843 to the War, by the adoption of the simple rule that the thirty-seven largest counties should have 2 members each, the remainder, 1; the total was also, curiously, fixed at 130, although, under the Constitution as it then stood, new counties might be created. In 1877 the creation of new counties was forbidden, and thus a return to the rule of 1843, slightly modified, recommended itself. The six largest counties now return 3 members each, the twenty-six next largest, 2, the remaining counties, 1 each, to a total, first fixed at 175; but in 1904 and again in 1908 this was raised to a present maximum of 184.

Georgia's neighbor, South Carolina, was the next State, in 1808, to adopt the following interesting rule. A double "ratio", as it came later to be termed, was adopted: first, 1/62 of the white population of the State; second, 1/62 of the total average taxes raised during

ately under-represented, the natural effect of limiting the

the preceding ten years. Each election district was entitled to 1 member for every full ratio of either sort, and for sums of remaining " fractions " of both, which, when added together, would form a unit. Each district was to have at least 1 member, in any case; and additional members were to be assigned to districts containing the largest unrepresented fractions of either sort, until a total of 124 should be reached. This very complete rule apparently worked so well before the War, that it has been continued since, with only such modifications as are involved in the change from a double to a single standard, and from the election district to the county. The ratio, that is to say, is now 1/124 of the population, and the residue of 124 members, after each county and each full ratio has been disposed of, is made up by representing the largest " surplus fractions ".

Kentucky, as will appear later, had devised, in 1799, a plan which, in its main outlines, resembled that common later in the North, but which included a peculiar treatment of " residuums " (" fractions," " remainders "). In 1817 this was elaborated by Mississippi. The total number was limited (24 to 36, until there should be 80,000 free white inhabitants; thereafter, 36 to 100; in 1832 the first half of the provision was dropped). The " ratio ", as usually in the North, might be any number that would yield this result. In the application of this ratio, however, the following rules were to be observed, in addition to the requirement that each county should have at least one member : If the residuums of two adjoining counties should together equal a full ratio, then the county containing the largest residuum should be given an additional member ; a city or town having a full ratio must be accorded separate representation ; the rule for shifted residuums held also as between this urban district and the balance of the county in which it lay. Alabama, two years later, adopted this same rule (originally 44 to 60 members, until there should be 100,000 whites ; thereafter, 60 to 100 ; in 1850, merely not to exceed 100), with the wise proviso, however, that cities or towns should not be accorded separate representation unless the balance of the county should also be left with a full ratio. This rule continued in both States until the War, and, with the urban provision omitted, was revived in Alabama until 1875 (total number of members not to exceed 100), when the shifted residuum was also dropped, and the Northern plan, in all its simplicity, was followed.

A more lasting modification of the South Carolina plan was devised by North Carolina, in 1835. The total was fixed (at 120) and the system of representing the largest surplus fractions was adopted. The ratio was to be determined. however, in the following manner :

total number of members was to produce a " ratio " of rep-

first, the counties containing each less than 1/120 of the enumerated population were given their separate single members; then the population of the rest of the State was to be divided by the remaining number of members. The purpose of this modification was of course to make sure that the system would work, since, under the original plan, it is theoretically possible for the required total to be reached before even all the full ratios are represented. No change has been made in this system.

Arkansas before the War, and since 1874, differs from the simple Northern plan only in having provided, prior to the War, that the ratio should be 500 free whites, until a total of 75 should be reached; since the War, that it should be 2,000 adult males, until 100 should be reached. The total was originally 54 to 100, and not above 75 until the State should contain 500,000 inhabitants; since 1874, 73 to 100.

Maryland has had much difficulty in hitting upon a satisfactory solution. In 1837 it modified the original Georgia plan, as follows: Counties containing under 15,000 of the enumerated population were to return 3 members each; under 25,000, 4; under 35,000, 5; all larger, 6; and Baltimore to return as many as the largest; specified counties, however, always to be entitled to at least 4, or to at least 5, irrespective of their population. This flagrant discrimination against Baltimore was to some extent remedied in 1851, when a total of 65 to 80 was prescribed, to be so apportioned that each county should return at least 2, and Baltimore always four more than the largest. Since 1864 still further changes have been made, which will be considered later.

Missouri, also, between 1849 and 1865, had an elaborate scheme aimed against the larger counties. The ratio was fixed at 1/140 of the enumerated population, and counties containing 3 full ratios were accorded 3 members each. Smaller counties were over-represented— all counties returning at least 1 member, and counties which contained 1¾ ratios returning 2; and larger counties were under-represented— an increase of 1½ ratios each being required for the fourth and for the fifth members, 2 ratios each for the sixth and for the seventh, 3 ratios for the eighth, 2 for the ninth, 3 each for the tenth, the eleventh and the twelfth, so that counties containing 24 ratios returned only 12 members. Still larger counties were to be represented "in the same proportion"; this probably meant (*cf.* Const. 1865, iv) that they were to return one additional member for every 3 ratios.

Florida, in 1868, adopted a simple plan, differing in some respects from that of any other State. Each county was to return one member " at large ", and one " additional " for every 1,000 registered votes; but no county to return more than 4. One member was also

resentation so large that, if each unit were to have at least

given to the Seminole Indians. Since 1885 the Indian representative has been dropped, the county maximum has been reduced to 3, and a maximum total of 68 members prescribed, with no fixed ratio. The retention of the expression " at large " indicates that the spirit of the provision secures, to each county having as much as a full ratio, either 2 or 3 members.

Ohio, in 1903, amending a "county union" plan devised in 1851 (*vide* p. 165, *infra*) now makes the county again the one unit of representation. The ratio is fixed at 1/100 of the population, and representation is based on full ratios, except in the case of the smaller counties, where the Missouri plan is adopted; every county, that is to say, is to have at least 1 member, and counties containing 1¾ ratios, 2 each. For unrepresented fraction of a ratio, an elaboration of the New England part-time representation appears: The biennial sessions of the decennial period are numbered, from one to five, and additional members are accorded for as many sessions as the fraction equals when multiplied by five; if the product equals 1, the member serves for the fifth session; if 2, for the fourth and third; if 3, for the first three sessions; and if 4, for the first four.

Finally, Iowa, since 1904, establishes the ratio by dividing the population by the number of counties; each county then gets 1 member, and each of the nine largest 1 additional, in case its population exceeds the ratio by three-fifths. The total number also may not exceed 108. Under this arrangement, Polk county, casting over 21,000 votes for President in 1908, is balanced by Dickinson and Osceola, casting together less than 3,500.

It will thus be observed that in five States — Georgia, Florida, Maryland, Missouri and Iowa—as well as in Ohio, in slighter degree, the more populous counties have been deliberately discriminated against under this plan.

References:

Pa. Const. 1790, i, 3, 4; 1838, i, 4 (until 1857).

N. Y. Const. 1777, 5, 16; Am. 1801, i, ii, iv; 1821, i, 2, 7 (until 1846).

Ky. Const. 1792, i, 6 (until 1799).

Tenn. Const. 1796, i, 2 (until 1834).

Ga. Const. 1798, i, 7, 25; Am. 1843, i, 7 (until the War); Const. 1877, iii, 3; * 1904, 1908.

Ohio Const. 1802, i, 2 (until 1851); Am. 1903, xi, 1, 2, 3.

S. C. Am. 1808; Const. 1868, ii, 4 6; 1895, iii, 3, 4.

Ind. Const. 1816, iii, 2 (until 1851).

Miss. Const. 1817, iii, 8, 9; 1832, iii, 8, 9 (until the War).

one representative, some very small fractions might thus secure full representation. This was felt in several States to be unfair; and since the limitation of total number was necessary, for reasons both of expense and of efficient operation, the plan was devised of uniting administrative districts, which contained less than the " ratio ", into special representative districts. New Hampshire, as early as 1784, had foreshadowed this method of treatment in its "classed" groups of towns, but Kentucky, in 1799, was the first to adopt it in connection with the periodic system. The plan has been introduced into twelve States in all, and survives in four: Maine, Tennessee, West Virginia and Texas. Since in some States the normal unit of representation was the town, in others the county, in still others both the county and the large urban district, the following types of representative districts resulted:

In Kentucky and Illinois, and in Texas until 1876: counties; urban districts; counties from which these urban districts were set off; groups of counties.

In *Maine:* towns; " plantations "; groups of towns or plantations.

In Virginia: counties; cities; until the War, towns; until 1850, boroughs; counties from which these urban districts were set off; groups of any of these normal units.

Ala. Const. 1819, iii, 8, 9; Am. 1850; Const. 1867, viii, 1; 1875, ix, 2, 3; 1901, 198, 199.

Mo. Const. 1820, iii, 2, 4; Am. 1849, iii (until 1865).

Md. Am. 1837, 10; Const. 1851, iii, 3; 1864, iii, 2, 4 (until 1867)

N. C. Am. 1835, i, 1; Const. 1868, ii, 6, 7; 1876, ii, 5, 6.

Mich. Const. 1835, iv, 2, 3, 4 (until 1850).

Ark. Const. 1836, iv, 34 (until the War); 1874, viii, 1.

Fla. Const. 1838, iv, 18; ix, 1; 1868, xiv; xvii, 7; 1885, vii. 3.

N. J. Const. 1844, iv, 3.

Tex. Const. 1845, iii, 29 (until the War).

Iowa Am. 1904, iii, 35.

In Massachusetts: cities; towns; groups of towns or (until 1840) " districts ".

In *Tennessee,* California, Ohio, *West Virginia,* Mississippi, and in *Texas* since 1876: counties; groups of counties.

This, however, was not all. One of the most character-- istic products of American political ingenuity is the " floating " or " flotorial " district: a grouping of counties, at least one of which is already separately represented, for the purpose of combining fractions of the representative " ratio ", and thus securing, for the group as a whole, an additional representative. The origin of the term is either that these new districts may be pictured as " floating " upon a substratum of already represented counties; or that, by a further refinement, the additional representative may be required to reside in each of the counties in turn, and so may be aptly termed a " floater "; or the term may have been first coined in allusion to the temporary character of such districts. The discovery that, under existing Constitutional provisions this device was permissible seems to have been made first either in Kentucky or in Illinois, since when its vogue has been greater in the South than in the North. It was forbidden, that is to say, in Illinois in 1848, in Iowa in 1857, and has never been introduced into Massachusetts, Maine, Ohio or West Virginia.

As regards the manner in which these various unions were to be formed, the great distinction is between the two New England States and the rest. In Maine and Massachusetts, as in New Hampshire, a town had the option between being grouped (in Massachusetts, of grouping itself) with any town or towns, or of taking part-time representation. Elsewhere, the Legislature—or, in Ohio, the Governor, Auditor and Secretary of State—determined the unions. In some cases, the absence of any requirement for separate county (or town) representation left the Legislature with a large measure of freedom in forming unions; but in other cases more or less elaborate rules govern both the formation of unions, and the apportionment of members to each unit thus resulting; and while occasionally—so in Texas, to-day—these rules have been designed to insure proportionate equality of representation, more often—so in Maine, Tennessee and West Virginia, to-day—they operate to the disadvantage of the more populous towns or counties.

Finally, it should be observed in connection with county unions, that Maine having evolved the notion of using the county as a superior unit of representation, its allotted members then to be distributed among the towns, *etc.*, Virginia, between 1830 and 1850 utilized four specified groups of counties in a similar fashion. These " distributing districts," as they may be termed, were permanent except as against a two-thirds majority of the Legislature, by whom they might be disregarded.[1]

[1] Virtually nothing more than limitation of total number of members appeared in:

Illinois, 1818-48 (27 to 36, until the State should contain 100,000 inhabitants).

Virginia, 1830-50 (134 members in all, divided among four great districts: 31 west of the Alleghenies; 25 between these and the Blue Ridge; 42 east of this and above tide-water; 36 on tide-water. If, however, by a two-thirds majority the great districts should be disregarded, a maximum of 150 was the only restriction). 1850—the War (152). 1870-76 (no limit). 1876-1902 (90 to 100).

Iowa, 1846-57 (26 to 39, until 175,000 whites; thereafter 39 to 72).

California, 1849-62 (24 to 36, until 100,000 inhabitants; thereafter 30 to 80).

Texas, 1868-76 (90).

Mississippi, 1868-90 (100 to 120).

In Illinois, the rule was extraordinarily free, reading merely that the total number should, at the stated times, " be apportioned among the several counties, or districts to be established by law, according to the number of white inhabitants ". In Virginia and Mississippi, it

3. *Obligatory subdivisions of administrative districts, without unions*

In none of the instances thus far treated is there any

was clear from other parts of the text that only the regular administrative districts—in Mississippi only the counties—might be joined to form these " districts ". Iowa and California expressly provided that they must be formed of contiguous, complete counties. In Texas, no warrant for unions appears but they appear in the accompanying provisional apportionment. The possible introduction of flotorial districts under these broad provisions is shown by the fact that such districts were later expressly forbidden in Illinois and Iowa, and appear in a provisional apportionment in the Virginia instrument of 1850. Here, also, two sets of part-time representatives, ingeniously alternating, so as to keep the total number of members the same, indicate the latent possibilities of these provisions.

An exception to the general rule of periodic rigidity appears in a Virginia requirement of 1830 (Const. iii, 4) that when a new county is created, or a city, town or borough has so increased as to be entitled in the opinion of the Legislature to separate representation, this shall be accorded, even if it is necessary to reapportion the entire great district. Compare, on a similar point, the Alabama, South Carolina and Florida provisions, *supra,* and that of Tennessee, *infra.*

Turning now to the more detailed provisions, we find, first, the shifted residuum rule of Kentucky. This differed from the Mississippi modification of the same, already described, in these respects: The total number of members was to be 58 to 100. The provision for an additional member, on a shifted residuum, making up a full ratio, applied only as between adjoining counties—not as between an urban district, and the balance of the county in which it lay. And not every county was entitled to one member. Instead of this, the least populous counties could secure separate representation only through the shift of residuum; if this did not work, then the Legislature was authorized to join two or more counties together. " Flotorials," apparently, might occur under this system, to a limited extent. This lasted until 1850.

Maine, in 1819, evolved the following cumbersome rule. The total number of members was to be provisionally fixed at some figure, between 100 and 150, and apportioned among the counties; under the original plan, the representation of each county was then to increase, in proportion to its increase in population, until a total of 200 should be reached, when a popular election was to decide what to do about it. Within each county, 1,500 is the minimum number of population below

reference to a possible division of the more populous coun-

which towns are not accorded full separate representation—provided this number will work; if it doesn't work, then a different figure is to be adopted. Towns and plantations containing less than the figure are to be "classed" into districts, containing that number; except that when any town or plantation determines against classification, the Legislature is authorized to give it a proportionate part-time representation. Larger towns are entitled to additional members, on an arbitrary rule, by which the "increasing number" is itself progressively increased, so as to discriminate against the larger towns; that is to say, 3,750 inhabitants are required for 2 members, 6,750 for 3, 10,500 for 4, 15,000 for 5, 20,250 for 6, 26,250 for 7; and no town more than 7. How this fixed scale is to be reconciled with a change in the determining 1,500 is not stated. The only change made in this rule was in 1841 to prescribe a flat total of 151 members.

Massachusetts, in 1836, saw no virtue in this use of counties for distributing purposes. To reduce the size of its chamber, it doubled its original minimal and mean increasing figures, establishing them at 300 and 450 ratable polls, respectively. For smaller towns, it introduced the part-time idea, with a formula by which the number of years was to be determined, in accurate proportion, and even extended this same idea to the unrepresented fractions of larger towns. Any two or more towns or "districts", however large or small, might unite themselves into a "Representative district", to be represented under the same rules as the towns. Four years later, the minimal and mean increasing figures were changed to 1,200 and 2,400 inhabitants, respectively, to be increased by 1/10 for every increase of 70,000 inhabitants in the State, over an assumed basis of 700,000. No part-time representatives were accorded to the larger towns, and for the smaller the formula was so changed as to give them representation for only three-fourths of the time to which they were proportionately entitled; on the other hand they might also elect a representative for the years in which property was appraised. This whole system was mercifully abolished in 1857.

Tennessee, meanwhile, in 1834, adopted a free plan, which provides, in addition to the limitation upon the total number (maximum of 75, until 1,500,000 inhabitants; thereafter maximum of 99) merely that every county having ⅔ ratio shall be entitled to one member. A technical improvement upon most other instruments also appears in the explicit declaration that the creation of new counties shall not affect existing representative lines until the regular reapportionment (Const. 1834, x, 5; 1870, x, 5). The "Ordinance" of the 1834 instru-

ties or cities, for representative purposes.   Except under

ment shows that under this system, which has never been changed, flotorials are permissible.

In Illinois, in 1848, a sliding total was provided (75 until the State should contain a million inhabitants; then 5 might be added, and, for every half-million increase, 5 more, until a total of 100 should be reached); flotorials were forbidden; separate representation of cities and towns authorized (not required) and additional regulations made, which, although not clearly expressed, would seem, in the light of the accompanying provisional apportionment, to bear the following meaning: All counties and districts to be represented only on full ratios credited to them; counties containing from 1 to 1¼ ratios to be separately represented; the excess over the ratio here to be credited to the nearest county or counties containing less than 1 ratio and the largest white population; these to be separately represented if they now are credited with a full ratio; otherwise to be combined with one another, or with counties containing over 1¼ ratios; counties containing over 1¼ ratios to be similarly combined with one another, if necessary, to prevent waste; but no county or district to return more than 3 members. A discrimination thus still existed against the more populous counties, though not so flagrant as if every county was to have at least one member. This lasted until 1870.

Three years later came Ohio, with another elaborate rule, the main features of which have already been described as still in force, and need not be repeated. The feature through the abolition of which, in 1903, the State reverted to the system of representing only counties, was this: Counties containing ½ the ratio were to be entitled to 1 member; those which at that time were smaller were formed into seven specified groups, each returning 1 member. If these union could subsequently be torn apart, so that each fragment could have ½ ratio, this was to be done. Similarly if an independent county should be found to have less than ½ ratio, it should be joined to the adjacent county having the smallest population, and this district represented under the same rule as for counties. (*Vide* p. 159, *supra*.)

Iowa, in 1857, set a maximum of 100 members, forbade flotorials, and discriminated against the more populous counties in the following flagrant manner: Counties containing from ½ to 1½ ratios return 1 member; all larger, 2; all smaller, to be formed into districts, comprising not more than four counties, returning 1 member in any case, and (probably) 1 more, under the same conditions as for counties. We have seen how, in 1904, this was replaced by a flat requirement of 1 or 2 for all counties.

the original broad Illinois provision, such divisions would

West Virginia entered with a still more elaborate plan. The total number of members was fixed at 47, subject to be increased by the inclusion of additional territory within the State. Divide the enumerated population by this figure, exclude fractions, and you obtain the ratio. Counties containing less than ½ ratio are to be joined to one or more contiguous counties, to form "delegate districts". Every delegate district and remaining county is to have a member for every full ratio, but 1 in any case. The additional members required to make up the fixed total are then assigned to the delegate districts or counties having the largest fractions, on the Carolina plan. Finally, the members chosen by the delegate districts must be residents within each of the included counties for a proportion of time, equal, as near as may be, to the proportionate population of the counties. This last crowning touch was removed in 1872, since when, also, the total number has been fixed at 65, subject to increase as before, and the determining fraction raised from ½ to ⅗.

Texas, the latest exponent of this system, provided, in 1876, a simpler and a fairer plan. The total is set at from 93 to 150 members, with the additional proviso that the ratio, to be obtained by dividing the population by this figure, must be at least 15,000; with the population as large as it now is, this proviso has no longer any significance. Counties are to be separately represented on full ratios; districts are to consist of contiguous counties; and flotorials are expressly authorized.

In six States, then—Maine, Tennessee, Illinois, Ohio, Iowa and West Virginia—the smaller towns and counties came to be favored even under this plan. In Maine, Tennessee and West Virginia, the discrimination, never very great, survives; in Ohio and Iowa it has been accentuated by a return to the system of granting a member to every county.

References:

Ky. Const. 1799, ii, 5, *6; (until 1850).

Ill. Const. 1818, ii, 5, 31, 40; 1848, iii, 6, 8-10 (until 1870).

Me. Const. 1819, ch. iv, part i, 2, 3; Am. 1841, iv.

Va. Const. 1830, iii, 2, 4, 5; 1850 iv, 2, 5, 6; 1870, v, 2, 4; Am. 1876, v, 2, 4 (until 1902).

Tenn. Const. 1834, ii, 5; Ordinance, v, Const. 1870, ii, 5.

Mass. Am. 1836, xii; 1840, xiii (until 1857).

Iowa Const. 1846, iii, "Leg. Dept.", 31, 32; Const. 1857 "Leg. Dept.", 35-37 (until 1904).

Cal. Const. 1849, iv, 29, 30 (until 1862).

not appear to be possible; although it must fairly be admitted that the language employed is not always so clear but that the Courts might uphold a contrary construction. In Louisiana, from the beginning, however, these divisions have been expressly permitted, and actually effected, and since 1845 they have in many cases been made obligatory. This development has occurred in six States, in five of which it survives, in connection with the original provision that each county must be accorded separate representation; and although in Massachusetts the existing "Representative districts " may be considered indifferently as unions of towns within the county, or as divisions of counties to be made without dividing towns, the details of the governing provision are such as to assimilate this system also, to that of its important neighbors New York and Pennsylvania.

As always, there has been much diversity. The saving clause in the original Louisiana instrument, prescribing, for a representative, residence " in the county for which he may be chosen *or in the district for which he is elected in case the said counties may be divided into separate districts of election "*, reflects merely the overlarge size of these early " counties ", which, as we have seen, were later superseded, in almost every respect, by " parishes ". Because of its late utilization for county purposes, however, the parish lacked that consecration, as at least one unit of representation, which almost everywhere else the county enjoyed. Hence it is not merely a coincidence that although, in 1845, Louisiana provided for proportionate representation of parishes, with the usual qualifications that each parish should return

Ohio Const. 1851, xi, 1-5, 11; Sched. 19 (until 1903).
W. Va. Const. 1862, iv, 2, 7-9, 14-16; 1872, vi, 6, 7, 10, 11.
Miss. Const. 1868, iv, 2, 33, 34 (until 1890).
Tex. Const. 1868, iii, 5, 7, 11, 39; 1876, iii, 2, 26, 28.

at least one member, it should have been the first of the
States to break a populous administrative district up. Not
merely, since 1845, have representatives been required to
be distributed among the several parishes *and election districts,*[1] but, until 1852, the left bank of Orleans parish was
divided into nine such districts, with boundaries defined in
terms of streets and " municipalities ". In 1852 this was
changed to an obligation imposed upon the Legislature to
divide the somewhat greater territory included in the same
description, into not more than ten districts; between 1868
and 1898 the Legislature would appear to have been free
to establish such districts or not, and in any parish that it
chose. In practice, however, it consistently maintained
them in New Orleans, and nowhere else, until finally, in
1898, the New Orleans " ward " was completely assimilated
to the parish elsewhere, as the original unit of representation—both parish and ward being still subject, it would appear, to subdivision by the Legislature at its own discretion.
Among the parishes and Representative districts, as they
happen to exist, members are then distributed by a simple
rule which makes no direct discrimination between urban
and rural districts.[2]

The State which has most nearly followed Louisiana is
Maryland, which, in 1864, required its Legislature to divide
Baltimore into three " Legislative districts ", " of equal
population and contiguous territory, as near as may be ",

[1] " Parishes and Representative Districts," 1868-79, and since 1898.

[2] Total number of members, 1812, 25 to 50; 1845, 70 to 100; 1868, 90
to 120; 1879, 70 to 98; 1898, 98 to 116.

Since 1845 each parish or district to have 1 member on every full
ratio, and additional fraction greater than ½, but each parish, and,
since 1898, each ward of the city of New Orleans, to have at least
one. Thus the only favoritism is to those parishes, if any, which are
less populous than the smallest New Orleans ward.

coördinate, for representative purposes, with the counties. Since 1867 the Legislature is empowered to alter the boundaries of these districts, " from time to time ", so as to preserve these conditions, and in 1901 their number was changed to four. The actual apportionment of members is made under a rule which discriminates against the Baltimore districts.[1]

The underlying idea in both these States was pretty clearly to give the minority party in each of the two cities a chance to return some members, instead of being virtually disfranchised. That minority representation should be fostered with especial care in the large cities is natural from every point of view. It is in large cities that unrepresented minorities are largest and the evils of the general ticket system are thus most clearly felt. Since also the minority party in the large city is apt to be the majority party in the State, in control of the Legislatures and of the entire process of framing Constitutional amendment, its interests have usually been first considered. This device of obligatory subdivision was, however, very quickly extended to counties; first, in 1846, by New York, and later by several States, among which it will be convenient for the moment to consider only those two in which the single member dis-

---

[1] In 1864 an extraordinary sliding scale of representation was introduced: first, 1 member for every 5,000 persons, or fraction greater than ½, until five members had been reached; then 1 for the next 20,000, or fraction greater than ½—that is to say, 1 member for the next 10,000, and none for the 10,000 after; then 1 member for each 80,000, or fraction greater than ½. Three years later this was abandoned for the present system: counties under 18,000 return 2; under 28,000, 3; under 40,000, 4; under 55,000, 5; all larger, 6; each Baltimore district returns the same number as the largest county. Since the State contains 22 counties, a little calculation will show that Baltimore, which now contains almost half the population, can never return more than a third of the representatives.

trict is not insisted upon, as well. These were New York's important neighbors, Massachusetts, and (after the War) Pennsylvania. In New York and Massachusetts all counties were required to be thus divided. Pennsylvania, after a period during which counties, unions of counties, cities, and divisions of cities, were all utilized, settled in 1873 upon the following plan: Cities of a certain size, and all counties, are to be represented separately; cities entitled, under the system of apportionment, to more than four representatives, and counties of over 100,000 population, must be divided into districts; other cities and other counties doubtless may be.

The successive steps in the formation of these divisions are, first, the determination of the number of representatives which the county or city as a whole is to return; and second, the actual division, by the districting authority, subject to such additional restrictions as may be imposed. As regards the first step, the same tendency that we have already seen so often reappears. It is not enough that, through a limitation upon the total number of members, coupled with a guarantee of at least one member to every county, the least populous sections are almost certain to be over-represented. In Pennsylvania, and, since 1894 in New York, mathematical rules are added which enhance the discrimination.[1]

[1] Virtually nothing more than a limitation upon total number of members appeared in New York, 1821-94 (128) and consistently in Massachusetts (240). In New York, the guarantee of 1 member was only to counties " as heretofore established and separately organized ", and excepted the county of Hamilton, which was to elect with Fulton county, until entitled to separate representation. In 1874, the re-enactment of the amended article extended the guarantee to the one new county organized since 1846; a saving clause was also added to explain that these provisions, particularly that in regard to Hamilton county, did not debar the Legislature from its complete control over

Once the number of members is determined, the divisions are made, in New York and Massachusetts, by local authorities, at such time as the Legislature determines (in the former State), or at specified dates (in the latter).[1] This division of functions was, of course, suggested by the process for the Federal house, in which Congress apportions, and each State Legislature districts. In Pennsylvania, however, the districting is performed by the Legislature itself.

county lines. In Massachusetts the counties, for representative purposes, were, in one special case, not absolutely identical with the existing administrative divisions.

The Pennsylvania rule of 1873 is very cumbersome. The ratio is fixed at 1/200 of the population. All counties return at least 1 member; counties containing less than 5 ratios return 1 member for every full ratio and additional ½; larger counties, 1 for every full ratio, only. Every city containing a population equal to a ratio elects separately its *proportion* of the county representation; what happens to fractions in such a case, no one knows.

In New York, since 1894, the guarantee of separate representation applies only to then existing counties, as before; one county has since then been created. The total is fixed at 150, and the first ratio is obtained by using this as a divisor. First one member is given to every county containing less than 1½ ratios (with the special exception for Hamilton, as before); then 2 members to every other county. Then, the smaller counties being thus made happy by an excess of representation which, in practice, amounts to six or eight members, the balance are distributed among the counties containing over 2 ratios, on the basis of their enumerated population—that is to say, on a new and larger ratio, the fractions or "remainders" over which are to be represented in the order of their size, on the Carolina plan, so as to yield the fixed total.

[1] In New York, by the Boards of Supervisors, in general. But in 1874, the Board of Aldermen was substituted in the city and county of New York; and in 1894, the Common Council, or body exercising its powers, "in any city embracing an entire county and having no Board of Supervisors"—i. e., in New York City.

In Massachusetts divisions are to be made by popularly elected special commissioners, or, in case the Legislature does not provide for these, by the County Commissioners, except in Suffolk county, and by the Mayor and Aldermen of Boston.

In New York, single-member districts, " as nearly equal in population as may be ", already familiar in connection with other Legislative bodies, were now first required for the lower house as well, with results which will be considered in a moment. Massachusetts, however, merely requires that not more than three members may be returned by any one district; Pennsylvania, not more than four. Apart from the size of the district, the following rules are to be observed. In New York, prior to 1894, districts were to consist of convenient and contiguous territory, without dividing towns; in Massachusetts, of contiguous territory, without dividing towns or city wards; in Pennsylvania, merely of compact and contiguous territory. Since 1894, however, New York has gone into much detail. Districts must be compact, without dividing towns or city blocks; they must not vary from one another more than one border town or block; nor more widely than the least discrepancy which would result from a redistribution of towns and blocks capable of being included within either of two districts; they must lie wholly within a Senate district, and the same number within each; or, if this is not possible, then the larger number must lie within the most populous, or the smaller number within the least populous, Senate district in the county.[1]

4. Obligatory single-member districts, following New York

The action of New York, in incorporating the principle of single-member districts in its instrument of 1846, marks

[1] References:
La. Const. 1812, ii, 4, 6; 1845, 8, 16; 1852, 8, 16; 1868, 20, 21, 22; 1879, 16, 18; 1898, 18, 20.
N. Y. Const. 1846, iii, 2, 4, 5; Am. 1874, iii, 5; Const. 1894, iii, 2, 4, 5.
Mass. Am. 1857, xxi.
Md. Const. 1864, iii, 2-5; 1867, iii, 4, 5; Am. 1901, iii, 2, 4.
Pa. Const. 1873, ii, 17.

a turning point in the way in which the problem of appor--
tionment was conceived.   Prior to the War with Mexico,
" apportionment " was pictured primarily as a distribution
of members among local districts already in existence; districts then might or might not be combined, for the purpose
of insuring a representation proportionate to their political weight; they might or might not be divided, for the purpose of preventing large voting minorities from being unrepresented.   This conception, as we have seen, lingered
for a time in the East.

In the West, on the other hand, the delimitation of representative districts began at once to be considered as the very
essence of " apportionment " and equality among such districts to be regarded as the ideal.   The Federal Apportionment Act of 1842,[1] in which, for the first time, single-member Congressional districts were made obligatory in every
State, undoubtedly had a powerful influence in causing this
type of district to be regarded as the norm.   If it was not
universally insisted upon, this was because other considerations came into play.   Either already existing representatives in the Legislatures and Constitutional Conventions felt
reluctant to deprive their constituents of advantages which,
under existing systems, they enjoyed; or the slight inequalities which resulted from the continued recognition of administrative lines were felt to be not as great an evil as the
danger of partisan gerrymandering which would exist, if
the apportioning body were free to make mathematically
equal divisions.   The existence of the party system of government, in other words, has caused modifications of the
single-member principle which in some cases are justifiable
on broad grounds, and in some cases are not, but which in
all cases are regarded by everybody as exceptions to the

[1] *Vide* ch. ix, sec. I, p. 219, *infra.*

normal and easily-understood single-district system. Such
being the habit of thought under which subsequent provisions have been drafted, such will be the best point of view
from which to approach them.

The new State of Wisconsin led off, in 1848, with the
only pure form of the obligatory single-district system for
the lower house that has ever existed. A total of from 54
to 100 members are provided, to be chosen by single districts, " such districts to be bounded by county, precinct,
town or ward lines, to consist of contiguous territory, and to
be in as compact form as possible ". The requirement that
the Legislature is " apportion and district " the members,
according to the enumerated population, throws a side-light
upon the changing meaning of the term " apportionment ".
From this State the idea of obligatory single districts has
spread to the five contiguous States of Kentucky, Michigan,
Illinois, Missouri and Kansas, as well as to California, and
(for a time) to Pennsylvania, but in all cases with important
modifications. Temporarily, in Kentucky and Pennsylvania, that is to say, it was applied only to urban districts;
while in the other cases, the system, although it has been
generally introduced, continues, as in New York, to revolve,
as it were, about the county, as upon a pivot.

The Kentucky system of representation, in force between
1850 and 1890, was a cumbersome grafting of the new idea,
with others borrowed from various sources, upon its own
original system. In the first place, ten groups of specified
counties were established as " distributing districts ", on the
Virginia plan, their permanence being protected by the requirement that in case new counties should be erected out
of territory lying within more than one district, such county
should be attached to that district which had the least number of qualified electors. The number of representatives
periodically distributed to each of these districts was then

to be redistributed among counties, the larger urban districts, and unions of counties, much on the original system. The additional complication now introduced was that if cities or towns should be entitled to more than one member, they must be subdivided into single-member districts, compact, composed of contiguous " squares ", and without dividing wards or municipal divisions except so far as necessary to equalize the districts.[1]

Somewhat similar was the system temporarily in force in Pennsylvania, between the original county and city plan, and the county, city, and subdivision plan already described as to-day existing. The unit here, between 1857 and 1873, was the county; the union of counties; and any city that might contain a sufficient enumerated population to entitle it to *more* than one member. Such a city was to be separately represented, and was also to be divided into single-member districts, of contiguous territory, as nearly equal in enumerated population as might be.[2]

---

[1] The total number of members was fixed at 100; these were to be apportioned among the ten districts, as with Maine counties, instead of being permanently allotted, as in Virginia. Cities and towns were to be given separate representation on full ratios, as always; but the Alabama qualifying touch was added, that the balance of the county must also be entitled to separate representation. The original plan of crediting residuums to adjacent counties was abandoned for the Carolina plan of representing the largest fractions in order of their size; this, of course, did away with any possibility of flotorials. Counties containing less than a full ratio were brought within the general principle; that is to say, if these fractions were large enough to obtain a member, before the whole number was used up, well and good. To guard against the possibility of failure, however, it was provided that a small county might be joined with an adjacent county or counties, to return one member. This system lasted until 1890.

[2] The total number of members was 100. Not more than 3 counties might be joined; counties containing as few as 3,500 " taxables " might be accorded separate representation; and it was expressly provided that no county might be divided. Flotorials would appear to be possible under this system.

In the other, and surviving, cases, the retention of the county as the original unit, by the divisions, and (usually) by the unions of which, approximately equal districts are to be secured, may be justified as a check upon partisan gerrymander. Michigan contains, next to New York, the oldest and the crudest system. This was one of the States in which, from the beginning, the simple county system had been modified by the requirement that only organized counties were entitled to separate representation, and that no county thereafter organized should be given separate representation until it should contain a full ratio.[1] The organized county, with such territory as may be attached thereto, has accordingly, since 1850, been the " pivot ". If entitled to more than one of the limited total number of members, it is to be divided into single-member districts by its Board of Supervisors, on the New York plan. Territory outside of separately-represented counties is to be divided by the Legislature into districts, as nearly equal in enumerated population as may be, without dividing towns or cities. In curious contrast, however, to the tendency in several other States, townships or cities, entitled to more than one member, are not to be divided, but are to elect by general ticket.[2]

In Kansas, no local action is provided, and each county is to have (as in New York) at least one member, no unions appearing. By an amendment adopted, however, in 1873, a county representative is to be admitted by the Legislature only if 250 legal votes were cast at the preceding general election, and a county in which less than 200

[1] *Vide* p. 154, note 2, *supra*.

[2] The total number is 64 to 100. Counties, *etc.*, containing one-half ratio have separate representation. Districts are to consist of convenient and contiguous territory, and the rule as to townships and cities appears to apply to the divisions of counties.

votes were cast is to be " attached to and constitute part of
the representative district of the county lying next adjacent
on the east." In Missouri also there are no unions, and the
single-member subdivisions, which are to be made by the
County Courts, as nearly equal in population as may be,
may be altered from time to time as the public convenience
may require; counties entitled to more than ten representatives, however (*i. e.,* St. Louis), are to be divided into
districts returning from two to four members each. In the
other three States, the total number of members is not
merely limited, but fixed; districts to the same number, as
nearly equal in enumerated population as may be, are to be
formed by the Legislature, and are to consist of complete
counties, or to lie wholly within a county.[1]

Additional rules in the four Middle States restrict the

---

[1] Kansas set merely a maximum of 100 members until 1873; since
then, of 125.

Missouri still establishes a permanent ratio of 1/200, giving to counties containing under 2½ ratios 1 member; under 4, 2; under 6, 3;
over 6, 4, and 1 additional for every 2½ ratios. New counties, however, are to be attached to the county from which the greatest amount
of their territory is taken, until they obtain a full ratio.

In Illinois the total is 51, this being also the divisor to be used in
determining the ratio. The districts are to be contiguous and compact,
and as nearly equal in population as may be, under the following limitations: No district shall contain less than ⅘ ratio; counties containing between 1¾ and 2 ratios may be divided into two; larger counties
into as many districts as they contain full ratios. These districts are
properly Senatorial districts, but are used also for the lower house,
under a system of minority representation.

California demands, in addition to the recognition of county lines,
only contiguous territory and a total of 80.

In Kentucky the total is 100. Counties, if united, must be contiguous; not more than two shall be united, unless the requirement of
approximate equality forbids; when inequality of population is inevi-
table (*i. e.* always) the advantage is to be given to the more extensive
(*i. e.* less densely populated) district. If the idea were to provide for
unequal growth, the arrangement should, of course, be just the opposite.

Legislature, and discriminate—not severely except in Missouri—against the more densely-populated counties.[1]

5. *Permissive single-member districts, with the county check*

In Indiana, since 1851, and later in the new States of Oregon, Utah and Oklahoma, the counties are the original units of apportionment, which are then to be grouped as convenient, and may or may not be subdivided; nor is there any requirement that the districts thus formed shall return each a single member. In California, also, before the obligatory rule went into effect, there was a transition period during which divisions of counties were merely permitted— here, however, into single-member districts, only.[2]

In Oklahoma, in case counties are divided, towns, and city wards which constitute single-voting precincts, may not be divided, and New York's rule for the location of border units has been copied. Flotorial districts would seem to be possible in all five States, including even Utah, which is the only one to provide that each county must have at least one member. The total number of members is of course everywhere limited; mathematical rules for their distribution appear only in Oregon and Oklahoma, and these

[1] References:
Wisc. Const. 1848, iv, 2-4.
Ky. Const. 1850, ii, 5, 6, 13; 1890, 33, 35.
Mich. Const. 1850, iv, 3, 4; * 1908, v, 3, 4.
Pa. Am. 1857, i, 2, 4 (until 1873).
Kans. Const. 1859, ii, * 2, 26; x, 1, 2; Am. 1873, ii, 2.
Ill. Const. 1870, iv, 6, "Minority Representation."
Mo. Const. 1875, iv, 2, 3, 7, 9; ix, 3.
Cal. Const. 1879, iv, 5, 6.

[2] These are the only States in which it is clear, by express grant, or by implication, that the Legislature may divide counties into representative districts at its own discretion. In some of the States, classified under sections 1 and 2, the same power may exist. *Vide* remarks at the beginning of section 3, pp. 163-7, *supra*.

discriminate against the more populous counties in Oklahoma.[1]

6. *Unrestricted formation of districts*

Finally, since the War, four Western States, and Virginia, have required their Legislatures to carve out districts, and distribute members among them, at the stated periods, free from any restrictions at all, other than a limi-

---

[1] Total number of members in Indiana, 100; in California, 30 to 80; in Utah, 36 to 90. In Indiana and California, districts not wholly within a county must consist of complete contiguous counties.

Oregon prescribes a maximum of 60 members. Fractions of over ½, resulting from division, are to be represented by a member, and a county not entitled to separate representation is to be attached to "some adjoining county." The evident intention of the rule is to disregard smaller fractions, instead of relying upon the flotorial device to equalize representation. It would seem, however, that if strictly applied, semi-flotorials — districts composed of two counties, one of which is separately represented—must sometimes be formed.

Oklahoma has a maximum of 109, with the Ohio fixed ratio of 1/100. Counties containing ½ ratio obtain 1 member; 1¾, 2; then 1 additional on every full ratio; but no county to take part in (*i. e.*, independently, or as part of a flotorial) the election of more than 7. For unrepresented fractions of a ratio, the Ohio elaborate part-time rule (*vide* p. 159, *supra*) is provided, with one change: if representation in only one of the five biennial sessions is secured, the particular session is not specified. The obsolete Ohio provision for detaching counties, entitled to representation, from districts already formed, and for joining undersized counties to form new districts (*vide* p. 165, *supra*) is also adopted with one modification: the county need not now be joined to its least populous neighbor. Flotorials, in spite of these apparent efforts to do away with them, appear in the accompanying provisional apportionment, in the shape both of "additional districts," composed of counties already represented, and of a county returning one member at large, in addition to single-district members.

References:
Ind. Const. 1851, iv, 2, 4, 5, 6.
Oreg. Const. 1857, iv, 2, 3, 5, 6, 7.
Cal. Am. 1862, iv, 3, 30 (until 1879).
Utah Const. 1895, vi, 3; ix, 2-4.
Okla. Const. 1907, v, 10, 12-16.

tation upon the total number of members, and a recognition (in Virginia, not expressed) of the proportionate principle.[1]

In these many variants of the original Pennsylvania plan a recent tendency to leave more and more freedom to the Legislature clearly appears. This reached its culmination in a group of instruments, next to be considered, in which the ideal of a rigidly periodic reapportionment has been itself abandoned.

III. DISCRETIONARY REAPPORTIONMENT

The rigidly periodic system of apportionment, exemplified in the preceding schemes, involves two essentials: first, the duty of the Legislature, or other apportioning body, to act at the stated intervals; second, its incapacity to act at any other time. The periodic duty is always clearly expressed; the intervening incapacity is often only to be inferred from this, and is subject to certain exceptions. Thus, in four Southern States the Legislature has been expressly authorized to make rearrangements incidental to the erection of new administrative units;[2] in Maryland, the

[1] In Nebraska, until 1875, the districts were required to be formed of contiguous territory, and as compact as might be.

Limitations of total number, and references:

Nevada (Const. 1864, iv, 3, 5; xv, 6, 13) maximum of 56.

Nebraska (Const. 1866, ii, 3, 5, 8) 39 to 75; (Const. 1876, iii, 2, 3) maximum of 100.

South Dakota (Const. 1889, iii, 2, 5) 75 to 135.

Washington (Const. 1889, ii, 2, 3) 63 to 99. For an indirect restriction, however, caused by the rule in regard to Senatorial districts, *vide* ch. viii, sec. ii, 6, pp. 211, 212, *infra*.

Virginia (Const. 1902, 42, 43) 92 to 100.

The original Illinois provision, in force between 1818 and 1848, was also very broad, requiring apportionment merely among "counties and districts." Undoubtedly, however, only unions of counties, or districts formed outside of organized counties, were contemplated.

[2] Virginia, 1830-50; Alabama, 1867-75; Florida, since 1885; South Carolina since 1895. *Cf.* also Mississippi since 1890, and New Mexico, p. 183, notes, *infra*.

Baltimore Legislative districts may be altered at any time; in Missouri, the subdivisions of any county may be so altered; in New Jersey, Maryland and Arkansas, finally, a general reapportionment may be made at any time, provided a fresh enumeration is made for this purpose.

The earliest direct assault upon the rigid periodic ideal came in the weakening of the original obligation to a mere authorization. In Minnesota, since 1857—for brief periods after the War, in Missouri, Arkansas and Georgia—recently in Mississippi and New Mexico—the apportionment may not be changed except at the stated periods, but need not be, even then. That is to say, if the Legislature is contented with the existing distribution of representatives, it is under no Constitutional obligation to make changes. The practical distinction, of course, between a Constitutional obligation, for the enforcement of which no sanction exists except the pressure of public opinion—and a Constitutional privilege, which is likely to be converted by this same public opinion, into a moral and political obligation—is not very sharp. From the purely formal point of view, however, there is all the difference in the world; and this difference is likely to have some influence, if not a decisive one, in practice. In New York, for instance, the Constitutional obligation to reapportion the Legislature, at the first session after the return of the Enumeration, in 1876 broke down, and it was not until 1879 that the Assembly was actually reapportioned; who shall say that the party majority would have even then made a change, which deprived it of six sure seats, if they could have used the Constitutional text to justify inaction? From a narrowly legalistic point of view, the attempt to impose positive duties upon the Legislature, without providing a legal remedy in case it refuses to act, is an absurdity, which leads to constant violations of such duties in practice. Looked at broadly, however, the reliance upon public opinion and the political remedy of the polls has been rather remarkably justified. If the letter of such provisions has been violated, the spirit has almost always triumphed in time; the people have shown themselves an occasionally dilatory, but on the whole efficient, guardian of the written Constitution. A change by which the Legislature, therefore, rather than the Constitutional instrument, is made the determining legal authority as to whether a reapportionment shall be made, is a considerable step in the direction of restoring to the Legislature its original control over its own composition.

In case the Legislatures of these States do make reapportionments, then, of course, rules are provided under which they must act. In Minnesota and in Arkansas, we have, in addition to a limitation upon the total number of members, only the requirement that, in the formation of Senatorial districts, Representative districts may not be divided.[1] In Georgia, the simple county unit, as always, appeared, with limitation upon total number of members only.[2] Missouri had a system of obligatory single-member districts, identical with that now in force, except that the discrimination against the more populous counties was even more severe.[3] Mississippi has a system of permissive single-member districts, under a strong county check, complicated by the Virginia-Kentucky device of permanent " distrib-

[1] For the restrictions upon the formation of Senatorial districts in these States, *vide* ch. viii, sec. ii, 6, 8, pp. 211-213, *infra*.

References:

Minnesota (Const. 1857, iv, 2, 23, 24) not more than 1 member for every 2,000 inhabitants.

Arkansas (Const. 1868, v, 7-9—until 1874) 82 members.

[2] Maximum of 175. Not even recognition of the proportionate principle was required. (Ga. Const. 1868, iii, 3—until 1877.)

[3] All counties return 1 member, or 1 for every 3 full ratios. (Mo. Const. 1865, iv, 2, 7, 8—until 1875.)

uting districts ".[1] New Mexico has apparently a county
union system.[2]

In addition to the foregoing there is a small group of
Western States, in which precisely the contrary development
has occurred. That is to say, the Legislature must reapportion at stated intervals, but may also do so " from time
to time, as public convenience may require ", and without
being subject to the expense or delay involved in taking a
fresh enumeration. The evolution of this Legislative privilege, which of course justifies a sincere partisan in voting
for a reapportionment whenever his party's interest appears
to demand it, is rather interesting.

In Missouri since the War, as has already been shown,
the obligatory single-member divisions of counties might
be altered by the County Courts, under the above rule, and
to this extent the prohibition upon change, except at stated
intervals, was already modified. The apportionment proper,
however, might be made only at the stated intervals by the
Legislature, which had itself no control over the subsequent
division of the larger counties into these " Representative
districts ", as they were termed. Now in 1876, the Constitutional Convention of the new State of Colorado, following
the prevailing customs of borrowing provisions from the
most recent convenient model, lifted bodily from the Mis-

[1] Three absolutely permanent districts are defined, in terms of counties as they then existed, among which from 100 to 133 members are
to be equally divided. Every county is to have at least one member,
and new counties may be represented at once, without waiting for the
regular apportioning session. The accompanying provisional apportionment shows that inequalities of a single member, among the distributing districts, are permissible, and that both subdivisions of counties and flotorial unions are allowed. (Miss. Const. 1890, 254, 256.)

[2] House of 49 members. "Each county included in each district
shall be contiguous to some other county therein," and newly created
counties to be annexed to some contiguous county, (* N. Mex. Const.
1911, iv, 3, " Apportionment ").

souri instrument of 1875 the clause in regard to changes in
Representative districts—perhaps only with the intention
of authorizing those special changes which are convenient
when new counties are created—and in 1889 Montana and
Wyoming did the same. But in these three States, the
county union system of representation was adopted, instead
of Missouri's obligatory single-district plan; the counties,
or unions of counties to be formed by the Legislature, were
the only Representative districts allowed; an authorization
to change them, at any time, was therefore equivalent to
permitting the Legislature to exercise its entire powers of
reapportionment at any time that it might wish to.[1]

If any doubt exists as to the effect of this provision in
making the Legislature capable, at all times, of exercising
powers, which, at stated times, are imposed upon it as a
duty, this doubt will perhaps be dispelled by examining the
provisions of still a fourth State, North Dakota. Here a
very remarkable system of representation appears. For the
upper house, the obligatory single-district plan, with county
check, has been adopted, the districts to be as nearly equal
as may be, in the number of inhabitants entitled to representation. Among these districts, a limited total of lower
house members is then to be apportioned, under no restriction at all as to the basis on which the apportionment is to
be made; while as to the time of apportionment, it is ex-

[1] Districts are to consist of complete contiguous counties, as compact
as may be. In Colorado, the total number of Senators and Representatives combined is to be from 75 to 100, and the number of Representatives is to be, as near as may be, two-thirds of the total. In Wyoming, the number of Representatives is to be from two to three times
the number of Senators, which itself is not limited. In Montana there
is no limit.

References:
Colo. Const. 1876, v, 45-47.
Wyom. Const. 1889, iii, 3, "Apportionment," 2, 3.
Mont. Const. 1889, vi, 2, 3.

pressly provided that both districts and apportionment shall be made at the stated intervals, but *may* be made at any regular session.[1]

Finally, the culmination of Legislative control is reached in Idaho and Arizona. In the Northern State, a modified county union system, under which separate representation is granted to each county, but flotorials are permitted, is in force, but the limited total of members is merely " to be apportioned as may be provided by law "; that is to say, neither basic principle, nor the time, is prescribed or restricted in any manner.[2] In Arizona no restriction of any sort appears, except an implied prescription of the county unit.[3]

IV. SUMMARY

To recapitulate: The seven States in which counties and unions of counties survive to-day as the only units of representation constitute a broken semi-circle running from Maine

[1] The number of Senators, and consequently of districts, is from 30 to 50; of Representatives, from 60 to 140; districts are to be compact, and to consist of complete counties, or to lie wholly within a county. By the accompanying provisional apportionment, 31 districts were defined, returning usually 2 members each to the lower house, but in six cases, 1, in four cases, 3, and in one case, 4 members. The intent of the provision is, doubtless, to enable the Legislature to make up, in the lower house, for inequalities which, because of the insistence upon county lines, must occur in the upper; or possibly, to permit an increased representation to rapidly growing counties, upon their estimated increase of population between two censuses. The actual language employed, however, would permit the most arbitrary distribution of members.

N. D. Const. 1889, 26, 29, 32, 35, 214.

[2] Total number, 36 to 60. Each county to be entitled to one member, and other districts (flotorials) to consist of contiguous complete counties. (Idaho Const., iii, 2, 4, 5.)

[3] Members must be residents of the " county from which elected." No limitation even upon their total number. (* Ariz. Const. 1911, iv, 2, 1, 2.)

(towns and unions of towns) in the extreme northeast, through West Virginia and Tennessee to Texas, on the Gulf, thence up through Colorado and Wyoming to Montana again on the northern border—the terminal moraine, so to speak, of a Continental movement originating in Kentucky and Illinois. In the Eastern one of the three sections into which the Union is thus roughly divided, lie the older, non-periodic systems, of five little States,[1] and an intermediate group of seven,[2] in which the periodic principle has been applied only to the county; by reversion, this intermediate system has also reappeared in Ohio and Iowa. The central area of disturbance is more notable, however, for two well-defined later movements, centering here: an insistence upon single-member districts, which appears in eight States here,[3] and in California to the West; and an almost complete removal of restrictions, which has broken through even the Allegheny barrier, appearing in six States in all, in all three sections.[4] In ten other States, lying usually on, or just outside, the " moraine ", conflicting tendencies have produced almost every conceivable variety of provision.[5] Independently of the above distinctions, the periodic principle has itself been weakened, in various ways, in half a dozen contiguous Western States,[6] and in Mississippi. Finally, either through the requirement that every county shall have at least one member, or in more flagrant ways, the less populous towns or counties are favored at the expense of the densely-populated counties or cities in

[1] N. H., Vt., Conn., R. I., Del.

[2] N. J., N. C., S. C., Ga., Fla., Ala., Ark.

[3] N. Y., Wisc., Mich., Ky., Mo., Kans., and, in modified form, Ill. and N. D.

[4] Minn., S. D., Neb., Nev., Wash., Va.

[5] Mass., Pa., Md., Miss., La., Okla., Utah, Idaho; also Ind. and Oreg.

[6] Minn., N. D., Mont., Idaho, Wyom., Colo.

twenty-one out of twenty-six States east of the Mississippi,[1] in five out of the eleven States between the Mississippi and the Rockies,[2] in two out of the eleven Rocky Mountain or Pacific States.[3]

Clearly the problem of the proper distribution of representatives is far from being solved. Apart from the technical diversity of these various schemes, which speaks for itself, the two most prominent tendencies—the increasing measure of control accorded to the Legislature itself, in some States, and the increasingly more detailed discrimination against urban communities in others—are really different expressions of one and the same attitude that rural legislators and rural delegates to Constitutional Conventions are beginning to assume. Either restrictions must not be imposed which will hinder them from perpetuating themselves in power; or restrictions must be imposed which will facilitate this same perpetuation. I speak, of course, with some exaggeration. Doubtless rural representatives sincerely believe in the superior virtue and intelligence of their own communities. But, with equal lack of doubt, the average urban dweller does not admit this claim; and though our situation is immeasurably superior to that which prevailed in England during the rotten-borough era, or to that which prevails in the German Empire and in Prussia to-day, yet we are rapidly drifting towards a state of affairs in which the attempts of rural communities to enforce this claim, against the preponderating physical and economic

[1] The scattered exceptions are New Hampshire, Massachusetts, Virginia, Indiana and Wisconsin.

[2] Favored in Iowa, Missouri, Kansas, Arkansas, and Oklahoma; not favored in the States to the north and to the south of this contiguous group.

[3] Favored, merely in that each county must have at least one member, in Utah and Idaho. Counties in this section of the Union are very large.

strength of the urban population, will create a top-heavy political structure. It is historically justifiable that urban communities should be under-represented to some extent. They were the last in the field, so of course they must expect to suffer. But if the discrimination should ever be felt to have been carried beyond a certain reasonable degree, the danger of a violent overturn can no more be avoided by us than it has been by other nations, the disfranchised majorities of which have sought, outside of law, a remedy for the law's injustice. The composition of the Legislature, it should be recalled, is of importance, not merely, and not principally, because the Legislature is the seat of residuary power under the Constitution. The composition of the Constitutional Convention itself is everywhere either determined by the Legislature, or is defined in terms of the Legislature's own districts.

Now, toward the solution of the real problem of representative distribution, no steps have been taken. Instead, the framers of Constitutions have frittered away their constructive powers in devising mathematically exact systems of proportionate—or disproportionate—local representation. There may have been a time when strictly proportionate local representation was worth emphasizing. But since local boundaries have become, except as between country and town, purely artificial, and matters of administrative convenience—since the representative has come to represent his party rather than his locality—proportionate local representation has been of value only in so far as it conduced to proportionate party representation. And since it does so conduce only in a rough-and-ready way, attempts at mathematical accuracy in the representation of each little section of the State, have been so much ingenuity wasted.

Let us define what the real problem is. It is not a strictly accurate proportioning of representation, to parties, even.

In a discussing body it is desirable that as many as possible shades of opinion and varieties of interest should be given vigorous voice. But as long as all matters of importance are decided by the preponderance of one compact party group, it does not matter seriously whether its majority is twenty or sixty. The problem before the rural Framer is not, even, whether urban communities, whose popular voting weight shall in the aggregate exceed that of half the State, shall or shall not be in a position to secure more than half the seats in Legislative chamber and Constitutional Convention. With the continued growth of town, at the expense of county, which is incidental to our development out of an agricultural into a manufacturing nation, rural predominance is doomed, if not in one way, then in another. His problem is to decide, merely, when and how he wishes urban communities to be thus masters of their own political destinies—and of his; whether he wishes it to occur fairly soon, and by ordinary Constitutional means—or somewhat later, and in a more violent manner; whether he wishes complete control over his own local affairs to pass into urban hands—or whether he had better begin to protect himself while he may, by a broad system of local charters.

It is not too soon to begin to consider this problem now, before it has really begun to press for solution. I repeat, that it is difficult to avoid the language of exaggeration. There is not, as yet, any deep-seated hostility between town and country. Rural representatives have not their feet upon the city's neck. That is the language of the electoral campaign, which no one really believes in. There is not a State in the Union to-day, outside of Delaware and the smaller New England States, in which the party whose strength lies chiefly in the cities is not liable, on some issue in no way connected with this, to find itself in complete control of the political machinery of the State. Our parties do not divide on sectional lines, as yet, and the bitterest partisan animosities are usually as a matter of fact to be found dividing inhabitants of the same city.   But for this very reason, the tendency which my recapitulation shows to exist in a large majority of the Eastern States, may well be pondered over by all parties now.   A lack of sympathy and mutual understanding between country and town, necessarily existing, for economic reasons, in some degree, may well become intensified, by a sense of political grievance, to the point where amicable adjustment is no longer possible.   A little historic insight will facilitate the adjustment.   It is to be hoped that nobody's neck will ever really be under anybody's foot.   But it is just as well to realize that laws, Constitutional or other, cannot run counter to underlying economic facts, and that in so far as anybody's neck will be underneath, that neck will not belong to a lusty urban body.   A livelier sense of the virtues of local self-government will be the natural result of this realization.   Once this attitude is reached, the importance of the Legislature as an organ of government will be greatly diminished, and it should be an easy matter to devise a plan by which all sections shall be equitably represented in the proposal of Constitutional changes, as they already are in the popular ratification.

I touch upon this point here because discrimination against the cities appears more commonly in connection with the lower house, though often more flagrantly in connection with the upper.   Further comment upon the structure of the Legislature as a whole can best be made after we have seen how its other branch is constituted.

CHAPTER VIII

DISTRICTS OF REPRESENTATION IN THE UPPER HOUSE

THE Colonial Council, out of which the State Senate developed, was appointed by Crown, Proprietor, or Royal Governor, except in Connecticut and Rhode Island, where "Assistants," together with their presiding officer, the Governor, were elected by the people by general ticket; and in Massachusetts, where they were elected by joint ballot of the Assembly and their own predecessors. Local representation was secured, if at all, only through a requirement of local residence; and this requirement, again, at the time of the Revolution, rested only upon custom or statute everywhere except in Massachusetts, where the Charter provided that, out of 28 "Councillors or Assistants", at least 18 should be inhabitants or landholders within the former colony of Massachusetts Bay, at least 4 within Plymouth, at least 3 within "Maine", and at least 1 within the territory between the Sagadahoc (Kennebec) and Nova Scotia (New Brunswick).[1] This organization, simplified by the elimination of the outgoing Council from the choosing body,[2] continued in force in Massachusetts until 1780; the Connecticut general-ticket system lasted for ten years after the adoption of a Constitution; that is, until 1828; and the similar Rhode Island body until 1842.

[1] Mass. Charter, 1691, Thorpe, p. 1879.

[2] Cushing, H. A., *History of the Transition from Provincial to Commonwealth Government in Massachusetts*, pp. 17, 175.

In tracing the development in the other States it will be convenient to discuss together all assemblages of local representatives which developed out of the Colonial Council, irrespective of whether the new organ retained the original mixture of executive, legislative, and judicial powers enjoyed by the Colonial Council, or whether it was reduced to a purely executive or to a purely legislative body. In all cases the problem was essentially the same: how to apply the consecrated principle of local representation to one, or sometimes to two, upper houses or organs, as emphatically as to the one beneath, and yet preserve some sort of distinction. One favorite method was to provide a longer tenure of membership, with or without the device, perhaps suggested by the Pennsylvania Frame of Government of 1683, of partial renewal. In New York and North Carolina, differing suffrage qualifications were for a time required. In other cases indirect election, an altered number of members to the district, or especially created districts, were invoked; and although of these three devices our particular concern is with the last, it will be impossible to separate the three in discussion.

The application of the principle of periodic reapportionment to the upper house lagged a trifle. Pennsylvania did not apply this principle to its upper house until 1790, Kentucky until 1799, nor Louisiana until 1845, although all had applied it from the beginning to the lower. In Massachusetts there was a delay of four years, between 1836 and 1840; Georgia waited from 1798 until 1868, and then applied the principle only in its discretionary form; while New Jersey, Maryland and South Carolina have never extended the principle upward. On the other hand, of the five States which do not apply the principle to the lower house, Connecticut adopted it, in its discretionary form, when it took up the locally-represented upper house in 1828; and Ver-

mont introduced the rigid form when, in 1835, it established
its first Senate. The ten later instances in which the principle has been modified are the same for both bodies, Connecticut and Georgia being, as it were, the connecting links
between the early and the late departures from the prevailing ideal.

I. EARLY TREATMENTS OF THE UPPER HOUSE

We have in the first place a group of instances in which
the principle of direct local choice was not introduced.
South Carolina, until 1778, had its Legislative Council
chosen by the lower house, in imitation of the surviving
Massachusetts Charter; instead, however, of the meagre
local representation which existed in this State, the choice
was to be made from among its own members.[1] Georgia,
until 1789, went its neighbor one better: the choice of its
Executive Council was to be made by the Assembly from its
own members, but the Councillors chosen were to be two
from each county entitled to full representation.[2] Maryland, until 1837, went both States several degrees better: it
erected a college of electors, separate from the lower house,
but composed in precisely the same manner, except that it
was half the size; this body was to choose, either out of its
own membership or not, fifteen Senators, local representation being secured by the requirement that nine should be
residents of the Western and six of the Eastern Shore.[3]
Kentucky's plan, until 1799, was a fusion of the two pre-

---

[1] Council of thirteen. Their seats were to be vacated, and filled by
fresh elections. S. C. Const. 1776, 2, 4 (until 1778).

[2] Their seats were to be vacated, but not filled up. It voted by counties; and when not engaged in examining legislation, only one member
from each county, in monthly rotation, was obliged to attend. Ga.
Const. 1777, 2, 25, 27 (until 1789).

[3] Md. Const. 1776, 14, 15 (until 1837).

ceding: an electoral college, an exact replica of the lower house as regarded numbers and mode of election, chose one Senator from each county.[1] Vermont got along until 1836 with a precise copy of Connecticut's general ticket system.[2]

These attempts to satisfy the people with local representation without direct election, or with direct election without local representation, were not destined to endure, and are of interest chiefly because of the light they throw upon two characteristic features of our present governmental structure. Maryland's electoral college was of course the prototype of our Federal Presidential machinery. And the reason why almost every State of the Union requires to-day that the members of both houses shall be residents of the districts by which they are chosen is undoubtedly because all through the Colonial period, local residence, in connection with the Council, was the only kind of local representation that existed. It was natural that, after the Revolution, this requirement should have become embodied in the fundamental law, should have continued to be imposed after local choice of Senators was accorded, and should have been extended by analogy to the lower house as well, where there never has been any reason for its existence.

A second method of attack was to accord local choice, without any regard to the voting weight of the localities. One obvious device was to give each county one Senator or

[1] Or at least one, until the number of counties should equal the number of Senators. This latter number was specified as 11, and one additional for every four representatives added to the existing 40. When the contemplated equality should be attained, new counties were to be considered as parts of the county or counties from which taken. Ky. Const. 1792, i, 8-15 (until 1799).

[2] Council of twelve, without local representation. Vt. Const. 1777, ch. ii, 17; 1786, 1793, ch. ii, 10.

Councillor, and this scheme, in all its simplicity, we find in operation in North Carolina until 1835;[1] in New Hampshire (for Executive Council only) since 1792;[2] in New Jersey throughout its entire history;[3] and in Rhode Island (applied to towns and cities) since 1842.[4] Its admirable efficacy in keeping Hudson County and Providence where they belong needs no emphasis of comparative figures.

In other States this general system was in force, but slight concessions were made to the one most populous city or county. Georgia gave each county one Senator from 1789 until 1843, when the Legislature was required to establish forty-six pairs of contiguous counties, making, with the single county containing the largest representative population, forty-seven, each of these " Senatorial districts " to return one Senator; any new county was to be annexed to " one of the districts from which it was taken ", so that the number would remain unchanged; this system lasted until the War.[5]   Louisiana, until 1845, specified eleven out of twelve " counties " as constituting one such district each; the twelfth county, however, was permanently divided into three districts, of which one was New Orleans city.[6]   South Carolina, in 1778, specified parishes or administrative districts, nearly identical with those for the lower house, each to return one Senator, except Charleston, to which two were accorded; a similar arrangement was made upon the change to specified election districts in 1790, and to unspecified counties in 1868; since 1895, however, all counties without

---

[1] N. C. Const. 1776, ii, 1 (until 1835).

[2] N. H. Const. 1792, part ii, 60.

[3] N. J. Const. 1776, 3; 1844, iv, 2.

[4] R. I. Const. 1842, vi, 1.

[5] Ga. Const. 1789, i, 2; 1798, i, 3; Am. 1843, i, 3 (until the War).

[6] La. Const. 1812, ii, 10 (until 1845).

exception are to return one Senator.[1] Maryland, in 1837, assigned one Senator to each county and to Baltimore city; in 1864, however, one to each of the three, or, since 1901, to each of the four, Baltimore Legislative districts.[2] The South Carolina discrimination amounts to comparatively little, and will in time amount to less, since Charleston is not growing so rapidly as the rest of the State. In each of the four Baltimore districts, on the other hand, an average of over 25,000 votes was cast for President in 1908, as against less than 2,000 in Calvert County.

Another class of modifications was induced by a desire to provide a proper basis for the system of partial renewal. Pennsylvania, until 1790, gave one Senator to each county and to Philadelphia city; these twelve units were then classed, as regards the beginning of the three-year term, into three permanent groups; as new counties were erected they were to be attached to adjacent groups.[3] Virginia established twenty-four permanent groups of counties, as districts to return one Senator each; then, on the basis of a four-year term, these districts were themselves to be classed into four " divisions " by lot; these were the forerunners of the four " distributing districts " which complicated the

[1] In 1776 there had been 28 parishes or districts. These were retained by Const. 1778, 12, for the Senate, although developed by division for the lower house (*vide* ch. vii, p. 141, *supra*). Const. 1790, i, 7, provided 35 election districts for the Senate, to 44 for the other chamber, and the two largest have double representation. By Am. 1808, the lower house districts are to be used, with double representation only for Charleston. By Const. 1868, ii, 8, similarly for counties. By Const. 1895, iii, 6, one Senator from each county, without exception.

[2] Md. Am. 1837, 2, 3, 11 (total number of Senators also fixed at 21); Const. 1851, iii, 2; 1864, iii, 3; 1867, iii, 2; Am. 1901.

[3] Pa. Const. 1776, 19 (until 1790).

lower house plan in 1830.[1] Delaware had a better idea. To meet the needs of its three-year term, it provided three Senators from each of its counties. When, in 1831, the quadrennial term for President had long made three-year terms seem incongrous, Delaware abandoned the partial renewal, but retained the three Senators. Finally, in 1897, it erected permanent single-member districts for Senators, as well as for Representatives, and on the same general plan, but discriminating even more severely against Wilmington.[2]

Attempts to provide for anything like genuine proportionate representation appear outside of the periodic States only in New Hampshire and Massachusetts. The first New Hampshire instrument—which also exhibits, very prettily, the transition from local residence to local choice, as the basis of local representation—specified, at varying figures, the representation which each of its five counties should have in its Council of twelve.[3] Then in 1780, New York having already blazed the path, Massachusetts provided that 40 " Councillors and Senators " should be chosen by Senatorial districts, to be formed by the Legislature " from time to time " to the number of not less than 13, and no district so large as to be entitled, on the basis of " public taxes paid ", to more than 6 Senators; these, by joint ballot with the lower house, were then to choose 9 Councillors proper, out of their own number so far as possible, but deficiencies from the people at large; not more

[1] Va. Const. 1776, Thorpe, p. 3816 (until 1830). *Cf.* p. 162, *supra.*

[2] In 1792, a two-thirds majority of the Legislature was authorized to increase the number of Senators. Since 1897 there have been 17 districts, of which 2 are in Wilmington; additional details precisely as for the lower house. Del. Const. 1776, 4; 1792, ii, 3; 1831, ii, 3; 1897, ii, 2. *Cf.* ch. vii, pp. 142, 143, *supra.*

[3] Five, two, two, two, and one. N. H. Const. 1776, Thorpe, p. 2452 (until 1784).

than two Councillors to be chosen from any one district; this lasted until 1840.[1] New Hampshire, in 1784, simplified this: 12 Senators were to be apportioned, among from 5 to 10 districts; two of them, together with three Representatives, were to be chosen by joint ballot for the Council.[2] Finally, since 1792, New Hampshire has required the formation, "from time to time", of single-member districts, as nearly equal as possible, on the basis of " direct taxes paid ", without dividing towns and unincorporated places; and has made its Councillors elective one by each county.[3]

Combining the preceding provisions with those in force for the lower house, we find additional support for the thesis, already sufficiently established, that mere territorial area is a factor of great importance in political development. The two smallest States, Rhode Island and Delaware, are the two in which the rural districts are most completely in control of both bodies, under antiquated systems of representation. In four out of the six next in size, they are similarly entrenched in one of the two houses—in Connecticut and Vermont, in the lower—in New Jersey and Maryland, in the upper. New Hampshire's system seems, on the surface, eminently fair, and indeed—in its definition of Senatorial districts in terms of taxes paid—even to favor the more populous sections; the absence of the periodic safeguard, however, is, from the technical point of view, fatal. Massachusetts is the only one of these small States which

[1] The seats of Senators chosen as Councillors were to be vacated, and filled up by the peculiar joint-ballot process provided for filling vacancies. Mass. Const. 1780, Part II, ch. i, sec. ii, 1, 4; sec. iii, 1, 4 (until 1840).

[2] N. H. Const. 1784, Thorpe, p. 2459 (until 1792).

[3] Twelve Senators until 1877; since then, twenty-four. The text requires the election of five Councillors, although there are now ten counties. N. H. Const. 1792, Part II, 25, 26, 27, 60; Am. 1877, ii, 25, 26.

accords to urban communities, under the periodic system, proportionate representation in both houses of the Legislature. Is the quality of Massachusetts' legislative output inferior to that of the other States?

II. PERIODIC REAPPORTIONMENT

The Connecticut Legislature is authorized to make its reapportionment at intervals of ten years, on the basis of population, as determined by the Federal Census.[1] The Vermont Legislature is required to make one, on the same basis, as determined either by Federal or State Census.[2] Among the States where both houses are subject to periodical reapportionment, the rules as to the apportioning body differ slightly in Missouri;[3] as to time, they differ at present only in Maine;[4] as to basis, only in a few obsolete instances[5]

[1] At the first session after the completion of the Census.

[2] The apportionment is to be made " after the taking of such census," which, by implication, may be ordered by the State at any time. The original language, self-contradictory on this point, was cleared up by an amendment adopted in 1850. This is the origin of the similar partial exception to the periodic principle which we have already noted in New Jersey, Maryland, and Arkansas. *Cf.* ch. vii, p. 146, *supra.*

[3] In case of failure by the Legislature to act, the Governor, Secretary of State and Auditor-General shall do so, within 30 days after its adjournment. (Mo. Const. 1875, iv, 7.)

[4] Representative apportionment, " at the several periods " of the State enumeration, required to be taken at intervals of from five to ten years. Senatorial apportionment, at dated intervals of ten years, merely.

In Iowa, 1846-57, the rule is obscure. From 1857 to 1904, the usual five-year action, at the first session after State of Federal Census, was required for the upper house; action at every regular session for the lower.

[5] In New York, prior to 1821, the basis was the same in terms ("number of electors"), but the electoral qualifications for the two bodies differed. In North Carolina, where also a freehold qualification was required (until 1856) for the Senate only, the five-year aver-

and in North Dakota.[1] In every instance in which the
Legislature has been merely authorized, and not positively
required, to reapportion the lower house at the stated intervals, it has the same discretion in regard to the upper
house, and it has this discretion for the upper house alone
in Connecticut, and, since 1877, in Georgia.[2] In every case
where the Legislature is empowered to act at other than
the stated intervals, the situation is the same for both houses.

Now as to the nature of the Senatorial district, under
either the rigid or the discretionary system. The painful
steps by which, for the lower house, the varying single-
member district has become to a large extent substituted for
the permanent town or county unit, did not need to be
taken here. Senates being an entirely modern invention, no

age of public taxes paid, in place of "Federal population" for the
lower house, was the basis before the War. In Louisiana the basis for
the upper house has been the entire population, since the first application of the periodic principle to this body, in 1845; for the lower house,
the number of electors (free white males) remained the basis until
1852. In Texas, 1868-76, the number of electors was the basis for
the upper house; no prescribed basis for the lower. Virginia's suggestion, in 1850, that a different basis might be adopted for the two
bodies, will also be recalled. And compare, outside the periodic States,
the population and tax-paying bases still co-existing in New Hampshire.

[1] For the upper house, "number of inhabitants entitled to representation," defined by N. D. Const. 1889, 121, as (1) Citizens of the United
States; (2) Aliens who have declared intention, 1½ years before the
election; (3) Civilized Indians, whose tribal relations have been for
two years severed. By an amendment adopted in * 1898 the second class
was dropped.
No basis for apportioning members of the lower house among the
districts thus formed. *Cf.* ch. vii, p. 184, *supra.*

[2] In Connecticut, no comprehensive reapportionment for the lower
house; authorized periodic reapportionment for the upper.
In Georgia, 1798 till the War, obligatory periodic reapportionment
for the lower house, none for the upper; 1868 to 1877, authorized
periodic reapportionment for both houses; since 1877, obligatory again
for the lower, authorized for the upper.

type of local district has had a consecrated right of representation in them. From the very beginning they have been State organs, rather than aggregations of local delegates, and although the system of local choice has undoubtedly been valued as incidentally assuring representation to different sections of the State, the main problem has always been how best to organize, for the election of the Senate as a whole, the whole body of State electors. This differing attitude towards the two houses has showed itself, among other ways, in the differing rules as to the total number of members. The original idea in regard to the lower house was that each locality should be represented—at first, arbitrarily—later, in proportion to its voting weight—the total of these representatives constituting the total size of the chamber; it was only as it was realized that a " ratio ", as small as the smallest locality, would make the total number inconveniently large, that limitations upon this total number were imposed, and small localities either combined, or the proportionate principle modified to their advantage. The Senate, on the other hand, as the successor of the Council, has always been pictured as containing a strictly limited number of members, so that the periodic process has never been an apportionment of *representatives* to the localities, but always a distribution of *members* throughout the State. For this purpose, the variable district from the beginning commended itself. Only in Vermont, and in Massachusetts for a time, has a fixed territorial unit clearly been adopted.

The single-member district, as the obvious perfection of the variable district, suggested itself at once. Single districts for the choice of Congressional Representatives were voluntarily formed by several State Legislatures, immediately after the adoption of the Federal Constitution. Single Senatorial districts, we have seen, have been prescribed since 1792 in New Hampshire. Here, however, another set of considerations came into play. Far the easiest way of defining Senatorial districts, on the basis of their enumerated population, was in terms of fairly large units, such as counties. It was also a most useful check upon partisan gerrymanders to insist that they should be so formed. Considerations of symmetry, to some extent local feeling as well, combined with one or both of these more practical arguments to inspire the feeling, in the larger States, that counties should not be divided. But if they were not to be divided, even approximately equal districts could often not be secured. Should proportionate equality be sacrificed to the single-member idea, or should the Legislature be permitted a wider freedom in the size and membership of the district? Should divisions be permitted which would make equality possible, but bring the risk of gerrymander in their train? Or should the whole problem be given up as insoluble, and every thing left to the honor of the apportioning body? Finally, was the same rule to be prescribed for the upper as for the lower house, or was a deliberate effort to be made to keep the two houses as dissimilar as possible?

The practical difficulty of the problem has resulted in its being solved in many different ways. Concerning these solutions it may in general be said that originally the two houses, because of their differing historical antecedents, were formed upon decidedly different lines, and that it is only recently that they have become, in several States, assimilated to one another. In so far, moreover, as this assimilation has occurred, it has been usually a matter of the lower house escaping from the bondage of traditional ideas, and assuming upper house characteristics.

1. *The permanent district*

This has appeared clearly in Vermont, where, since 1836, Senators are apportioned among the counties, in the same manner as Representatives in several other States; and in Massachusetts, where, between 1840 and 1857, the then established Senatoral districts were utilized as permanent units.[1] These are instances, of course, of the lower house practice influencing the upper. In Arizona, also, it would appear that the county is to remain the unit for both houses.[2]

2. *Simple unions*

The first instruments of New York, Ohio, Indiana, Illinois and Maine did not expressly provide that Senatorial districts were to be formed only by grouping contiguous and undivided counties (or, in Maine, towns). Such was the undoubted intention, however, and the technical defect was remedied by Pennsylvania, in 1790, and by all other States which have since adopted this system. It was a natural and common method, which survives in nine States to-day, widely scattered.[3]

In two of these surviving States, Tennessee and Colorado, the county union plan is provided for the lower house as well. In the case of Tennessee, however, we must be on our guard against assuming that it means the same thing as applied to the two houses. As applied to the lower house, it means that the county is the normal unit, unions of small

---

[1] In Vermont (Am. 1836, iv; 1850, xxiii), total of 30 Senators, at least one to each county, and remainders represented in order of size.

In Massachusetts (Am. 1840, xiii), total of 40 Senators, and at least one to each district (until 1857). Total of 9 Councillors, to be chosen by joint ballot, and not more than one from each district (until 1855).

[2] Under the provision regarding the qualifications of members. No other restriction of any sort, for either house. (*Const. 1911, iv, 2, 1, 2).

[3] Maine—Florida—Indiana, Tennessee—Iowa—Colorado, New Mexico —Idaho, Oregon.

counties being formed only in exceptional cases. As applied to the upper house, it means that the districts normally consist of county groups, which, when practicable, are made of such a size as to return a single Senator; it is only exceptionally that a district returns more than one Senator, or consists of a single large county. In Colorado and New Mexico, the two systems are assimilated in theory, but the smaller size of the lower house district makes the exceptions more likely to occur in practice.[1]

[1] Virtually no additional provisions, other than limitation upon total number of members, appear in:

New York, 1801-21 (32 Senators).

Ohio, 1802-51 (⅓ to ½ number of Representatives).

Indiana, 1816-51 (⅓ to ½ Reps.) ; since 1851 (max. 50).

Mississippi, 1817 to the War (⅓ to ½ Reps.).

Illinois, 1818-48 (⅓ to ½ Reps.).

Maine, since 1819 (total of 20, to be increased according to the increase in the lower house, up to a maximum of 31).

Missouri, 1820-65 (14 to 33).

Texas, 1845 to the War (19 to 33).

Iowa, 1846-57 (⅓ to ½ Reps.) ; 1857-1904 (max. 50) ; since 1904 (50).

California, 1849-62 (⅓ to ½ Reps.).

Florida, 1868-85 (¼ to ½ Reps.) ; since 1885 (max. 32).

Virginia, 1870-76 (no limit as to number of Senators; max. 40 *districts*) ; 1876-1902 (33 to 40 Senators).

Colorado, since 1876 (approximately ⅓ of an aggregate ranging from 75 to 100).

Idaho, since 1889 (18 to 24).

New Mexico, since 1911 (24).

In Maine, the districts are to "conform, as near as may be, to county lines." In Florida, until 1885, one Senator was accorded to the Seminole Indians. In Virginia, the districts are formed by grouping counties, cities and towns. In Colorado they must be compact.

The earliest detailed provision appeared in New York, in 1777. The total number, provisionally set at 24, was to be increased up to a maximum of 100, under the same unworkable rule as was provided for the lower house. In 1801 this was abandoned for the flat total mentioned above, without other restrictions. In practice, the number of "Great Districts" was never changed from the number originally provided—four—although their boundaries were frequently shifted.

3. *Obligatory single-member districts, without divisions*

The attempt to obtain approximately equal districts, re-

Pennsylvania, in 1790, with a total of from ¼ to ⅓ the number of Representatives, provided that no district should return more than 4 Senators. In 1838 a further step in the direction of the single member system was taken, through the requirement that no separate county or city should return more than 4, no grouped district more than 2 Senators. This lasted until 1857.

Tennessee, in 1796, required from ⅓ to ½ the number of Representatives, and no district to return more than 3 Senators. Since 1834, the total is not to exceed ⅓ that of the lower house, there is no limitation as to size of district, and fractions lost by counties in the apportionment for the lower house are to be made up to them in the upper, "as near as may be practicable."

In Connecticut, from 1828 till 1901, from 18 to 24 Senators were to be chosen in from 8 to 24 districts, lying wholly within counties, no town to be divided, and no county to have less than 2 Senators.

In North Carolina, from 1835 till the War, a flat total of 50 appeared. Residuums were to be shifted to undersized adjacent counties, in imitation of the original Kentucky lower house provision, so as to give these separate representation if possible.

In Oregon, finally, the total is to be from 16 to 30, and approximately ½ the number of Representatives. As with the lower house, fractions exceeding ½ ratio are to be represented.

References:

N. Y. Const. 1777, 10, 12; Am. 1801 (until 1821).

Pa. Const. 1790, i, 4, 6, 7; 1838, i, 4, 6, 7 (until 1857).

Tenn. Const. 1796, 3, 4; 1834, ii, 6, 1870, ii, 6.

Ohio Const. 1802, i, 6 (until 1851).

Ind. Const. 1816, iii, 6, 1851, iv, 2, 5, 6.

Miss. Const. 1817, iii, 10, 13; 1832, iii, 10, 13 (until the War).

Ill. Const. 1818, ii, 5, 6 (until 1848).

Me. Const. 1819, iv, Part ii, 1, 2.

Mo. Const. 1820, iii, 6 (until 1865).

Conn. Am. 1828, i, ii (until 1901).

N. C. Am. 1835, i, 1 (until the War).

Tex. Const. 1845, iii, 10, 31 (until the War).

Iowa, Const. 1846, iii, 6, 31, 32; 1857, iii, 34, 35, 37; Am. 1904, iii, 34.

Cal. Const. 1849, iv, 6, 29, 30 (until 1862).

Oreg. Const. 1857, iv, 2, 3, 6, 7.

Fla. Const. 1868, xiv; 1885, vii, 2, 4.

Va. Const. 1870, v, 3, 4; Am. 1876, v, 3, 4 (until 1902).

turning a single member each, and yet preserve county lines
intact, was first made by Kentucky in 1799, and survives
in this naked form in Alabama and Georgia to-day.[1]   In
view of the large number of Senators which it has been
thought necessary to provide, this necessarily leads to inequality of representation.   The general principle, therefore,
modified by a permission accorded to exceptional counties
or districts to return more than one member appears in
Arkansas and Ohio.[2]   New York, between 1821 and 1846,

Colo. Const. 1876, v, 46, 49.

Idaho Const. 1889, ii, 2, 5.

N. Mex. Const. 1911, iv, 3, "Apportionment."

[1] No additional provision other than limitation upon total number in:

Kentucky, 1799-1850 (24 Senators, and one additional for every
three Representatives added to the existing number of 58).

Alabama, since 1819 (¼ to ⅓ number of Representatives).

Florida, 1838—the War (¼ to ½ number of Representatives).

Georgia, since 1868 (44 Senators).

Virginia introduced, in 1830, two distributing "Divisions," corresponding to the four "Great Districts" for the lower house. The
one to the west of the Blue Ridge was to return 13, the one to the
east, 19 Senators, counties, cities, towns and boroughs being grouped
for this purpose into single member districts. If, by extraordinary
majority, these divisions should be ignored, a maximum of 36 Senators was set. From 1850 till the War, counties, cities and towns were
merely to be grouped into 50 single member districts.

In Illinois, between 1848 and 1870, 25 single member districts were
to be formed, under the lower house mathematical rule, which discriminated slightly against the urban districts, and with the same
authorization to accord separate representation to cities and towns
containing the requisite population.

References:

Ky. Const. 1799, ii, 6, 11, 12 (until 1850).

Ala. Const. 1819, iii, 10, 11; 1867, viii, 3; 1875, ix, 1, 4; 1901, 197, 200.

Va. Const. 1830, iii, 3-5; 1850, iv, 3, 5, 6 (until the War).

Fla. Const. 1838, ix, 1-3 (until the War).

Ill. Const. 1848, iii, 6, 8-10 (until 1870).

Ga. Const. 1868, iii, 2; 1877, iii, 2.

[2] Arkansas started (Const. 1836, iv, 31-33) with a requirement of

profiting by Delaware's example, enumerated eight districts, to return four Senators each, of whom one to be elected each year, on the partial renewal plan; somewhat similar arrangements appeared in Michigan for a time, and in West Virginia, to-day, the advantage of course being that these larger districts can more easily be made equal.[1]

from 17 to 33 Senators, and not more than 25 until the State should contain a population of 500,000; the ratio, meanwhile, to be 1,500 free white males, and each district to contain, "as nearly as practicable" an equal number of free whites, with a special exception for Washington county. This did not survive the War. It was revived, however, in 1874 in the following form:—Total number, 30 to 35; each Senator to represent an equal number "as nearly as practicable." (Const. 1874, viii, 2, 3).

Ohio, since 1851 (Const. 1851, xi, 6-10) fixes a ration of $1/_{35}$; Hamilton county to be one district, returning 3 Senators; the remaining counties to be grouped into 32 single member districts. The lower house rules as to according part-time representation on remainders, and annexing districts, containing less than $3/4$ ratio, to adjacent districts, are repeated; also as to separation of counties from an existing district, except that here a *full* ratio is required in both parts. *Cf.* ch. vii, pp. 159, 165, *supra*. The rule discriminates very slightly against Hamilton county.

[1] By New York Const. 1821, i, 5, 6, until 1846, there were to be eight districts, each returning four Senators. This was in order that one might be elected each year, for a four-year term.

By Mich. Const. 1835, iv, 2, 6, until 1850, the total number was to be $1/3$ that of the Representatives, "as nearly as may be"; and there were to be from four to eight districts, to elect an equal number annually, "as nearly as may be."

By West Virginia Const. 1862, iv, 2, 4, 5, 13, 16, a total of 18 Senators, subject to increase if the State should be enlarged, were to be chosen, two each, on the partial renewal plan, from 9 equal and compact groups of counties, and not both from the same county; any district might at any time be divided by county lines or otherwise, into full single member districts. In 1872 (Const. 1872, vi, 2, 4, 11) this last feature was dropped, and the figures changed to 24 Senators and 12 districts.

4. *Obligatory single-member districts, with occasional divisions*

Another solution, devised by Louisiana in 1845, at the time that divisions of Orleans parish for lower house purposes was made obligatory, was to permit this parish to be divided for upper house purposes also. The obligation to form single-member districts was later removed, and a somewhat similar Pennsylvania requirement of single-member districts only in Philadelphia is also obsolete. To this period belongs, however, the existing Massachusetts provision permitting any city to be divided in the formation of a general single-district system.[1]

---

[1] The total number in Louisiana before the War was 32; 1868-79, 36. Newly created parishes were to be attached to any contiguous district. The original rule was that Orleans was to have 4 Senators, and the ratio for the rest of the State to be obtained by dividing the rest of the population by the rest of the Senators—the rule later introduced into North Carolina for the lower house. No parish was to return more than four Senators, and no grouped district more than two—the Pennsylvania Senatorial rule of 1838. And districts to return two Senators were not to be formed, if an enumerated population within ⅕ of a single full ratio could be secured. In 1852, Orleans was given 5 Senators. In 1868, its representation was not fixed, and the ratio was to be obtained by dividing the entire population by the entire number of Senators. This lasted until 1879.

Pennsylvania, in 1857, amended its rule of 1838 by the requirement that Philadelphia was to be divided into single member districts, of contiguous territory, without dividing wards.

Massachusetts, in 1855 provided that 8 single member districts should be formed for *Councillors*, without dividing towns or wards, and that, in case 40 Senatorial districts should later be provided, Councillor's districts should consist of contiguous groups of 5 of these. Two years later these Senatorial districts were provided, to be formed without dividing towns or wards, and, as nearly as might be, without running over county lines.

References:

La. Const. 1845, 15, 16; 1852, 15, 16; 1868, 28-29 (until 1879).

Pa. Am. 1857, i, 2, 4, (until 1873).

Mass. Am. 1855, xvi; 1857, xxii

5. *Obligatory single-member districts, with divisions of large counties*

Eleven States, following New York in 1846, permit counties entitled to two or more Senators to be divided. The original intention of the rule may have been to permit this only for the formation of districts wholly within the county. The rule does not so state, however, in New York until 1894, in Kentucky until 1890, and to-day in Michigan and North Carolina, and it was not so interpreted in the New York apportionments, for instance, of 1875 and 1892, when parts of New York county or Kings were joined with adjacent counties. The modern phrasings prevent these anomalies. New York has recently made a very stringent discrimination against its largest city.[1]

[1] No additional limitations, other than that of total number, in:
New York, 1846-94 (32 Senators and districts).
Michigan, since 1850 (32).
North Carolina, since 1868 (50).
California, since 1879 (40).
North Dakota, since 1889 (30 to 50).
Kentucky, since 1850, has required 38 districts. Until 1890, the rule as to separate representation of urban districts, on full ratios, applied to both houses. Since then, the rule that districts having the larger territory are to be given the advantage, in whatever inequality results from the enforced recognition of county lines, is applied to both houses. *Cf.* the fairer Tennessee rule, under which inequalities are to cancel each other, p. 205, *supra.*

In Missouri, since 1865, there are to be 34 districts, and compact subdivisions of counties entitled to more than one member are to be made by the County Court, or, since 1875, by the Circuit Court, precisely as for the lower house. This is the only instance of local action in the formation of Senatorial districts.

For the Illinois rule regarding the formation of 51 districts, *vide* ch. vii, p. 177, *supra.*

In Pennsylvania, since 1873, 50 compact districts are to be formed on a ratio of 1/50. Counties containing ½ to ⅘ ratio, which adjoin counties entitled to one or more Senators, and all counties containing ⅘ to 1 ratio, *may* be given separate representation. A separate

In several of these States, the single-member system is

Senator (apparently) *must* be given to all counties containing 1 to
⅗ ratios, and separate representation to larger counties on the basis
of one Senator to every full ratio and additional ⅗, but no county or
city to have more than ⅙ of the whole; and counties not entitled to
more than one Senator may not be divided. ⅙ of 50, in whole numbers, in 16%; Philadelphia in 1910 contained over 20% of the population.

New York, in 1894, applied the rule for the formation of compact
districts, without dividing towns or city blocks, and with border
units to be distributed so as to make the parts as nearly equal as
possible, to the upper as well as to the lower house (*vide* ch. vii,
p. 172, *supra*).   An extremely interesting mathematical rule governing the apportionment proper is also provided.   A fixed ratio
of 1/50 is prescribed, and a distinction made between counties having
less, or more, than 3 ratios.   Those containing less may, by implication, be represented on less than full ratios.   Those containing more
—and only New York county, Kings, and Erie can contain more,
for many years to come—may not be; and no one of them shall ever
have more than one-third—no two counties, " or the territory thereof
as now organized, which are adjoining counties or are separated only
by public waters " (i. e. New York and Kings counties) shall ever
have more than one-half—of the total number of Senators.   It is in
the determination of what this total number shall be, however, that
language has been most skilfully employed to veil its real significance.
The total number is to be 50, unless, on any apportionment, one of
the larger counties, as above defined, shall be entitled to an increase,
in which case it shall receive the additional Senator, or Senators, *and
the total number be correspondingly increased*.   This looks, at first
glance, as though some concession were being made to the larger
counties here, to make up for what they suffer by the rest of the
provision.   A moment's reflection will show, however, that if, instead
of this rule, the total number of Senators were fixed, not only
would the larger county obtain its addition, but the smaller group
must lose a corresponding number; the effect of the rule is at once
to keep the existing number of rural Senators intact, and to grant
to the larger counties one-half the benefit to which their more rapid
growth would equitably entitle them.   New York and Kings, with
an actual combined population (including aliens) of over 48% of
the State, have to-day 20 out of 51 Senators.   A little figuring will
show that when their enumerated population is 60% of that of the
entire State—when they cast a majority in the popular vote of, say,
half a million—the positive restriction upon the number of their Sena-

prescribed also for the lower house, but differences in the manner of recognizing administrative lines makes the two systems identical only in California and Kentucky. In Illinois and North Dakota the Senatorial districts are utilized for the lower house, but not so as to return a single member.[1]

6. *Free formation of single-member districts*

Of the preceding single-member States, New York is the only one to insist upon harmony between the lines of upper and lower house districts. Wisconsin, in 1848, followed by Minnesota and Washington, limit the single-mem-

---

tors will still not need to be invoked, because even without it, they will not be entitled to half the Senate.

Connecticut, since 1901, requires 24 to 36 single member districts, to lie wholly within towns, or to consist of groups of complete towns lying wholly within a county, and no county to have less than one Senator.

In Oklahoma, the rule for border units, etc., based upon that of New York, applies to both houses. The number of Senators starts at 44, but, in further imitation of New York, in case any county is found entitled to 3 or more Senators, its representation, and the total number of Senators, is to be increased accordingly. Doubtless $1/_{44}$ is intended to be a fixed ratio, although not so stated.

References:

N. Y. Const. 1846, iii, 2-4; 1894, 2, 4.

Mich. Const. 1850, iv, 2, 4; * 1908, v, 2, 4.

Ky. Const. 1850, ii, 5, 13-15; 1890, 33.

Mo. Const. 1865, iv, 4-8; 1875, iv, 5, 6, 9.

N. C. Const. 1868, ii, 3, 5; 1876, ii, 3, 4.

Ill. Const. 1870, iv, 6.

Pa. Const. 1873, ii, 16, 18.

Cal. Const. 1879, iv, 6.

N. D. Const. 1889, 26, 29, 214.

Conn. Am. 1901, xxxi.

Okla. Const. 1907, v, 9.

[1] System of minority representation in Illinois; no system at all in North Dakota.

ber requirement only by the proviso that lower house districts are not to be divided. Texas has no limitation at all.[1]

Wisconsin, alone of these four, requires the single-member system for the lower house also.

7. *Permissive single-member districts, with the county check*

Groups and divisions, both, were permissible in California for a time after 1862, and to-day in Mississippi and Utah. Groups, and permissive divisions of Orleans parish, only, survived in Louisiana, in 1879, the removal of the single-member requirement. Montana curiously permits divisions but forbids unions of counties.[2]

---

[1] Wisconsin (Const. 1848, iv, 3, 5), ¼ to ⅓ number of Representatives.

Minnesota (Const. 1857, iv, 2, 23, 24), not more than one Senator to every 5,000 inhabitants.

Texas (Const. 1876, iii, 2, 25, 28), 31 Senators.

Washington (Const. 1889, ii, 2, 6), ⅓ to ½ number of Representatives.

[2] By California, Am. 1862, vi, 6, 30, (until 1879), the total number was ⅓ to ½ that of Representatives, and any county might be divided to form single member districts.

By Louisiana Const. 1879, 17, 1898, 19, the total number of districts—first, 24 to 36—then 36 to 41—are to be formed of complete parishes, except in the case of Orleans. There is not even any requirement that the parishes shall be contiguous.

Montana (Const. 1889, v, 3, 4; vi, 2, 4) does not limit the number, requiring merely that new counties are to be entitled to one Senator, and that a Senatorial district shall not consist of more than one county. That it need not consist of an entire county is clear from the use, elsewhere, of the words "county or district."

Mississippi (Const. 1890, 35, 42, 255, 256) makes the total number 30 to 45, apparently to be equally divided among the three lower house distributing districts. There are no other restrictions, and the accompanying provisional apportionment shows that flotorials (very rare for the upper house) are here permissible.

In Utah (Const. 1895, ix, 4) the total number of Senators is to be 18 to 30, and ⅓ to ½ of the Representatives. Counties are to be divided only to contain districts wholly within them.

8. *Unrestricted formation of districts*

Since Nevada showed the way in 1864, no direct territorial restrictions have been provided for either house in this State, Nebraska, South Dakota and Virginia. And no restrictions upon the formation of upper house districts, only, appear, in surviving instances, in Kansas and Wyoming.[1]

III. SUMMARY

The relative frequency of the single-member requirement, applied to twenty-two Senates to-day, as against, strictly speaking, only seven lower houses, is to be ascribed, in part, as already pointed out, to the absence of historical tradition standing in the way, and in part simply to the smaller number of Senators. The association of the representative with a single district was made most easily, and most promptly, in the case of Congressmen, where only a few broad districts were needed; next, for the Senate, at a period when the number of Senators was smaller, the distribution of population more equal, than now, and approximately equal districts could thus be formed without division of the more populous centers; last of all, it was sought in a few States to apply the idea to the lower house, to which end divisions

---

[1] Kansas (Const. 1859, ii, *2; x, 1-3) maximum of 33; (Am. 1873, ii, 2) maximum of 40.

Nevada (Const. 1864, iv, 4, 5; xv, 6, 13) ⅓ to ½ number of Representatives, with aggregate maximum of 75.

Nebraska (Const. 1866, ii, 3, 5, 8) 13 to 25; (Const. 1875, iii, 2, 3) 30 to 33.

Texas (Const. 1868, iii, 12, 34—until 1876) 19 to 30.

Mississippi (Const. 1868, iv, 4, 35—until 1890) ¼ to ⅓ number of Representatives.

Arkansas (Const. 1868, v, 7-9—until 1874) 26 Senators.

South Dakota (Const. 1889, iii, 2, 5) 25 to 45.

Wyoming (Const. 1889, iii, 2, 3, "App.", 2) ⅓ to ½ number of Representatives.

Virginia (Const. 1902, 41, 43) 33 to 40.

of counties were indispensable. Since then, as the size of
the Senate has increased, and the size of the districts correspondingly diminished, divisions of counties have been
in greater or less degree permitted for this body also, in
many States; in others, another way out of the difficulty has
been sought, or the proportionate ideal has been sacrificed;
while, in a few, administrative lines have been ignored altogether.

This last solution may be discarded at once, as afford-
ing the apportioning body altogether too much scope for
the display of partisan spirit. Of the others, none are fitted
to secure satisfactory results. The difficulty is not with the
single-member system, which is an admirable conception in
itself. It is good that districts should be approximately
equal, to the end that unrepresented minorities—the de-
feated parties in the popular campaign—may everywhere
be about the same in size. It is good that each of these districts should return only one member, upon whom local
attention may be focussed. The trouble is with the number
of districts which, under present conditions, must be formed
in a territory already permanently divided into counties.
The smaller the Senatorial district, the harder the task of
packing counties into it. The obvious remedy is a great de-
crease in the number of Senators, say to ten or twelve, in the
formation of whose great districts urban lines, as having
a genuine local significance, shall be recognized first of all;
county lines secondarily, merely as a conventional check
upon gerrymander.

Turning now to the structural distinctions between the
two houses, it will be observed that here, too, there is almost
no agreement among the States. The Senate is always
smaller in size than the lower body, or, better expressed,
the lower house is always larger. Incidental allusion has
been made to the device of a longer Senatorial term, with

or without a system of partial renewal; this distinction is
common, though not universal. As regards definition of
district, and numerical representation of the district when
formed, the system in a few States is the same for both
houses; in most, either through historical accident or de-
sign, it is not; and in some cases this difference of system
results in the urban districts being accorded proportionately
equal representation in one of the two houses, but not in
the other.

The elevation of this latter distinction into a deliberate
structural principle is an insidiously tempting idea. Urban
house checking rural house, and through this nice balance
of conflicting interests—"because of the necessary movement of things"—just and wise action being somehow
taken by both, is Montesquieu's theory of government expressed in modern terms; and, from the point of view of
urban communities, would be, at worst, a bad means to a
thoroughly desirable end. Just as surely as deadlocks, once
broken, can never be renewed—just as surely as British
Crown and Lords have become hopelessly subordinate to
the Commons—just so surely, after an intervening period
of friction, more or less severe, the rural house would find
itself at the mercy of that house in which the real power
of the community resides, or—as appears far more likely—
both houses alike would be overwhelmed by the rising tide
of Initiative and Referendum. This latter movement is
only one of many indications that the institution of two
Legislative chambers, with equal and coördinate powers,
has ceased to rest upon a firm basis of popular affection and
respect; if it is to endure, it must be reformed. But it must
be reformed on lines which will enable the popular majority, upon its sober second thought, to secure anything
and everything it wants. On no principle less extreme than
this can a lasting system of government be founded. We

may, of course, regard the bi-cameral Legislature as an institution that has outlived its usefulness. If that be the
case, there is no need to spend much thought upon its composition. It does not work so badly but that, with a little
patching here and there, it will carry us through until superseded by an entirely new system. But if it seems worth pre-
serving, it must be made as responsive to the general popular will as the substitute offered. That substitute at present
appears to be direct popular government, so-called; and
although this is a misleading term, since the people can
never act except upon propositions placed before them, it
will be noted that the upbuilding of organizations, temporary or permanent, by which Initiative petitions can be
framed, is in the nature of things more easy in urban than
in rural communities. We do not need to depend, then,
upon generalities to support the proposition that cities, as
they increase in strength, will infallibly, in one way or another, control the State. We can point out the particular
way in which this is likely to occur, in case rural Legislators do not recede from their entrenched positions.

Once let it be admitted that the true interests of all sections will be best preserved by according to cities their full
proportionate representation in Legislatures and Constitutional Conventions, it is difficult to see why any distinction
other than that of terms of service should be made in the
structure of the two houses. Restore the dignity of each
house by reducing the total membership of each to a point
where election by one's fellow citizens becomes a signal
honor. Define a single set of great districts by lines that
coincide, so far as this may be done, with genuine economic
distinctions. Give the one house a short term, fitting it to
reflect the passing popular mood, which is often mistaken in
the concrete action it demands, but always worth considering as evidence that some action is needed. Give the other

a long term of service—rather longer than at present—partially renewed at intervals not too long, fitting it to delay and to revise, but not permanently to block, action which is insistently demanded.   And protect minorities, wherever their local interests can be divided from those of the community at large, by broad charters of self-government. Even if direct popular government, so-called, comes to be applied to the most important issues in the State, the business of government is increasing at such a rate that there will always be plenty left to do for a bi-cameral Legislature that is fitted to do it.

CHAPTER IX

MISCELLANEOUS DISTRICTS OF REPRESENTATION

I. CONGRESSIONAL DISTRICTS

By Article I, Section 4, of the Federal Constitution, " The times, places and manner of holding elections for senators and representatives shall be prescribed in each State by the Legislature thereof; but the Congress may at any time, by law, make or alter such regulations, except as to the place of choosing senators."

Whether under this provision the State Constitution has any jurisdiction at all over Congressional elections is not clear; and the authority of Congress itself to determine such a fundamental point as the nature of Congressional districts is by no means free from question. If Congress may provide for a system of single-member districts, in general terms, why may it not define these districts outright, and distribute the State representation arbitrarily among them? If Congress, without power to determine suffrage qualifications, may require that these districts shall be equal in population, why may it not provide that they shall be equal in amount of taxable property, or of taxes paid to the Federal government? However this may be, eleven States, beginning with Virginia in 1830, have at one time or another professed to impose Constitutional restrictions upon their Legislatures in the formation of Congressional districts; and although Congress has never passed any permanent law upon the subject, it has since 1842 regularly

218   [610

supplemented its apportionment acts by single-member provisions.

The original Virginia provision, in force until 1850, required merely the apportionment of Congressmen among
the counties, cities, boroughs and towns, as nearly as might
be according to their Federal population. Its effect was
thus merely to prevent divisions of administrative districts,
although after 1842 it must be read in the light of Congress's own action.[1]

The Federal apportionment act of 1842,[2] crystallizing a
practice that had been common, though not universal, since
the beginning, imposed merely the single-member system,
in general terms. The act said nothing about equality
among the districts. Subsequent acts, of which that of
1882[3] may be taken as an example, go more into detail.
and introduce important modifications. Here the districts,
if newly formed, must contain " as nearly as practicable an
equal number of inhabitants "; existing districts may be retained, however, and additional members, if any, elected at
large; or, where the representation is decreased, the whole
number may be elected at large—under a strict reading of
the text, indeed, *must* be elected at large, if the Legislature
does not act before the next election. This change in the
Federal practice explains some of the diversities in the
State provisions, while in other cases the influence of provisions affecting the structure of the Legislature will be discerned.

Counties not to be divided.

This requirement has been imposed by Iowa from the

[1] Va. Const. 1830, iii, 6 (until 1850).
[2] U. S. Laws, June 25, 1842.
[3] U. S. Laws, February 25, 1882.

beginning, by California until 1862, and by South Carolina, less clearly, since 1895.[1]

Counties, cities and towns not to be divided; single-member districts, equal and compact.

So in Virginia, from 1850 till 1902.[2]

Counties, grouped counties, or subdivisions of counties.

So in California, from 1862 till 1879.[3]

Single-member districts, equal.

So in Alabama, from 1867 till 1875.[4]

Districts not to be changed.

So in Arkansas, from 1868 till 1874.[5]

State to be districted after each Congressional apportionment.

So in three Far Western States, which entered the Union with only one representative each.[6]

---

[1] In Iowa and California the counties must be contiguous.
Iowa Const. 1846, iii, 32; 1857, iii, 37.
Cal. Const. 1849, iv, 30 (until 1862).
S. C. Const. 1895, vii, 13.

[2] Equal, as nearly as may be, in Federal population, before the War; in population, afterwards. Va. Const. 1850, iv, 13, 14; 1870, v, 12, 13 (until 1902).

[3] Cal. Am. 1862, iv, 30 (until 1879).

[4] Ala. Const. 1867, viii, 6 (until 1875).

[5] The first Legislature might, however, redistrict. Ark. Const. 1868, xiv, 1 (until 1874).

[6] The Colorado practice is not to interpret this as equivalent to a requirement of single-member districts.
Colo. Const. 1876, v, 44.
Wyom. Const. 1889, iii, "App." 1.
Utah Const. 1895, ix, 1.

Unions of lower house districts.

California, in 1879, made a valiant effort to harmonize its three sets of variable districts. 40 Senatorial and 80 lower house single-member districts are provided, each to consist of counties, grouped counties, or subdivisions of a county; and although it was not expressly required that each Senatorial district should comprise two for the lower house, it was obviously hoped that such might usually prove a practicable arrangement. The Congressional districts, however, are positively required to consist of compact groups of lower house districts, and county lines are in general to be rigidly observed; but after districts have been formed within the larger counties upon full ratios, then the residue of the county may be attached to adjacent counties; in plain English, San Francisco and Los Angeles county are to have as many districts as can be formed within them, but the surplus population is not to be deprived of its claim to representation. So long as California's total representation in Congress is 8 (as now) or 10, this is a very pretty system; when uneven figures come in, then of course it breaks down, so far as the proportionate system is concerned, unless Congress permits additional members to be elected at large; the provision itself does not require fresh districting after each apportionment.[1]

Single-member districts, equal and compact.

This is the provision finally adopted by Virginia.[2]

Besides the seven widely-scattered States in which these varying *restrictions* upon the Legislature survive, the two Dakotas provided that, until otherwise provided by law,

---

[1] Cal. Const. 1879, iv, 27.

[2] " As nearly as practicable an equal number of inhabitants." Va. Const. 1902, iv, 55.

Congressmen shall be elected at large; a provision apparently superfluous when these States entered the Union with only a single Representative, but serving the purpose now of perpetuating the general ticket system, in default of Legislative action to the contrary. These are now the only States in which Congressional districts, based upon either an old or a new apportionment, might exist but actually do not.[1]

2. JUDICIAL DISTRICTS OF REPRESENTATION

In seven States, including one obsolete instance, districts of territorial representation in the highest Court, not corresponding to any obligatory division of judicial powers or duties within these lines, have come into existence. While occasionally, as we shall see, this system of districting was preceded by one in which the districts served a double purpose, a deliberate attempt was finally made in all these States to pattern their Courts somewhat after the Legislative model—to introduce local representation for its own sake, that is to say, into an organ possessing State-wide jurisdiction. This little group of States, for the most part lying on or near the Mississippi river, includes all where districts, additional to those already discussed, have served, so far as the instrument provides, a purely representative purpose. Provisions affecting the formation of districts like those of the New York Supreme Court, for instance, where the territorial lines affect not only the choice of Judges, but also their individual powers or duties after they are chosen [2] —or like the Maryland Circuits, which are now utilized also

---

[1] N. D. Const. 1889, 214.

S. D. Const. 1889, xix, 1.

[2] In this case, the requirement that they shall reside within the district—not to be confused with a residential qualification for election.

as the basis of the Court of Appeals—have already been discussed under the general head of Major Judicial Districts.[1]

The movement, if it may be dignified by this name, started in Mississippi in 1832, in connection with an early introduction of the as yet uncommon principle of direct popular election of Judges. Given the determination to have a Court of three elected Judges, it was a very natural development that the Legislature should be required to divide the State into three districts, each to return one Judge; and the similarity of this small body to the typical Senate was still further enhanced by applying the principle of partial renewal. Maryland and Louisiana, twenty years later, when the extreme democratic wave was at its height, adopted the same system, except that in Maryland there were four specified districts, of which Baltimore city was one, and no provision for partial renewal; in Louisiana, four Judges and districts, and an additional Chief Justice elected by the State at large.

Such was the situation in these three States before the War. Then a curious development took place, illustrating the tenacity of old customs. Maryland, in 1864, substituted election by the State at large, but required the Judges to be chosen, one each, from the districts, of which, Baltimore being divided by wards, five were now defined; three years later this was abandoned for a system by which Circuits and Circuit Judges were utilized. The other two States, in their Reconstruction instruments, reverted to appointive Judges, in the same number as before, but here also Mississippi has always made the proviso, which Louisiana also in 1879, imposed, that the Judges shall be appointed *from* separate territorial divisions. In Mississippi there has been no further change, and the system is simple and

---

[1] *Vide* ch. v, sec. iii, pp. 105 *et seq., supra.*

symmetrical; the Legislature is apparently free to change or to leave untouched the three districts. The Louisiana instruments, however, have defined the districts, in terms of parishes, and, in place of an additional Chief Justice to be chosen from the State at large, have required two Judges to be chosen from the district in which New Orleans is included; finally, in 1904, the elective system was revived upon this basis; the partial renewal system, also, has gradually lost its original symmetry, until now elections for a full term occur at the Congressional election following any vacancy.[1]

Meanwhile another pair of States, Illinois and Kentucky, showed a tendency to economize districts, in contrasting manners. Illinois in 1848 provided for three "Grand Divisions" by a method already described, within each of which the Court must hold one annual term; provisionally, also, the Judges were to be elected within these, but the Legislature might substitute election by general ticket; this being, in other States, the favorite method. Kentucky, two years later, did just the reverse of this: districts of election and of partial renewal were prescribed; the number of Judges, originally four, might be reduced to three and (probably) increased at will, in which case the districts were to be changed, presumably under the original restrictions. These restrictions were that the districts should consist of complete counties, and be equal in voting population. The Legislature then, it was provided, might or might not require that the Court should hold its sessions in one or more of these districts.

The distinction between the two States, as regards place of sessions, has endured. Illinois still has its " Grand Divi-

[1] Miss. Const. 1832, iv, 2; 1868, vi, 2; 1890, 145.
Md. Const. 1851, iv, 4; 1864, iv, 17 (until 1867).
La. Const. 1852, 64 (until the War); 1879, 83; 1898, 87; Am. 1904, 87.

sions ", while the Kentucky Court, except in emergency, sits
at the capital.   In both States, however, districts of election
now appear, in connection with a haphazard system of judicial tenure.   In Illinois, since 1870, there are to be seven
Judges, each elected by a district, the boundaries of which
may be changed only at a Legislative session next preceding an election, and subject to the restriction that districts
must be compact, and as nearly equal in population as possible without dividing counties.   In Kentucky there are to
be from five to seven districts, according to the number of
Judges; these districts may be changed every ten years, or
whenever the number of Judges is changed; the rule for the
original formation of these districts, which is presumably intended to apply permanently, is the same as in Illinois.[1]

Finally, Indiana, since 1851, followed by South Dakota
and Oklahoma, provide for the election of Judges by the
people at large; each Judge to be chosen however (as in
Misissippi, under the appointive plan) from a separate district.   In Indiana five to seven districts are to be formed
of contiguous territory and of equal population, without
dividing counties, but no provision is made as to times of
redistricting.   South Dakota requires merely from three to
five districts.   Oklahoma has no restriction.[2]

Similar to the above are provisions in Ohio and Louisiana for the election of lower Judges.   The Ohio Common
Pleas districts, themselves to consist of three or more counties, are to be subdivided, for purposes of election, in the
first instance, into three parts, compact, as nearly equal in
population as practicable without dividing counties; in each

[1] Ill. Const. 1848, v, 3; 1870, vi, 5.
  Ky. Const. 1850, iv, 4; 1890, 113, 116.
[2] Ind. Const. 1851, vii, 2, 3.
  S. D. Const. 1889, v, 6, 11.
  Okla. Const. 1907, vii, 3, 22.

of which one Judge is to be elected; changes in the subdivisions, as in the districts themselves, are to be made by a two-thirds majority of the Legislature, under a grant of power apparently broad enough to sweep away the entire system.[1] Louisiana has also provisionally divided its two recent rural circuits into three districts each, for the purpose of electing partially renewed Courts of three Judges.[2]

3. GUBERNATORIAL DISTRICTS OF REPRESENTATION

Maryland's Governor, until 1837, as originally in all the Southern States, was chosen by joint ballot of the two houses. The strongly-marked geographical features of the State, which we have seen reflected in the requirement that the Western and Eastern Shores should have distinct sessions of the highest Court, distinct Treasurers and Registers of the Land office, and distinct groups of Senators under a system of indirect election, would naturally make the Governor's place of residence a matter of more significance than in other States. This led to the Constitutional requirement, between 1837 and 1864, that the Governor should be chosen, by vote of the entire State, for a term of three, or later four years, from each of three specified districts, in rotation.[3]

4. ADMINISTRATIVE DISTRICTS OF REPRESENTATION

Virginia and Louisiana, in the last decade before the War, provided for Boards of Public Works, which, unless abolished by three-fifths vote of the Legislature, were to

---

[1] Ohio Const. 1851, iv, 3, 15.

[2] La. Am. 1906, 100.

[3] The Eastern Shore was one district; Baltimore city was grouped with the southern counties, and Baltimore county with the northwestern. Md. Am. 1837, 20; Const. 1851, ii, 5 (until 1864).

Cf. also the use made by Mississippi, since 1890 (Const. 140) of its lower house districts in the gubernatorial election.

consist of three, or in Louisiana of four, Commissioners, to be elected on the partial renewal plan, in districts to be formed so as to contain, as nearly as might be, an equal number of voters.[1] These did not survive the War. Since then, however, the instruments of Louisiana, and of three other States, have applied the principle of territorial representation to various types of Boards. At first, electoral districts were prescribed, but, as in some judicial examples, already noted, the principle of district representation has survived a centralization of the selecting authority.

(a) *Boards of Education*

Alabama, in 1867, provided a Board of Education whose members were to be elected, two each, by the Congressional districts, with a Superintendent of Public Instruction, elected at large, as its presiding officer. Since 1875, control over common schools has been vested in the Superintendent alone, but two Boards of Trustees, for the two State Universities, are constituted on a similar plan, except that members are now appointed by central authority from the districts.[2]

(b) *Boards of Railroad Commissioners*

Boards of three members, charged with the supervision of railway, or of transportation systems, to be elected by the voters of districts, appear in California, Kentucky and

[1] Va. Const. 1850, v, 14, 18 (until the War).

La. Const. 1852, 130, 134 (until the War).

[2] The Boards consist of two members from the Congressional district in which the respective University is situated, and one from each other district, together with the Superintendent and Governor. Appointments are made by the Governor, or—for one of the two Boards, since 1901—by the surviving members, subject in both cases to the approval of the Senate.

Ala. Const. 1867, xi, 1, 4; 1875, xii, 9; 1901, 264, 266.

Louisiana; in Kentucky, however, the Legislature is authorized to substitute election at large, with or without continued representation of the districts. The districts themselves are in California merely required to be made as nearly equal in population as practicable, with no provision for maintaining equality; in Kentucky, provisional districts are specified, which the Legislature is authorized to change so as to equalize their population; in Louisiana they are permanently specified in terms of parishes.[1]

(c) *California Board of Equalization*

This taxation board consisted, in 1879, of members to be elected one by each of the (four) Congressional districts, with the Controller as *ex officio* member. In 1884, the State having meanwhile become entitled to two additional Congressmen, it was provided that the districts should be the Congressional districts, as established in 1879, or that the Legislature might form four fresh districts, " as nearly equal in population as practical ".[2]

(d) *Miscellaneous Louisiana Boards*

Since 1898, Louisiana also provides for a Board of Appraisers, to assess the property of corporations engaged in transportation, and a Board of Agriculture and Immigration, each to consist of members apointed by central authority, one from each Congressional district. It is also provided that the State Board of Health shall consist of " representative physicians from the various sections of the State ".[3]

---

[1] Cal. Const. 1879, xii, 22.
Ky. Const. 1890, 209.
La. Const. 1898, 283, 289.
[2] Cal. * Const. 1879, xiii, 9; Am. 1884.
[3] Corporation Appraisers are appointed by the Governor, Lieutenant-

5. DISTRICTS OF REPRESENTATION WITHIN COUNTIES

Justices of the Peace are sometimes chosen by precincts, with jurisdiction over the entire county, and merely an obligation to reside within their respective districts. County authorities are sometimes formed by aggregating individual Justices of the Peace into Courts of Quarter Sessions, or individual town Supervisors into Boards, or by utilizing Justices' precincts as districts of choice for independent Commissioners. All such distinctions are outside the scope of this study. In four States, however, including three where the provision survives, purely representative districts have been introduced into counties. Mississippi, having already a Constitutionally established county authority of five elected Commissioners, provided in 1852 that they should be elected " by districts "; these lasted until 1898, when they were converted into full Justice's precincts, though still utilized for the original purpose.[1] Texas, since 1876 has provided for electoral " Commissioners precincts," four in number, independent of the four to eight Justice's precincts also established; these districts to be formed by the county authority.[2] Florida, in 1885, required the Legislature to provide for the division of each county into five districts, from which separate Commissioners were to be appointed; five years later, however, the County Commissioners themselves were to form these districts, which were to be as nearly as possible equal in population, and to be

Governor, Treasurer, Attorney-General and Secretary of State; members of the Board of Agriculture and Immigration by the Governor and Senate; for such an unimportant function as the care of the public health, the Legislature is free to devise the system, subject to this sacred principle of territorial representation.

La. Const. 1898, 226, 296, 307; Am. 1902, 226.

[1] Miss. Am. 1852, iv, 20; Const. 1868, vi, 20 (until 1890).

[2] By the County Court, in the first instance; subsequently by the

full electoral districts.[1]   Kansas merely requires three electoral districts.[2]

6. DISTRICTS OF REPRESENTATION WITHIN CITIES

City wards, already discussed, are of course in their origin representative districts for the Council, but have received Constitutional recognition in connection with their administrative use, in the process of conducting popular elections.[3]

7. SUMMARY

These provisions may be summarized as a crude imitation of those affecting Legislative districts.   The general principle of requiring single-member districts is adopted, but no safeguards are taken to prevent these districts from becoming, in the course of time, widely unequal.   Is the general principle a sound one, subject to correction in detail in subsequent Constitutions or amendments?   I think not.   As regards Congressional districts, it is true that the single-member system is a convenient means for preventing large minorities from being submerged, and ought not to be allowed to degenerate into a system whereby some or all Congressmen may be elected at large—ought rather to be extended, so far as this can conveniently be done, to the choice of Presidential electors.   Control over these matters, however, is vested, by the Federal Constitution, not in the States, but in the State Legislatures; whether State Constitutions can pass upon them at all is therefore at least open to grave question.   In the other cases there is no good reason for any sort of a district system, whether crude or elaborate,

Commissioners Court, consisting of these four Commissioners with the County Judge as presiding officer.

Tex. Const. 1876, v, 18.

[1] Fla. Const. 1885, viii, 5; * Am. 1900.

[2] Kans. Am. 1902, iv, 2.

[3] *Vide* ch. iv, sec. ii, p. 89, *supra.*

whether combined with district election or independent of
the same, whether imposed by the Constitution, as in the
few instances which have come under our survey, or introduced by the Legislature at its own discretion.   The end
in view is unexceptionable—political office is not to be
monopolized by a small section of the State; in matters of
concern to all sections, the State is to be as broadly as possible represented.   This, however, is the precise end which,
under the conditions of party government, appointing or
nominating authorities can most surely be trusted to aim
at, for themselves.   Nothing is more essential to party wel-
fare than the wide appeal.   Patronage is distributed so as
to build up the organization in counties where it is weak.
The ticket is framed in such a manner as to appeal to the
widest possible variety of voters.   Among the many criti-
cisms to which the professional politician is subjected, this
one, at least, has never been heard—he has never been
charged with not paying sufficient attention to considerations of political availability, whether racial or geographic.
He has hard enough work as it is to build up a civil service
which shall satisfy local claims and at the same time be in-
dividually efficient.   The enforced recognition of artificial
lines tends merely to make this a little harder.

The demand that the section of territory, broad or small,
in which we reside, or in which our interests lie—with
which, in one way or another, we have come to have personal associations—shall be represented in those who govern it, is one of the strongest of human instincts.   It is this
feeling which, over large territories, stimulates loyalty to
the native-born king rather than to the foreign conqueror.
It is this feeling which, operating on a smaller scale, demands that this same king's subordinates—or those authorities who have come to share his powers—or those, finally,
who have ousted and replaced him—shall, in a more par-

ticular sense, be our neighbors. It affects equally the choice of officials having purely local powers, and the composition of organs of broader jurisdiction—Sheriffs and Justices in the American county, as earlier in the English shire—Legislatures in the State, following Councils and Assemblies in the Colony, and Lords and Commons in the original model. When conditions are favorable, it takes the form of demanding this representation, not merely for one's locality, but for oneself, but in periods of centralized authority frequently survives the loss of self-governing privileges. It is a feeling which cannot successfully be withstood, and is perhaps the distinguishing feature of civil as opposed to military government—of a system which, resting upon common acquiescence, endures until, by the slow diffusion of ideas, the subject wakes up to the realization that he wants a change—as opposed to one which only the immediate threat of physical force keeps standing.

But although the instinct itself is ineradicable, the territorial limits to which it is applied are capable, it would seem, of an almost indefinite expansion. The traditions of the English House of Commons are so glorious that we are a little too apt, I think, to look upon a body organized on that general model as the last word of democratic development, and to forget that, although originally devised as a method by which local districts might adjust with one another their respective fiscal responsibilities, its most important use was as a means for securing common action to a large community of feeling. Broad party lines obliterated narrow sectional divisions, while, as between parties themselves, acquiescence in majority rule was a symptom of that broader unity which included the entire nation. Neighborliness, in short, under the shadow of Commons and the Crown, broadened into patriotism.

Now, the Commons was an indispensable means of securing this broad community of feeling, in any other shape than a blind subjection to royal authority. With us, however, the device of narrow sectional representation is no longer needed. We have learned, in popular elections covering areas larger than the entire United Kingdom, to acquiesce in the results of majority rule and to feel ourselves, however the election goes, always a united people. The agregation of district representatives is the middle stage in an organic development of which the first form was the people of a small Teutonic community in direct control of its own local affairs; the second, the election of representatives, for purely local purposes, by this people. Taking up the process at the point to which England had brought it, our genius for political organization enabled us to place, side by side with the aggregation of these representatives, a single one—the Governor—elected by the people of the entire State. Finally, completing the cycle, we have in the Referendum, first commonly applied to changes in the Constitution itself, this large community directly exercising governmental functions. It is in the habits of thought engendered by these last two operations that our political unity now rests. Local districts of representation have reverted to their original use as a means of reconciling such local animosities as, in the shadow of this general unity, still exist, and in order to have any value for this purpose should correspond to real differences in local interests and feeling. In the Union as a whole such differences, for historical reasons, still exist as between the States. Within the States, in a few cases, distributions of mountain and plain constitute fairly well-defined local areas. Broadly speaking, however, the distinction between urban and rural communities is the important one within each State. Whether we are dealing with Legislative or Administrative bodies, whether the districts are for jurisdictional purposes, or for electoral purposes, or for the purpose of securing local representation without local election, any system which fails to recognize the prime distinction, in problems and in spirit, between a stretch of farm lands and a congested town, may be condoned as an unimportant survival of old ideas, but is quite without justification in reason.

CHAPTER X

Conclusion

PROBABLY the most vivid impression left with the reader of the preceding pages will be one of extreme confusion. This effect is somewhat enhanced by the comparative method of treatment. The situation in no single State is as bad as in the Union as a whole. It must be admitted however that there is great evidence of a doctrinaire adoption of scattered ideas, and little evidence of any attempt to create a comprehensive and harmonious system, intelligently adapted to present-day problems. What is true in regard to the particular topic of governmental structure which we have singled out for discussion here, is equally true of the field as a whole, and would be still more tediously evident if we were to extend our survey into the realms of statutory experiment. By far the greater number of existing provisions are the products of manhood suffrage, working under the practical limitations imposed by a rigidly bi-party system. Shall we say that after two generations of trial—I take the Mexican War as marking, roughly, the maturity of the system—under conditions unusually favorable so far as concerns material prosperity and freedom from external pressure—the best contribution which democracy has been able to make to the problem of providing a proper form of government for large territorial areas has been to take a few inherited ideas, tack on a few general principles pushed to the extreme, and then, with no discernible unifying aim except that of keeping big cities under, trust to Heaven and our own good sense to make the product work satisfactorily?

This would be a somewhat depressing conclusion, alike for those of us who earnestly believe that our democratic foundations are the only ones upon which a permanently great nation can be built, and for those whose colder reason finds no difficulty in abandoning this faith, but is unable to discover any practicable means whereby we may be made less democratic. Various general qualifications of our censure suggest themselves. Two generations are a small period in the life of a people attempting a task which, on this scale of magnitude, has never been faced before. The War between the North and South had a demoralizing influence beyond what any but the most disastrous foreign conflict could have brought; and although manhood suffrage is perhaps responsible for the actual call to arms, it was not responsible for the institution which clove the nation wide apart in spirit. If we compare our State governments with those built upon superior strata of the social whole, we shall not find these latter much superior in simplicity and technical finish, if I may use the term; and I much doubt if the lower strata are so well satisfied under them. I think also that one who reads attentively the story of structural development which I have tried to tell, will find, amidst much perfunctory detail, flashes of real constructive ability. And even our tendency to make frequent change, dashing madly after the latest political panacea, is only an extreme form of an openness to new ideas, which, emptied into the crucible of experiment to-day, are of solid assistance to us to-morrow.

In addition to these general observations which, with many others, suggest themselves, two points seem to me to deserve especial consideration.

One is, that a very large part of the confusion into which

our system of local districts has fallen has been due to the bankruptcy of the county system of government. The county was formed at a period when means of communication were immeasurably inferior to those of to-day, and, partly because of its use as a unit of representation, has tended to become rather smaller than larger. It is to-day so obviously ill-adapted to the purpose of a prime dividing line between coördinate officers of the central government, that it is hard for us to adjust ourselves to the conception that it played a part in our administrative machinery, for a time, analogous to that played in modern France by the *département*. Its officers were appointed by the central authority. Only 12 counties, for instance, existed in New York, at the time of the Revolution (besides two in Vermont) as against 61 to-day; 12 in Pennsylvania, as against 67; 34 in North Carolina, as against 97; 8 in Georgia, as against 146. It was a perfectly practicable arrangement at the time to distribute governmental functions among the comparatively small number of appointive subordinates. Later the impulse of local self-government, always more easily applied to small units than to large, placed these officials upon a popular basis, so that to-day we never think of the county as being primarily a division of the State, but always as a purely local unit. Hence, when the movement towards centralizing governmental functions began, and large administrative divisions were sought, none were ready to hand, and Congressional districts had to be impressed into service, or new and strange districts created. Hence the necessity of compounding counties into judicial circuits or districts. Hence the anomaly of large cities forming counties, or even groups of counties, by themselves. Hence much incidental confusion in the systems of representation.

Now, manhood suffrage did not create the county system.

It had to take it as it found it. Few nations have had the advantage of modern France, in being able to lay out the territorial bases of its government upon a *tabula rasa*. And manhood suffrage has to get along with this system as best it may to-day. The mind recoils from the practical confusion which would result from the attempt to convert the counties, with all their subdivisions, cross-divisions and overlapping sets of unions, into a symmetrical gridironed system. All that can be done, then, is to make the best of conditions which, when all is said and done, are not much worse than exist in Prussia and England to-day. If these conventional lines, which have lost all contemporary significance, cannot be obliterated, at least they may be utilized in a rational manner.

The other point worth emphasizing is that a very simple explanation exists for the chaos and, from the point of view of the dominant city-dweller, the unfairness, of the prevailing Legislative structure. Provisions affecting the composition of the Legislature are what they are, because they have been drafted by members of already constructed Legislatures.

That the Legislature cannot be trusted to determine the rules of its own being, we have always assumed as axiomatic. And the wisdom of laying down Constitutional rules of apportionment, and the beneficial working of these rules in the main, are clear from a comparison of our districting with, say, the quite simple but grossly unfair distribution of seats now provided for the German Reichstag. As often, when we drop the ideal standard, and test our institutions by those of foreign lands, we find ourselves in a surprisingly healthy condition. The reason why, however, we are in some danger of losing our comparative advantage is that Constitutional Conventions have been constructed on the model of one or both houses of the Legislature, and that the existing system of districts has thus been in a sense self-perpetuating. It is not in human nature for representatives, chosen in numerous small electoral divisions, to look with favor upon a reduction in total number which would relegate a good part of them to political obscurity. It is not in human nature for a rural clique, accustomed to deal with urban problems according to their own ideas as to what is best, to face with equanimity the prospect of urban domination. Hence districts have always grown smaller, never larger, in territorial area. Hence the existing distribution of seats has rarely been changed so as to correct injustice to the towns, and has frequently been changed so as to prevent equal representation in future.

This explanation, once clearly understood, is so complete that the reasoning is likely to be carried too far. It may be argued that not only has this been true in the past, but that it must be so in the future too; that we cannot hope to change human nature, and that the fundamental fallacy of a democratic system of government is thus revealed; that a benevolent despot, imposing justice upon others, is at least a logical conception, even if it is not often realized; but that the notion of a people ruling themselves is a vicious circle in thought. No man can lift himself by his own bootstraps. There must be something outside himself on which he can depend. This something, in our government, has turned out to be, so it may be argued, a self-perpetuating oligarchy, working under cover of representative government primarily in its own interests. It is the dawning realization of this sad truth, so one is tempted to think, that has produced the current outcry against machine government and " bosses ".

Apart from the question of why it can be assumed that the benevolent despot, also, will not possess human nature, it seems to me that experience reveals one simple fact which is quite sufficient to shatter any such chain of reasoning. I refer to the conduct of elective office-holders after an adverse election. No one who is familiar with the crimes which in past generations have been committed by men who possessed political power and wished to retain it, could have believed, if he did not see it daily occurring before his eyes, that by the peaceful process of recorded votes political overturns could ever be effected. It is contrary to human nature, but it happens. It is not, of course, the system of government which secures this result. It is the pressure of public opinion. That is the "something outside" on which democracy depends for its successful working and for its continuance. Once let public attention be fastened upon the composition of the Legislature, and parties will tumble over themselves in their haste to secure popular favor.

The two especial weaknesses, then, of our State system of political subdivisons are their complexity, and the manner in which they discriminate against urban centers. The first evil is the more difficult to remedy, and the less important. For although, as I have previously pointed out, symmetry and simplicity have a genuine practical value, in opening the door of intelligent political discussion to a larger body of citizens, still, life is necessarily a complex thing, and we have to get along with it as we find it. Life is not, however, necessarily an unfair thing, and equal representation as between town and country cannot but seem to the average city-dweller, once his attention is turned to it, as a necessary complement of equal voting power as between man and man, and to have its roots in simple justice. Speaking in a purely political sense, it would not in the least be necessary to pay any attention to the views of the average city-dweller, either about justice or about anything else, if there were not so many of him. Being, however, the important personage that he is, his conception of rights and wrongs is going to be the one that will prevail, and we shall have to accept it even if we think it faulty. This acceptance is important; and it is bound to come; there remain only the questions of detail and of method. In the opinion of the writer, the change from a centralized State government, to a system of broad local charters, for rural and urban territory alike, would so diminish the importance of the Legislature, that the precise composition of this body would with little friction settle itself, along lines dictated by economic conditions.

BIBLIOGRAPHICAL NOTE

I. DOCUMENTARY FIELD

The Secession and early Reconstruction instruments have been excluded from the survey, on the ground that, having proved to be without force, as against Congressional action, they are more appropriately to be classed with the organic laws of Federal territories than with genuine State Constitutions. Early Iowa and Kansas instruments, more or less formally adopted, but superseded prior to the admission of these states into the Union, have been omitted, on this same general principle. To have included proposed, but unratified, instruments or amendments, would have expanded the documentary field to unworkable dimensions. The revived Massachusetts Charter, in force until 1780, the early instruments of South Carolina, and the War Ordinances of Missouri, have, on the other hand, been included, as expressions of the original plenary or residuary powers of these States, even though not, strictly speaking, Constitutions. For the purpose of completing the Continental development of the United States, it has seemed best also to include the recently adopted instruments of New Mexico and Arizona, in spite of the fact that, at the moment of writing, these States have not yet been admitted into the Union.

Provisional determinations, expressed in the Constitutions, but not restricting the Legislatures, or restricting them only for a limited term of years, have of course been omitted.

II. TEXTS

F. N. Thorpe's *The Federal and State Constitutions* (7 vols., Government Printing Office, 1909) is an indispensable mechanical aid to the student of State Constitutions. When the time is ripe for a fresh collection, incorporating the new material which will have accumulated by then, it is greatly to be hoped that the editor will be more conscientious. For criticism of Thorpe's collection, see Professor J. F. Jameson, in the *American Historical Review* for October, 1909, and Professor W. F. Dodd in the *American Political Science Review* for February, 1910.

Authorities needed to supplement Thorpe are arranged below under the several States. All are actually required, in order either to cor-

242   [634

rect his grosser errors and omissions, to elucidate obscurities due to his unsystematic arrangement, or to carry the survey beyond the year (usually 1906) at which his compilation stops. No attempt has been made to verify his text, to change the dates attached to complete instruments, nor—except in one or two glaring instances—to correct errors in proof-reading. On the other hand, I have not confined myself to the particular provisions included in the subject-matter of this study, but have considered the needs of the student of State Constitutions in general. I cannot believe that I have discovered all the errors, and shall be grateful to have my attention called to those I have overlooked.

The italicized year under each State denotes the year to the end of which the survey has been made. When no reference follows, my authority for declaring, both that amendments printed as proposed by the Legislature were ratified by the people, and that no more recent amendments have been adopted, is the Secretary of State for the commonwealth in question. In this connection, my thanks for prompt and full response to enquiries are especially due to Hon. W. T. Smithers, Sec. of State for Delaware; Mr. John A. Lapp, Legislative Reference Librarian, Indiana State Library; Hon. W. C. Hayward, Sec. of State for Iowa; Hon. F. C. Martindale, Sec. of State for Michigan; Hon. P. D. Norton, Sec. of State for North Dakota; Hon. J. Frederick Parker, Sec. of State for Rhode Island; Hon. H. W. Goodloe, Sec. of State for Tennessee; Hon. B. O. James, Sec. of State for Virginia; and Hon. R. C. Myrick, Dep. Sec. of State for Vermont.

Mr. H. M. Lydenberg, of the New York Public Library, has rendered me a great service in giving me access to its shelves during the period of removal to the new building; while to Mr. Franklin O. Poole, Librarian of the Association of the Bar of New York City, my obligations are quite incalculable.

ALABAMA

For amendment to the instrument of 1901, adopted in 1908, affecting the power of the State to engage in works of internal improvement, see MS. copy in N. Y. Bar Association Library.

1910 (ibid).

ARIZONA

For the instrument of 1911, see House Doc., 61st Cong., no. 1423.

ARKANSAS

For original of amended article VII, sec. 20, of the instrument of 1868, see Thorpe, App. p. 4157.

Professor Dodd points out that Thorpe's amendments 2 and 3, to the instrument of 1874, were knocked out by the Courts.

For Initiative-Referendum amendment, adopted in 1910, see Ark. Session Laws, 1909.

1910.

CALIFORNIA

For the original instrument of 1879, and for all amendments to the same, see the compilation of Constitutions, etc., issued by the Secretary of State, 1909.
The amendments given as to be submitted in 1910 were all adopted.
1910.

COLORADO

For amendments omitted by Thorpe, and for subsequent amendments, prior to 1910, see *The Revised Statutes of Colorado*, Denver, 1908.
For amendments adopted in 1910, see Colo. Session Laws, 1909, 1910.
1910.

CONNECTICUT

Article XXXIII of amendments was adopted at the same date as the preceding article.
1910.

DELAWARE

For Bill of Rights of 1776, see *The Constitutions of the several independent States of America*, London, 1783.
The date of the amendment to the instrument of 1792 is Feb. 5, 1802 (*Laws of the State of Delaware*, Wilmington, 1829).
For an amendment to the instrument of 1831, adopted in 1893, see Del. Session Laws, vol. 19.
Article IX, secs. 3 and 6, of the instrument of 1897, as given by Thorpe, are the provisions as amended in 1903. For the unamended provisions, see *Journal of the Constitutional Convention*, 1897.
For Registration Fee amendment, adopted in 1907, see Del. Session Laws, 1907.
1910.

FLORIDA

For amendments to the instrument of 1885, adopted 1900-04, see *The General Statutes of the State of Florida*, St. Augustine, 1906.
For amendments to article V, adopted in 1910, see Fla. Session Laws, 1909, marked copy in N. Y. Bar Association Library.
1910 (ibid).

GEORGIA

For amendments to the instrument of 1877, omitted by Thorpe, and for subsequent amendments, see *The Code of the State of Georgia*, Atlanta, 1911.
1909 (ibid).

IDAHO

For Am. 1894, XVIII, 6, see Idaho Session Laws, 1893.
Am. 1896, XVIII, 6; 1898, XVIII, 4, 7, 9; 1902, XIII, 2; 1906, V, 18; VI, 2; are given by Thorpe without date.
For Am. 1900, IX, 11, and Am. 1906, VII, 9, see *The Revised Codes of Idaho*, Boisé, 1908.
For amendments adopted in 1908, see Idaho Session Laws, 1907, checked by *N. Y. State Library Yearbook of Legislation*, 1908.
1908 (ibid).

ILLINOIS

Thorpe conceals the instrument of 1848 under the running headline of the preceding instrument of 1818.

Of seven amendments adopted to the instrument of 1870, the first three and the fifth are incorporated in Thorpe's text, the unamended provisions appearing in the notes below. For the fourth, see p. 1052.

For Chicago Government amendment, adopted in 1904, see *The Revised Statutes of the State of Illinois,* Chicago, 1905.

For Canal amendment, adopted in 1908, see Ill. Session Laws, 1907, checked by *Yearbook of Legislation.*

1908 (ibid).

INDIANA

For the originals of amended provisions in the instrument of 1851, see Thorpe, pp. 1094-5, "Article IV, sec. 22, In relation to fees and salaries," has reference merely to that paragraph of the section. (Cf. *Statutes of the State of Indiana, Indianapolis,* 1876).

When no date is given for amendments inserted in the text, read "1881". (Cf. *Burns' Annotated Indiana Statutes,* Indianapolis, 1908). No amendment since 1881.

1910.

IOWA

For Eminent Domain amendment, adopted in 1908, see *Iowa Official Register,* 1909-10.

1910.

KANSAS

For the originals of amended provisions, see *General Statutes of Kansas, 1909,* Topeka, 1910.

The provisions given by Thorpe, as to be submitted in 1906, were all adopted. *(ibid).*

1909 (ibid).

KENTUCKY

In article II, sec. 6, of the instrument of 1799, Thorpe omits the following between lines 11 and 12: "may not have a sufficient number of qualified electors to entitle it to one representative, and when the adjacent county or counties may" (*The Kentucky Statutes,* Louisville, 1909).

1908 (Yearbook of Legislation).

LOUISIANA

For abrogation of article 50, of the instrument of 1868, in 1870, see Report of the Secretary of State, 1902.

For the unamended instrument of 1879, and for amendments to the same, see *ibid.*

For amendments to the instrument of 1898, adopted in 1908, see *Constitution and Revised Laws of Louisiana,* N. O., 1910.

1909 (ibid).

MAINE

For the unamended instrument, see Thorpe, App. p. 4159.

For amendments adopted prior to 1877, see Thorpe, App. p. 4179.

For amendments adopted 1877—1902, see Thorpe, p. 1664.

For Initiative-Referendum amendment, adopted in 1908, see Me. Session Laws, 1907.

N. B. Pages 1646 to 1664 of Thorpe give the instrument as amended in 1876, with revised numbering of sections, officially adopted in that year. My references, unless otherwise noted, are to the original numbering.

1910.

MARYLAND

For omitted amendments to the instrument of 1776 (including an important suffrage provision), and for omitted words in Am. 1799, VI (St. Mary's county, " three " districts; Frederick county, " seven ") see *The American's Guide*, Philadelphia, 1832, or later editions of this manual.

1910.

MASSACHUSETTS

For amendment affecting the tenure of Justices of the Peace and Notaries Public, adopted in 1907, see Mass. Session Laws, 1910.

1910 (ibid).

MICHIGAN

For the unamended instrument of 1850, see Thorpe, App. p. 4204.

For amendments adopted prior to 1877, see Thorpe, App. p. 4235.

The substance of most amendments adopted between 1877 and 1905, inclusive, may, with a little trouble, be discovered from Thorpe, pp. 1944-74, by using the footnotes, and the Summary, pp. 1974-80. Note that article X, 10 was first amended in 1903; and article XIV, 9, in 1893.

For six amendments, however, to article VI, 6, from 1881 to 1903 inclusive, see Mich. Session Laws, 1881, 1883, 1885, 1889, and 1903.

For an amendment to article IX, 1, adopted in 1882, see Mich. Session Laws, 1883.

For article IV, 49, in its original form, as adopted in 1893, see *The Compiled Laws of the State of Michigan*, Lansing, 1899.

For three amendments adopted in 1907, see Mich. Session Laws, 1907.

For the instrument of 1908, see *Manual of the Constitutional Convention of Michigan, 1907.*

For an amendment affecting the bonded indebtedness of counties, adopted in 1910, see Mich. Session Laws, 1909.

1910.

MINNESOTA

For the unamended instrument of 1857, see *The Public Statutes of the State of Minnesota*, St. Paul, 1859.

For amendments made prior to 1873, see *The Statutes at Large of the State of Minnesota*, Chicago, 1873.

For amendments made 1873-88, see *The General Statutes of the State of Minnesota*, St. Paul, 1888.

For Municipal Charter amendment, in its original form, as adopted in 1896, see Minn. Session Laws, 1897.

Other amendments, prior to 1906, may be found in Thorpe, scattered through the text.

For amendment affecting power to tax, adopted in 1906, see *Revised Laws of Minnesota, Supplement, 1909*, St. Paul, 1910.

1909 (ibid).

MISSISSIPPI

For Donation amendment, adopted in 1908, see Miss. Session Laws, 1908.

1908 (ibid).

MISSOURI

For important Judiciary amendment to instrument of 1875, adopted in 1884, see *The Revised Statutes of the State of Missouri*, Jefferson City, 1909.

On p. 2274, for " sec. 7 ", read " sec 6 ", and omit Am. 1900, sec. 1, declared invalid by the Courts (*ibid*).

On p. 2275, for " sec. 2 " (*bis*) read " sec. 12 " (*ibid*).

For amendments adopted since 1902 see *ibid*., or Mo. Session Laws, 1909.

1910.

MONTANA

The Initiative-Referendum amendment, given by Thorpe as to be submitted in 1906, was ratified. (*The Revised Codes of Montana of 1907*, Helena, 1908).

For Tax Limitation amendment, adopted in 1908, see Mont. Session Laws, 1907, checked by *Yearbook of Legislation*, 1908.

1908 (ibid).

NEBRASKA

For Railway Commission amendment, adopted in 1906, see *The Compiled Statutes of the State of Nebraska*, Lincoln, 1909.

1910.

NEVADA

For the unamended instrument, see Nev. Session Laws, 1866.

For Initiative-Referendum amendment, adopted in 1904, and for Taxation amendment, adopted in 1906, see *Constitutions of the U. S. A. and of the State of Nevada*, Carson City, 1910.

1909 (ibid).

NEW HAMPSHIRE

No amendment since the last given by Thorpe.

N. B. References are to the paragraphs as numbered in the unamended instrument of 1792. Paragraph XI having dropped out in 1889, all after this now bear official " article " numbers one below the paragraph number.

1910.

NEW JERSEY

For the Election Act of 1807, equivalent to a change in the Constitution, see Elmer, L. Q. C., in *Proceedings of the New Jersey Historical Society*, series ii, vol. ii; and compare *Laws of the State of New Jersey*, Trenton, 1821, pp. 740-2.

For the unamended instrument of 1844, see Thorpe, App. p. 4186.

For amendments adopted in 1875, see Thorpe, App. p. 4201.

For article IV, sec. 7, par. 2, and article V, sec. 12, as amended in 1897, see Thorpe, pp. 2604 and 2608.

1910.

NEW MEXICO

For the instrument of 1911, see Senate Doc., 61st Cong., no. 835.

The reference on p. 2681 of Thorpe is erroneous. *Cf.* p. 2687.

NEW YORK

For the unamended instrument of 1894, and for the development since then, see the annual New York *Legislative Manual*.
1909 (*ibid.*, 1910).

NORTH CAROLINA

For amendments to the instrument of 1868, adopted in 1873, see N. C. Session Laws, 1872-73. (For fact of ratification see Appleton's Annual Cyclopedia, 1873, p. 554).
For the unamended instrument of 1875, see N. C. Session Laws, 1876-77.
For amendments adopted 1880, see N. C. Session Laws, 1879.
For amendment adopted 1888, see N. C. Session Laws 1887.
For amendments adopted 1900, see *Revisal of 1908 of North Carolina*, Charleston, 1908.
1908 (*Yearbook of Legislation*).

NORTH DAKOTA

The dates of the six amendments given by Thorpe are as follows: 1894, I; 1898, II, 121, 127; 1900, III, 76; IV, 179; 1904, V (now known as VII), 176; 1906, VI, 162 (not in existing official instrument). Compare N. D. Session Laws.
For present amendments 1906, V, 215; VI, 215; VIII, 162; 1908, IX, 158; X, 89, see North Dakota *Legislative Manual*, 1909.
For amendments to sections 158 and 216, adopted in 1910, see N. D. Session Laws, 1909.
1910.

OHIO

For originals of amended provisions in the instrument of 1851, see Thorpe, App. pp. 4157-8. Disregard upper half of p. 4157.
Article XVII of this instrument, as given on p. 2937, is a fragment of an Elections amendment, adopted in 1905. For the complete article, see *The General Code of the State of Ohio, Cincinnati*, 1910.
1910.

OKLAHOMA

For the Constitution, see Thorpe, App. p. 4271.
For the " Grandfather " amendment, adopted in 1910, see ?
1910.

OREGON

For amendments adopted in 1908 see *Constitution of the State of Oregon and Official Register*, Salem, 1908.
For those adopted in 1910 see marked copy of Referendum Pamphlet of 1910, in N. Y. Bar Association Library.
1910 (*ibid*).

PENNSYLVANIA

For originals of amended provisions of instrument of 1873, see Thorpe, p. 3152.
For amendments adopted in 1909, see *Supplement to Purdon's Digest of the Statute Law of the State of Pennsylvania*, Philadelphia, 1910.
1910.

RHODE ISLAND

For articles XIII, XIV and XV of amendments, adopted in 1909, see R. I. Session Laws, 1909.
1910.

SOUTH CAROLINA

For amendments to the instrument of 1868, adopted subsequent to 1880, see *Code of Laws of South Carolina*, Columbia, 1902.

For amendments to the instrument of 1895, adopted prior to 1902, see *ibid.*

For amendments adopted in 1903, 1905, 1907, 1908, 1909, see Session Laws of those years.
1910 (Session Laws, 1910).

SOUTH DAKOTA

For amendments IX, 7; V, 23; XI, 1; XXI; adopted in 1906, see S. D. Session Laws, 1905, checked by *Yearbook of Legislation.*
1908 (ibid).

TENNESSEE

No amendments to instrument of 1870.
1910.

TEXAS

For an amendment to the instrument of 1845, adopted in 1850, see *A Digest of the Laws of Texas*, Phila., 1850.

The amendments to the instrument of 1868, stated by Thorpe to have been ratified in 1873, were really ratified in 1874. (Tex. Session Laws, 1874.)

For amendment to article VII, adopted in 1908, see Tex. Session Laws, 1907, checked by *Yearbook of Legislation.*
1908 (ibid).

UTAH

For amendments adopted in 1906, see *The Compiled Laws of the State of Utah*, Salt Lake City, 1907.

For Taxation amendment, adopted in 1908, see Utah Session Laws, 1907, checked by *Yearbook of Legislation*, 1908.
1908 (ibid).

VERMONT

No amendment since the last given by Thorpe.
1910.

VIRGINIA

For a change in the suffrage requirement in 1785, equivalent to a change in the Constitution, see Chandler, J. A. C., *History of Suffrage in Virginia.*

For an amendment to the instrument of 1870, adopted in 1894, see Brenaman, J. N., *History of Virginia Conventions*, 1902.

For amendments adopted in 1901, see Va. Session Laws, 1899-1900.

For County Officers amendment to the instrument of 1902, adopted in 1910, see Va. Session Laws, 1908.
1910.

WASHINGTON

For Religious Freedom amendment, adopted in 1904, see *Remington and Ballinger's Codes and Statutes of Washington*, Seattle, 1910.

For Woman's Suffrage and Gubernatorial Succession amendments, adopted in 1910, see *ibid.*, marked copy in N. Y. Bar Association Library.

1910 (ibid).

WEST VIRGINIA

For the unamended instrument of 1876, see Thorpe, App. p. 4235. Note that in the instrument as amended, pp. 4033 et seq., the word " not " has been inserted into article VI, sec. 6.

Amendments are to be found partly in pp. 4033-63, and partly in pp. 4063-4.

1908 (The Code of West Virginia, St. Paul, 1906, Supplement, 1909).

WISCONSIN

For Special Legislation amendment, as originally adopted in 1871, see *Wisconsin Statutes of 1898*, Chicago, 1898.

For amendments adopted in 1908, see Wisc. Session Laws, 1907, checked by *Yearbook of Legislation*, 1908.

1908 (ibid).

WYOMING

Sections 13-21 of article VI are officially numbered " Elections ", secs. 1-9 (*Revised Statutes of Wyoming*, Laramie, 1899).

1908 (Yearbook of Legislation).